STAGING
SHAKESPEARE

About the Author

Brian Kulick is the Chair of the Graduate Theatre Program at Columbia University. He was the Artistic Director of Classic Stage Company where he directed *Galileo* with F. Murray Abraham, *The Tempest* with Mandy Patinkin, and *The Forest* with Dianne Wiest. He commissioned and co-directed poet Anne Carson's award-winning *An Oresteia*, collaborated with composer Duncan Sheik on productions of Brecht's *Caucasian Chalk Circle*, *Man's A Man*, and *Mother Courage,* and produced CSC's much-lauded Chekhov Cycle with Alan Cumming, Maggie Gyllenhaal, Ethan Hawke, Joely Richardson, Peter Sarsgaard, John Turturro, and Dianne Wiest. He also made CSC the home for playwright David Ives, whose *Venus in Fur* transferred to Broadway and was nominated for a Tony Award for best play. Prior to this, he was an Artistic Associate and then Associate Producer for the Public Theatre where he directed Tony Kushner's adaptation of *A Dybbuk,* as well as acclaimed productions of *Twelfth Night, A Winter's Tale,* and *Timon of Athens* at the Delacorte Theater in Central Park. He is the author of *The Secret Life of Theatre, The Elements of Theatrical Expression,* and *How Greek Tragedy Works.*

STAGING SHAKESPEARE

A Director's Guide to
Preparing a Production

Brian Kulick

methuen | drama
LONDON · NEW YORK · OXFORD · NEW DELHI · SYDNEY

METHUEN DRAMA
Bloomsbury Publishing Plc
50 Bedford Square, London, WC1B 3DP, UK
1385 Broadway, New York, NY 10018, USA
29 Earlsfort Terrace, Dublin 2, Ireland

BLOOMSBURY, METHUEN DRAMA and the Methuen Drama logo are trademarks
of Bloomsbury Publishing Plc

First published in Great Britain 2022

Cover design by Ben Anslow
Cover image: *Shakespeares Will* (© Lordprice Collection / Alamy Stock Photo)

A catalogue record for this book is available from the British Library.

A catalog record for this book is available from the Library of Congress.

ISBN: HB: 978-1-3502-0103-3
       PB: 978-1-3502-0102-6
       ePDF: 978-1-3502-0104-0
       eBook: 978-1-3502-0105-7

Typeset by RefineCatch Limited, Bungay, Suffolk
Printed and bound in Great Britain

To find out more about our authors and books visit www.bloomsbury.com
and sign up for our newsletters.

To my son Noah who, along with an assist from Shakespeare,
taught me how to move from a "Theatre of No" to a "Theatre of Yes"

CONTENTS

List of Illustrations   ix

Acknowledgments   xi

INTRODUCTION "For It Hath No Bottom": Shakespeare and the Vertigo of Multiple Meaning   1

PART ONE "It Shall be Inventoried": A Brief Look at Shakespeare's Dramatic World   7

1 "Now Sir, What is Your Text?": Which Shakespeare? Which Text?   9

2 "And There is Much Music": Reading the Visible and Invisible Score of Shakespeare   31

3 "Wherefore Are These Things Hid?": Pattern Recognition in Shakespeare's Plays   63

4 "Your Actions Are My Dreams": Structure and Shakespeare   79

5 "Stand and Unfold Yourself": Revelation of Character in the Works of Shakespeare   95

PART TWO "What Means This, My Lord?": Toward a Fourfold Reading of Shakespeare 113

INTRODUCTION Standing in the Textual Garden of Forking Paths 115

6 "To Sing a Song That Old Was Sung": Plain Readings 119

7 "You Speak a Language That I Understand Not": Allegorical Readings 130

8 "A Natural Perspective That is and is Not": Analogical Readings 136

9 "Is Not This Strange?": Abstract Readings 142

PART THREE "Come, Give Us a Taste of Your Quality": Practical Matters 149

10 "What Say You?": Finding the Rhyme between Shakespeare, Yourself, and Your Time 151

11 "The Fall of a Sparrow": Shaping Shakespeare 156

12 "Brave New Worlds": Designing Shakespeare 165

13 "The World Must be Peopled": Auditions 187

14 "Resolve You For More Amazement": The First Day of Rehearsal and Beyond 197

Appendix "Volumes That I Prize Above My Dukedom": Some Helpful Secondary Texts to Have at Hand 199
Notes 201
Index 212

ILLUSTRATIONS

1   *Timon of Athens* (Public Theater 1996). Set sketch by Mark Wendland.   169
2   *Timon of Athens* (Public Theater 1996). Set sketch by Mark Wendland.   170
3   *Timon of Athens* (Public Theater 1996). Set sketch by Mark Wendland.   170
4   *Timon of Athens* (Public Theater 1996). Set sketch by Mark Wendland.   171
5   *Timon of Athens* (Public Theater 1996). Set sketch by Mark Wendland.   171
6   *Timon of Athens* (Public Theater 1996). Set sketch by Mark Wendland.   172
7   *Timon of Athens* (Public Theater 1996). Costume renderings by
    Mark Wendland.   173
8   *Timon of Athens* (Public Theater 1996). Costume renderings by
    Mark Wendland.   173
9   *Pericles* (Public Theater 1998). Set sketch by Mark Wendland.   175
10 *Pericles* (Public Theater 1998). Set sketch by Mark Wendland.   176
11 *Pericles* (Public Theater 1998). Set sketch by Mark Wendland.   177
12 *Pericles* (Public Theater 1998). Set sketch by Mark Wendland.   178
13 *Pericles* (Public Theater 1998). Set sketch by Mark Wendland.   179
14 *Much Ado About Nothing* (Berkeley Rep. 2001). Set sketch by
    Mark Wendland.   180
15 *Much Ado About Nothing* (Berkeley Rep. 2001). Set sketch by
    Mark Wendland.   181
16 *Much Ado About Nothing* (Berkeley Rep. 2001). Set sketch by
    Mark Wendland.   182
17 *Much Ado About Nothing* (Berkeley Rep. 2001). Set sketch by
    Mark Wendland.   183
18 *Much Ado About Nothing* (Berkeley Rep. 2001). Set sketch by
    Mark Wendland.   183

ACKNOWLEDGMENTS

None of what you are about to read would have ever been written if it wasn't for the benign intervention of Rosemarie Tichler, who started me on this Shakespearean path some twenty-five or so years ago. At that time, Rosemarie was at the Public Theater and went to see a play I directed Off-Broadway. Somehow she got it in her head that I, who had never directed Shakespeare before, could do so for the New York Shakespeare Festival in Central Park. Then there was Tony Kushner who, together with Rosemarie, assailed George C. Wolfe, the then artistic director of the Public Theater, to hire me. George went to the trouble of schlepping all the way to Cincinnati to check out another show of mine. Ultimately, and thankfully, he agreed with Tony and Rosemarie. At that point, it became a matter of which Shakespeare and when. All of this was answered by the great visionary director Richard Jones, who was slated to direct *Timon of Athens*. At the last minute Richard needed to pull out because a big Broadway musical he was developing had been given the green light. As a result I got *Timon* and Richard ran off to do *Titanic, The Musical!* I suppose, in many ways, I owe my entire career in Shakespeare to Richard and the musical sinking of that famous ship. Next in need of thanks is the entire staff of the Public Theater who, each in their own way, gave me a crash course in directing Shakespeare. This began with George and extended all the way to the extraordinary casting directors, Jordan Thaler and Heidi Griffiths, who assembled an amazing team of seasoned Shakespearean actors for the production. It was this immensely gifted and generous group of artists who became a kind of communal Virgil, leading me through the hell, purgatory, and heaven of directing a Shakespeare play in Central Park during one of the worst heat waves in recorded history. I ended up getting a serious case of sunstroke, survived to finish the show, and have been hooked on Shakespeare ever since.

Between that initial encounter and today stands a much larger constellation of actors, designers, producers, dramaturges, assistant directors, and even critics who have continued to teach me about the strange and mercurial process of translating Shakespeare from the page to the stage. One key figure who was at the center of much of this work was the prodigiously gifted actor Michael Cumpsty. I met Michael on *Timon* and he went on to play other titular roles in my productions of

Richard II, Richard III, and Hamlet (for which he won a well-deserved Obie Award for outstanding performance). Most of what I know about Shakespeare comes from watching and working with Michael. This knowledge was further augmented by the rigorous engagement of an army of young graduate directors who've taken a Shakespeare course that I've taught at Columbia University over the past two decades. At the end of the day, I'm never quite sure who taught who more. I sometimes suspect I have been the greater beneficiary of these encounters since I've had the opportunity to see and be inspired by their endlessly inventive scene work. I would like to particularly single out the directors and dramaturges of the class of 2018 who were so instrumental in helping me find the spark and arc for this book. These amazing students included Daniel Craig Adams, Mark Barford, Emily Boyd, Josh Brown, Miriam Gill, Mikhaela Derva Mahony, Elizagrace Siobhan Modrone, Kaitlin Anne Premus, Jeffrey Paige, Cole Josset Stern, Stephen C. Smith, Annie Wang, and Katherine Wilkenson.

I would also like to thank such dear friends and colleagues as Anne Bogart, Barry Edelstein, Oskar Eustis, Nancy Keystone, Marike Sprint, Jonathan Vandenberg, Kim Weild, Mark Wendland, and William Worthen. These kind souls braved the earliest drafts of this work and reminded me that there was still much more to be mined. Then there was the keen eye and equally keen minds of Jonathan Seinen and Rakesh Palisetty, who kept watch over all my wandering sentences and vanishing prepositions. I am also very much indebted to the unflagging support of Meredith Benson at Bloomsbury. She has been there at every crucial juncture of this book's development, gently guiding it from the roughest of manuscript pages to the finished book that you now hold in your hands. Finally, and perhaps most importantly, there is my wife Naomi, who has been by my side all these years. I wouldn't have made it anywhere, including the end of this sentence, if it wasn't for her love and support.

INTRODUCTION

"For It Hath No Bottom": Shakespeare and the Vertigo of Multiple Meaning

The Call

The phone rings. You answer it and learn that you got the job. Several months from now you're going to stage a play by Shakespeare. Now . . . what do you do? I mean what do you do after that initial burst of adrenalin has passed through your body and you realize you haven't a clue as to what the play is really about, or what you might want to do with it? How exactly do you prepare for such an equally wonderful and daunting task? *How indeed.* That's the central question of this little book which you now hold in your hands. It grows out of decades of preparing for Shakespeare productions and watching others do the same. Its simple wish is to save the reader from some of the panic, wasted time, and fruitless paths that I have experienced, or watched others succumb to during my days as an assistant, then as a director, and now as a producer and teacher. There is no sure recipe for success, but there are a series of things that I have found helpful for myself, my colleagues, and my students. These are a variety of methodologies which can help mitigate some of the stresses and strains that a young artist might feel as they prepare for their first professional encounters with Shakespeare. This can be challenging since we often feel that Shakespeare, as one of his character's famously says, "Speaks a language I understand not."[1] In this respect, there are things we can do, as artists, to "learn" how to speak Shakespeare's particular language. Jorge Louis Borges, the great Argentine poet, use to say it was impossible to translate Shakespeare into Spanish, or any language for that matter. As far as

Borges was concerned, Shakespeare did not even speak English. Shakespeare spoke Shakespeare. This is a unique lexical world which Borges called "Shakespeare-ese." It is a language we must become fluent in. It should not be confused with learning how to speak Shakespeare's verse (which we will also do) but involves how to comprehend the language of image, action, pattern, and structure that is unique to the plays of this extraordinary playwright. It is a body of work that the philosopher Ludwig Wittgenstein likened to:

The Stuff of Dreams

Wittgenstein famously lamented that, after years and years of studying the works of Shakespeare, they still made absolutely no sense to him; or rather, if there was any sense to be made, it was the kind found in dreams. In other words, as far as poor Ludwig was concerned, the whole Shakespearean affair was complete and utter nonsense. But let's let Wittgenstein speak for himself; here he is confiding in his notebook:

> Shakespeare and dreams. A dream is all wrong, absurd, composite, and yet at the same time it is completely right: put it together in this strange way it makes an impression. Why? I don't know. And if Shakespeare is great, as he is said to be, then it must be possible to say of him: it's all wrong, things aren't like that—and yet at the same time it's quite right according to a law of its own. It could be put like this too: if Shakespeare is great, his greatness is displayed only in the whole corpus of his plays, which create their own language and world. In other words he is completely unrealistic. Like a dream[2]

It is hard to hear the word dream and not think of Bottom in *Midsummer Night's Dream*, who boasts:

> The eye of man hath not heard, the ear of man hath not seen, man's hand is not able to taste, his tongue to conceive, nor his heart to report what my dream was ... It shall be called "Bottom's Dream," because it hath no bottom...[3]

Bottom is not alone in this bottomless sensation, Rosalind reports a similar sense of vertigo in *As You Like It*; here is what she reports to her cousin about her sudden, completely unexpected love of Orlando:

> O coz, coz, coz, my pretty little coz, that thou didst know how many fathom deep I am in love. But it cannot be sounded; my affection hath an unknown bottom, like the Bay of Portugal.[4]

Along with love, there is also its distant cousin: grief. Listen to Titus of *Titus Andronicus*, after he has lost his daughter, his hand, and two of his sons:

Is not my sorrow deep, having no bottom?
Then be my passions bottomless with them."[5]

And so, Shakespeare is, for Wittgenstein and many of us, as bottomless as our dreams, our loves, and our griefs. Not to mention fraught with danger, since it is so very easy to get lost, drown, or just have one's heart broken working on these otherworldly plays. So there's the bottomless problem: no matter how hard we work, we are never going to get to the bottom of the meaning of a Shakespeare play. Switching metaphors, we can think of a Shakespeare text like a room. You enter it and say to yourself, "How lovely, how spacious." Then you notice a door. You open it and discover another room with another door. You open that door and there's yet another room with another door that leads to more rooms, with more doors which you continue to open and enter. Pretty soon you realize, "My God, all these rooms and doors stretch to infinity!" And now you begin to understand that you're not in a room, or a house, or even a factory; but rather, a magnificent, ever-expanding palace of multiple meaning. It is an interior that reveals itself to be as vast and varied as entire continent. A veritable "undiscovered country" and you are part of some great, ongoing cartography project that has been charged with mapping this still uncharted authorial expanse. And it is right then that you sense how easy it is to lose your way in this infinite palace of meaning. So what's a young theatre director supposed to do to avoid getting lost? That's where this book comes in, as a kind of "one-stop shopping" for all those interested in understanding how Shakespeare works; or, put another way, it's:

Everything You Always Wanted to Know About Shakespeare But Never Even Thought to Ask

The goal of this book is to take the reader through this crucial period of preparation and help them focus on such issues as:

- What Shakespeare's life, work, and world can tell us.
- What patterns to look for in the text.
- What techniques might help unpack Shakespeare's verse.
- What approaches might unlock certain hidden meanings.
- What literary lenses might bring things into sharper focus.

- What secondary sources might lead to a broader contextual understanding.
- What thought experiments might aide in visualizing the play.

Ultimately, this book wants to draw back the curtain and show the reader how the antique machinery of Shakespeare's theatre works. In full disclosure, I do not subscribe to any one school of interpretation. I came of age between the demise of New Criticism and the rise of Post-Structuralism. I was never a true believer in either literary cause. I, like many of my generation, developed an allergic reaction to any critical "ism" that promised to be the one and only path to understanding. Art, and certainly Shakespeare, has a way of outsmarting such aesthetic hubris. The best I can do is look at this vast legacy of critical theory, not as a series of fallen gods, but as tools for an interpretational toolbox. I don't particularly care where these tools come from, or if they are mutually exclusive from one another, as long as they can help with a provisional understanding of a work at hand. And so I am more than happy to use a hammer from Heidegger, a wrench from Lacan, and even a chainsaw from Derrida. I'm open to any approach as long as it helps me build a temporary house of understanding. It is this theoretical eclecticism that I want to bring to the infinite meaning-machine of Shakespeare.

The imaginative time span of this book is from the moment you learn that on such-and-such date you will begin rehearsing such-and-such Shakespeare play. The clock starts ticking the moment you put down the phone and stops when you arrive at the rehearsal hall and open up the text to begin your first table read. So much of what will be the success or failure of a director's project rests on this work that is done before rehearsals even begin. Part One of the book is an inventory of sorts, attempting to give the reader a crash course in all things Shakespeare. In other words, everything the director would need to know in order to fully understand the way a Shakespeare play can mean. It begins with a quick tour of the Shakespeare canon and groups the plays into distinct stages of an ever-shifting worldview. From there it moves to such issues as Shakespeare's Quartos vs. Folios, the nature of Shakespeare's verse, pattern recognition in Shakespeare's plays, and the larger structural issues that pertain to Shakespeare's plots and characters. Having covered these basics, we can move to Part Two of the book. This section deals with issues of interpretation and asks the reader to consider Shakespeare's plays from four interpretative vantage points. These are a plain, an allegorical, an analogical, and an abstract reading of the text. Such a multi-pronged approach allows us to circle the text and reach something of a three-hundred-and-sixty-degree understanding of the play's potential meanings. Part Three finally turns our attention to the more practical matters of how all this work can help a director with the cutting, designing, and auditioning of a given Shakespeare play.

These are the things that this book wants to tease out and coax into the light of day. It favors the how rather than the why of Shakespeare; especially since

Shakespeare's why likes to play hide and seek, posing questions that will always exceed our answers. Believe it or not, that is as it should be. That's what brings us back, generation after generation, to the same set of plays, hoping that each time we might get a little closer to the work's ultimate meaning. And so, without further ado, let's get started. The clock is ticking.

PART ONE

"It Shall be Inventoried": A Brief Look at Shakespeare's Dramatic World

1 "Now Sir, What is Your Text?": Which Shakespeare? Which Text?

When someone says, "I'm doing Shakespeare", I always want to immediately ask them, "*Which* Shakespeare?" In other words, is it Early Shakespeare (*Two Gentlemen of Verona* to *Henry V*), Middle Shakespeare (*As You Like It* to *Antony and Cleopatra*), or Late Shakespeare (*Pericles* to *The Tempest*)? Even though these plays are all ostensibly by Shakespeare (sometimes with a little help from Christopher Marlowe, or Thomas Middleton, or even the tavern owner George Wilkins), they are all *very different Shakespeares.* Not that we have any real idea of who Shakespeare was. Do not be fooled by the wealth of biographies that have emerged from the nineteenth century all the way to the day before yesterday. When you get right down to it, there is probably five pages of actual biographical data on this fellow named William Shakespeare, and what makes up the rest of these books is historical padding, summaries of the plays, and a whole host of surmises. The little actual biographical evidence we have is mostly due to a handful of legal documents. Thank God Shakespeare seems to have been litigious in nature or we would know virtually nothing about the man. Not that we necessarily know that much more about any of his colleagues. Biographies, at that time, were reserved for monarchs, murderers, or martyrs. No one, at least not in England, was paying any real attention to the lives of writers, especially writers of so ephemeral and seemingly irredeemable an art as theatre. And so Shakespeare remains something of a mystery. Borges once quipped, "We worship Shakespeare, and we know as little about Shakespeare as we know about God."[1]

Be that as it may, we are left with a body of work, some thirty-seven or so plays, that when placed side by side begin to tell a larger story of sorts. It is the story of a particular writer's ever-evolving relation to the world. We could call this thirty-seven-volume work, "Portrait of an Artist as an Ever-Evolving Eye." It is a vision that, over the course of a lifetime, looks at the world from four very distinct vantages points. These ways of being-in-the-world rhyme with William James's four stages of humankind. This is a system James first articulated in his majestic *Varieties of Religious Experience.* He names these stages: Once-Born, Twice-Born, The Sick Soul, and (what I will rechristen) The Reborn. Let's briefly unpack each of these categories of being and then relate them to the phases of Shakespeare's canon. We will begin with:

Once-Born

From *Two Gentlemen of Verona* to *Henry V*

Shakespeare tells us, via Jaques in *As You Like It*, that there are seven stages of man. William James, the nineteenth-century philosopher and sometimes transcendentalist, reduces these stages down to four. He calls the first stage "once-born" and describes it in the following fashion: "In many persons, happiness is congenital and irreclaimable. 'Cosmic emotion' inevitably takes in them the form of enthusiasm and freedom. I speak not only of those who are animally happy. I mean those who, when unhappiness is offered or proposed to them, positively refuse to feel it, as if it were something mean and wrong."[2] James goes on to give us a brief catalog of those that he designates as "once-born." This includes the Ancient Greeks, the Romans, Saint Augustine, Saint Francis, the young Rousseau, Diderot, "many of the leaders of the eighteenth century anti-Christian movement," Walt Whitman, and a certain Theodore Parker, who he quotes as writing in a letter: "I have swum in clear sweet waters all my days; and if sometimes they were a little cold, and the stream ran adverse and something rough, it was never too strong to be breasted and swum through."[3]

Those who are "once-born" are, to carry this metaphor further, robust swimmers, seemingly unperturbed by whatever rough waters might come their way. They do not lose sight of the other shore, and swim resolutely onward, in the belief that they will reach it. This is very much the case of many of the characters that we find in Shakespeare's early comedies and histories. Yes, the lovers of *Love's Labour's Lost*, *Much Ado About Nothing*, and *A Midsummer Night's Dream* all meet with a series of dire complications, but everything—ultimately—ends on a positive note, with everyone being made all the better for weathering such hardships. The same is true for Shakespeare's histories which, if we look at them in the order that they were penned, chronicle a movement from the darkness of the three parts of *Henry VI*, through *Richard III*, toward *Henry IV Part 1* and *Part 2*, ultimately reaching their glorious apotheosis in *Henry V*. There are also characters who do indeed resist the siren call of the once-born. There are such dramatic personages as Titus, Shylock, Don John, and—to a lesser extent—Jaques. But these discordant figures are outnumbered by a veritable army of lovers and warriors who swim onward, against the current, resolute in their goal. These are such figures as Andrew Aguecheek, Antipholus, Berowne, Bianca, Bolingbroke, Bottom, Catherine, Celia, Caesar, Claudio, Clarence, Demetrius, Dogberry, Doll Tearsheet, Don Alonso, Dromio, Duke Senior, Falstaff, Feste, Flute, Friar Lawrence, Hal, Helenia, Hermia, Hero, Hotspur, Jessica, Juliet, Kate, Lysander, Lancelot, Maria, Oberon, Olivia, Orlando, Orsino, Petruchio, Phoebe, Pistol, Portia, Puck, Mistress Quickly, Peter Quince, Richard II, Richard III, Romeo, Sebastian, Sir Toby, Titania, Theseus, Touchstone, Tybalt, and so on.

Now, I know what you're thinking. You're thinking, "Wait a minute, back up a bit. Just before Romeo did you *actually* add Richard III to the list of those who are 'once-born.'? In what universe is such a taxonomy possible?" Let me attempt to explain, beginning with warriors in general and then the specifics of a dramatic personage like Richard III. James believes that the consciousness of the warriors of ancient Greece and Rome may be "full to the brim of sad mortality," yet they still comport themselves very much within a "sunlit world" of order.[4] He cites the following passage of Homer to support his argument. It is the moment when Achilles is about to slay Lycaon, Priam's young son. He hears the boy beg for mercy and responds, "Ah, friend, thou too must die: why thus lamentest thou? . . . There cometh morn or eve or some noonday when my life too some man shall take in battle, whether with spear he smite, or arrow from the string."[5] James goes on,

> Then Achilles savagely severs the poor boy's neck with his sword, heaves him by the foot into the Scamander, and calls to the fishes of the river to eat the white fat of Lycaon. Just as here the cruelty and the sympathy both ring true, and do not mix to interfere with one another, so did the Greeks and Romans keep all their sadnesses and gladnesses unmingled and entire ... This integrity of instinctive reactions, this freedom from all moral sophistry and strain, gives a pathetic dignity to ancient pagan feeling.[6]

This is true for many of the warriors who carve their way through Shakespeare's bloody tetralogy. Some do succumb to the dark undertow of war; but most make it safely to shore, where they believe history will reward them for their actions. Even as problematic a character as Richard III has something of the once-born in him. How so? Once-borns, to switch metaphors, run undeterred to the finish line. If they should stumble, fall, and skin their knee, they pick themselves back up and continue running until they reach their goal. Richard, we could say, has been crippled by such a fall, tripped up by mother nature herself, which has kept him from fitting in. He is the first to tell us, in the greatest of detail, about his resulting disfigurement:

> I, that am curtailed of this fair proportion,
> Cheated of feature by dissembling nature,

Deformed, unfinished, sent before my time
Into this breathing world scarce half made up,
And so lamely and unfashionable
That dogs bark at me as I halt by them;
Why, I, in this weak piping time of peace,
Have no delight to pass away the time,
Unless to spy my shadow in the sun
And descant on mine own deformity.[7]

Now, most folks who had suffered Richard's fate might call it a day. They have suffered a great fall and they quietly retire to the sidelines. But Richard is not one of those people. Not only does he stand back up, but he resumes the race, telling us:

And therefore, since I cannot prove a lover
To entertain these fair well-spoken days,
I am determined to prove a villain
And hate the idle pleasures of these days.
Plots have I laid, inductions dangerous,
By drunken prophecies, libels, and dreams,
To set my brother Clarence and the King
In deadly hate the one against the other.[8]

It is this resilience that makes him one of the once-born. At first, there is something unnervingly infectious about this malice; we know we shouldn't root for Richard and yet, somehow, we can't help ourselves. Perhaps it is his once-born exuberance that distracts us from the mayhem he unleashes. Eventually, though, it catches up with us, and even with Richard himself. This brings us to the shores of:

The Twice-Born

Richard III, Richard II, Rosalind, Brutus, Beatrice, Benedict, and, of Course, Our Friend Hamlet

There is a fascinating moment late in Act 5 of *Richard III* where Richard wakes from a troubled sleep and asks himself: "What do I fear? Myself? There's none else by. / Richard loves Richard; that is I am I."[9] This last line, "I am I," is the Folio reading. This is, no doubt, a sly allusion to the moment where Moses asks God what his chosen people should call him and God responds simply, "Tell them I am who I am." This is also not that far off from Popeye, the 1920s cartoon character who identified himself as, "I yam what I yam." All three responses—those of God, Richard III, and Popeye—are very much in sync with the resolutely assured ego of

William James's once-born community. There is little room for doubt when one is once-born; things are simply what they are, end of story. But there is an earlier Quarto version of this line by Richard III which has Richard saying: "Richard loves Richard; that is I and I."[10] At first glance this difference might strike one as rather inconsequential; after all, it is just a little shift from "am" to "and"; but the resulting ramifications are actually enormous. To say "I am I" is to resolutely assert one's sense of self; but to say "I and I" opens up a breach between these two "I"s. There is one "I" and now it seems there is another "I" set in opposition to the first. How would one stage this Quarto version where we find Richard saying "I and I"? Perhaps we might have Richard looking into a mirror. There is one "I" that looks *into* the mirror and another I that looks *out from* the self-same mirror. Are they still the same "I"? Can Richard look into the mirror expecting to see his reflection and discover something or someone entirely other that is reflected back to him? Richard may think of himself as justified in his vengeance; but when he looks in the mirror, perhaps he sees another Richard: Richard as monster. Suddenly, there is a schism between these two Richards; a schizoid crack emerges in his consciousness. James quotes the author Alphonse Daudet, who experiences a similar splitting of self in what Daudet calls "Homo duplex." This is how Daudet describes this condition:

> The first time that I perceived that I was two was at the death of my brother Henri, when my father cried out so dramatically, "He is dead, he is dead!" While my first self wept, my second self thought, "How truly given was that cry, how fine it would be at the theatre." I was then fourteen years old. This horrible duality has often given me matter for reflection . . . how it sees into things, and how it mocks![11]

Think of such characters as Beatrice and Benedick in *Much Ado About Nothing*, who seem to carry on a similar bicameral relationship to love. They are the opposite of their young counterparts, Hero and Claudio, who are very much of the once-born variety, giving over fully to their oceanic feelings of love. Not so with Beatrice and Benedict, who are constantly aware of such romantic behavior as somehow ridiculous. They possess Daudet's second self, constantly mocking such emotions as love. It is from this detached vantage point that they can protect themselves and laugh at the once-born foolishness of others. And yet, they too are ultimately pulled by the gravitational force of eros which rends them in two, making them both critic *and* actor. This catches both by surprise. Benedick asks himself if he may be "converted" into a lover like Claudio; his tentative answer is, "I cannot tell; I think not."[12] But as the play progresses, he cannot help but find himself more and more under the spell of Beatrice until we find him composing a love sonnet. Here we see Daudet's Homo duplex in the moment of composition. Benedick enters singing: "The God of love / That sits above / And knows me, and knows me. . ."[13]

But he cannot sustain this performance that is better suited to the once-born. He will forever be twice-born, and he quickly moves from actor in his own love story to critic, deploring his inability to express himself in rhyme: "I have tried. I can find out no rhyme to 'lady' but 'baby'; an innocent rhyme. For 'scorn', 'horn'; a hard rhyme. For 'school', 'fool'; a babbling rhyme; very ominous endings. No, I was not born under a rhyming planet, nor I cannot woo in festival terms."[14] Similar challenges beset Beatrice who, when Benedick finally blurts out to her, "I do love nothing in the world so well as you. Is that not strange?"[15] responds in the language of the perfect twice-born/divided soul: "As strange as the thing I know not. It were as possible for me to say I loved nothing so well as you. But believe me not. And yet I lie not. I confess nothing, nor I deny nothing. I am sorry for my cousin."[16] Benedick, being a twice-born, knows a fellow twice-born when he sees one, and concludes from Beatrice's response, "By my sword, Beatrice, thou loves me."[17] What is true of Beatrice and Benedick is equally true of their dramatic cousin Rosalind in *As You Like It*. She is perhaps all the more divided, since she is tasked with being a woman who has to play being a man who (for Orlando's sake) is playing a woman. If that doesn't divide a self, I'm not sure what will.

And so, we begin to see that those who are once-born have a harmonious constitution which is balanced from the beginning. Their impulses are consistent with one another, every thought aligning behind the subject's will, ready to march wherever that will commands without a second thought. Those who are twice-born lack such inner consistency. The twice-born, in short, suffers from a certain discordancy, a riven psychic constitution. This is the trajectory of Richard III in Acts 4 and 5 of his play. We can see it at work on Brutus caught in the interim between "the acting of a dreadful thing / and the first motion" where "the state of man / Like to a little kingdom, suffers then / The nature of an insurrection."[18] The same chaos of thought can be found in the mind of Richard II as he sits alone in his cell awaiting death. Here, he tells us at the top of Act 5 that his mind cannot help but beget:

> A generation of still-breeding thoughts,
> And these same thoughts people this little world,
> In humours like the people of this world;
> For no thought is contented. The better sort,
> As thoughts of things divine, are intermix'd
> With scruples, and do set the word itself
> Against the word.[19]

This brings us to the shores of *Hamlet* where our noble Prince is equally torn between conflicting voices in his head. This tempest of thought finally winnows down to his famous existential dichotomy of "To be or not to be." When we reach *Hamlet*, we have arrived at the moment where if the contraries inherent in this divided state exist for too great a length of time, we begin to see how they can rend the psyche asunder, plunging a character like Hamlet into the abyss of what James calls:

The Sick Soul

From *Hamlet* to *Timon of Athens*

Some fortunate souls are able to remain once-born throughout their entire lives, many of us become twice-born, and a select few fall prey to what James calls the sick soul. This state usually comes upon us from out of the shadows, often when we least expect it. This how James sets the stage for the arrival of this sad fate:

> A chain is no stronger than its weakest link, and life is after all a chain. In the healthiest and most prosperous existence, how many links of illness, danger, and disaster are always interposed? Unsuspectedly from the bottom of every fountain of pleasure, as the old poet said, something bitter rises up: a touch of nausea, a falling dead of delight, a whiff of melancholy, things that sound a knell, for fugitive as they may be, they bring a feeling of coming from a deeper region and often have an appalling convincingness. The fuss of life ceases at their touch as a piano-string stops sounding when the damper falls on it. Of course the music can commence again; and again and again—at intervals. But with this the healthy-minded consciousness is left with an irremediable sense of precariousness. It is a bell with a crack.[20]

Or, as Hamlet famously explains to his friends Rosencrantz and Guildenstern:

> I have of late, but wherefore I know not, lost all my mirth,
> forgone all custom of exercises and, indeed, it goes so heavily
> with my disposition that this goodly frame the earth seems to
> me a sterile promontory, this most excellent canopy the air,
> look you, this brave overhanging firmament, this majestical
> roof fretted with golden fire, why it appeared nothing to me
> but a foul pestilent congregation of vapors.[21]

This is the new struggle that faces many of the characters that occupy this phase of Shakespeare's dramaturgy. It is a struggle that is perhaps best dramatized in *Twelfth Night*. It is here, with this play, that we can witness the all-out war between the first-borns (Viola, Sir Toby, Sir Andrew, Feste, and Maria) versus the sick souls (Olivia, Orsino, Malvolio, and Antonio). Scholars disagree over whether this comedy, which swings between joy and sorrow, precedes or follows *Hamlet*. What they can all agree on is that *Twelfth Night* is the last unequivocal victory of the once-borns over the sick souls and marks the end of Shakespeare's first phase as a writer. We will have to wait until Shakespeare's late Romances for the once-borns to once again carry the day. Yes, there are the alleged "happy endings" of *Measure for Measure* and *All's Well that Ends Well*, but thanks to the immense irony and ambiguity that infuses the finales of these works, one needs those scare quotes to prop up the phrase *happy ending* so that it does not completely collapse in on itself. Gone, in this phase, are any real once-borns. At best we have a handful of twice-born characters like Angelo and Isabella (*Measure for Measure*) or Helena (*All's Well*), but the rest of Shakespeare's characters from this period are pulled into the black hole of the sick soul.

After *Twelfth Night*, it is Hamlet's view of the dramatic terrain that now dominates the plays of Shakespeare. Here, all the color and vibrancy feels as though it has been squeezed from the world, leaving in its wake a desiccated black-and-white no-mans-land where a diaspora of sick souls wander about lamenting and raging against the impenetrable heavens. This sad processional includes: Barnardine, Bertram, Claudio, Coriolanus, Cressida, the Duke, Edmund, Froth, Gloucester, Goneril, the Ghost of Hamlet's father, Hamlet, Helena, Iago, Lady Macbeth, Lear, Macbeth, Mad Tom, Ophelia, Oswald, Othello, Parolles, Pander, Pompey, Regan, Seyton, Troilus, and, of course, those three weird sisters, aka the Witches.

The reign of the sick soul can begin innocently enough. It can be a mild melancholy, the likes of which Hamlet describes. It can be exacerbated by the thought of betrayal, as in *Othello*. It can, if left to fester, grow into madness as with Lear or Lady Macbeth, the latter of whom, we are told by her physician, "is troubled with thick-coming fancies / That keep her from her rest."[22] And on the other side of this madness? The final and most dreadful stage of the sick soul? Macbeth himself, who tells us:

> I have liv'd long enough: my way of life
> Is fall'n into the sere, the yellow leaf;
> And that which should accompany old age,
> As honor, love, obedience, troops of friends,
> I must not look to have; but in their stead,
> Curses, not loud, but deep, mouth-honour, breath,
> Which the poor heart would fain deny, and dare not.[23]

We are a stone's throw away from Macbeth's "To-morrow, and to-morrow, and to-morrow / Creeps in this petty pace from day to day / To the last syllable of recorded time"[24] and his final view from the abyss of nihilism: "It is a tale / Told by an idiot, full of sound and fury / Signifying nothing."[25] Aye, there's the rub: *signifying nothing*. Nothing matters any more: morals, the future, life itself, all are meaningless. Macbeth's nothing is the sibling of Lear's "never, never, never, never, never," which he howls to heavens in his fifth act. This is the universe of eternal negation, a world illuminated by Julia Kristeva's *Black Sun*. We have reached the deepest depths of the sick soul. This is where you will find Shakespeare's final victim, Timon of Athens, who tells us, before he takes his own life: "Lips, let four words go by and language end / What is amiss, plague and infection mend / Graves only be men's works and death their gain / Sun, hide thy beams. Timon hath done his reign."[26]

One would think, or at least surely understand, that Shakespeare, having reached these depths of despair, might want to put aside his pen for good and follow the advice of Hamlet, leaving the rest to silence. But he does not. He picks up his pen again and stages one final war between the sick souls and the once-borns. These final battles are now known as Shakespeare's Romances. It is a term he never employed but it has been offered up by scholars to help us see how these final plays are linked in a series of themes that goes against the current of Shakespeare's middle phase. In all honesty, we do not know if Shakespeare's psyche had gone through some significant sea-change (a word Shakespeare coins in his *Tempest*), or if he is just following the whims of his audiences, who seem to have lost patience with the tragic mode and now flock to the tragi-comedies of Beaumont and Fletcher. We will never know whether this shift is heartfelt or calculated; whether it is motivated by a change in Shakespeare's outlook or an eye toward box-office receipts. Regardless, these plays lead us to the new stage in Shakespeare's work that we could designate as a kind of:

Rebirth

From Pericles to Prospero

To be what I am calling reborn (and not to be confused with being "born again") is a state that James describes as being *regenerated*. It is to receive grace, and to gain assurance in the world again. It is a process where the sick soul becomes unified and the world returns to its former vibrancy, often all the more so for having been away for so very long. The sick soul is reborn and the fallen world is re-enchanted. This "new birth" can, as James tells us, be produced by the irruption into the individual's life by some new stimulus or passion.[27] This could be love, faith, a newfound vocation, or a change of location. The transformation can be sudden, but is usually gradual in nature. James cites Tolstoy, who tells us that one spring day, while walking alone in the forest, there arose in him a re-awakening to life, a sudden realization that the God that he thought had abandoned him was actually there, all about him; that this so-called God was simply *life itself, the life that flowed within and around him*. From that moment on, he explains:

Things cleared up within me and about me better than ever, and the light has never wholly died away. I was saved from suicide. Just how or when the change took place I cannot tell. But as insensibly and gradually as the face of life had been annulled within me, and I had reached my moral death-bed, just as gradually and imperceptibly did the energy of life come back. And what was strange was that this energy that came back was nothing new. It was my ancient Juvenile force of faith, the belief that the sole purpose of my life was to the better.[28]

This is the trajectory of the Romances. Here, the battle between the once-borns and the sick souls is waged one final time. The army of the first-borns include the formidable dramatis personae of Camillo, Cerimon, Belarius, Florizel, Gonzalo, Gower, Hermione, Imogen, Marina, Miranda, Paulina, Perdita, Simonides, and Thaisa. They are matched by such sickened souls as Alonso, Antiochus, Antonio, Autolycus, Bawd, Bolt, Caliban, Cleon, Dionyza, Iachimo, Leontes, Pericles, Polixenes, Posthumus, Prospero, and Sebastian. But in these final plays, it is the once-borns who now carry the day. Here, all sick souls are reborn and all fallen worlds are re-enchanted.

The operative end point of this process from sick soul to rebirth is wonder. This is the final destination of Shakespeare's Romances. These are dramatic realms "for men to see and, seeing, wonder at"[29], where "wonder and amazement"[30] reign supreme and "marks of wonder"[31] are everywhere, engendering a "notable passion of wonder"[32] in all. Where people are known to look upon one another and exclaim, "Oh you wonder"[33] and report that "such a deal of wonder is broken out" everywhere.[34] Wonder, as I have written elsewhere, is our response to the things that animate our imagination. This became something of a sixteenth-century phenomenon with the sudden profusion of what were called wonder cabinets. Here one could find exhibited a host of man-made and natural curiosities that were striking and remarkable, thereby engendering the wondrous. Heidegger designates wonder as one of humankind's basic attunements toward life (along with anxiety, boredom, and love). For Heidegger, wonder is not just reserved for what is out of the ordinary, but for the very ordinary itself. Wonder is at its most sublime when it takes the very things that have been dulled by the habits of our day-to-day quotidian existence and returns to them their essential uniqueness; or, as Heidegger puts it, "The most usual—whose usualness goes so far that it is not even known or noticed in its usualness—this most usual itself becomes, in wonder, what is most unusual."[35] Heidegger goes on to tell us, "In wonder, what is most usual of all and in all, i.e., everything, becomes the most unusual."[36] Thanks to wonder, everything is unique by the brute fact that it simply *is*. Aye, there's the rub: *is-ness*. Wonder returns us to *the magnificent is-ness of the world*.

Take Shakespeare's *The Winter's Tale*. Paulina, to protect Hermione from her vengeful husband, tells Leontes that his wife has died of a broken heart. Paulina allows this protective ruse to continue over sixteen years, long enough for Leontes to repent for his destructive behavior. Having done so, Paulina invites Leontes to see a statue of his wife. This, of course, is yet another of Paulina's ruses, for Hermione merely pretends to be a statue to see if her husband has indeed changed from his jealous and destructive ways. If so, then he would be worthy of her forgiveness. It is this dramatic conceit that sets the stage for the work of wonder that is about to overtake the play. It forces Leontes to marvel at this so lifelike statue and ask such questions as "What was he that did make it?"[37] And "What fine chisel could ever yet cut breath?"[38] It is hard, when hearing such questions, for us not to answer, "The Gods above." Here, the numinous and the quotidian meet and become one. Breath, this simple act, is indeed something of a miracle when you stop and think about it. But we rarely do, thanks to the deadening force of habit. The great irony of all of this is that such insights are always *in sight*; we are just dulled by the force of habit from seeing them.

Shakespeare's Romances are rigged for such recognitions which, when you get right down to it, are re-cognitions of ourselves and the world that envelops us. The result is a re-enchanting of that world, a momentary return to the rush of first-ness which must have filled Adam and Eve as they walked together in the Garden of Eden; or, when we as children first encountered the world beyond our crib, in all its sublime and infinite mystery. The Romances give us a glimpse of that long-lost Garden-of-Eden state, before we fall back once again into the blind habit of the day-to-day, a routine that dulls us from such appreciations. This makes seeing a Shakespearean Romance all the more necessary. For in these last plays, Shakespeare finds a way to reconnect us to the gift of being. It is at such moments that the heroes of the Romances will exclaim: "This, this: no more. You gods, your present kindness / Makes my past miseries sports"[39] or "If this be Magic, let it be an art / Lawful as eating."[40] Although *Much Ado* is not a Romance, it possesses perhaps one of the best articulations of the telos of these late plays. It comes toward the end of the fifth and final act of the play. Benedick enquires of Beatrice:

BENEDICK
    . . . And now tell me, how doth your cousin?
BEATRICE
    Very ill.
BENEDICK
    And how do you?
BEATRICE
    Very ill too.[41]

And it is here, right here, at this very moment, that Benedick utters what might as well be the very credo of this final phase in Shakespeare's work. It is only six little words, but they sum up the entire project of Shakespeare's Romances:

BENEDICK
Serve God, love me, and mend.[42]

It is that last monosyllabic word that perhaps says it all. If we were tasked with finding one word to sum up the Romances, and perhaps all of Shakespeare, this last little word just might be our best candidate: *mend*. There are of course three more Shakespeare plays after *The Tempest*: *Two Noble Kinsmen*, *Henry VIII*, and the now lost *Cardenio* (portions of which some scholars believe still remain in Lewis Theobald's reconstruction, which goes by the awkward Restoration title of *Double Falsehood*). These last works, each fascinating in their own right, are primarily collaborations with John Fletcher who, after Shakespeare's retirement to Stratford, was being groomed to become the new house playwright for the King's Men. These works become harder to categorize, since they seem to be less about Shakespeare's evolving dramatic sensibility and more about a senior author lending a hand in polishing a play or two for his old friends.

And So . . .

After working on several Shakespeare plays, I realized it was immensely helpful, for me, to know where the play I was working on was situated within the overall corpus of Shakespeare's plays. The more of the canon I worked on, the more associations I could draw across plays, which, as Wittgenstein points out, "create their own language and world."[43] Eventually I began to feel more and more that what were early, middle, and late plays were best defined by James's human stages from once-born, through twice-born and sick soul to rebirth. This larger picture helped me understand the fundamental shifts in Shakespeare's vision and how this comes to bear on the meter, language, and behavior of his plays. A character's diction and disposition changes radically from stage to stage. One can take a dynamic like jealousy and see how a given character's reaction to this state of being changes from play to play. Take the once-born stage of Claudio in *Much Ado*, through the multiple stages of the divided self of Othello, to the very apotheosis of the sick soul in Leontes of *The Winter's Tale*. It is the same emotion, but its manifestation in each case is deepened by where these characters are situated within the spectrum of James's stages of being. This was particularly true in how these characters express themselves in verse, becoming more and more complex from play to play and character to character. Claudio, who is once-born, sounds very much like a stock figure in a perfectly regulated world of iambic pentameter; but Othello's verse is constantly shifting, just as he is shifting within his twice-born consciousness; this finally leads to the sick-soul-dom of Leontes, whose verse sounds more like stream of consciousness (what he himself calls "chopped logic"[44]), as if anticipating such modernist authors as James Joyce. In short, it is the same emotion, but it could not be more different in terms of character and expression. This is one of the reasons that I have grown weary of what I call the one-size-fits-all approach to speaking Shakespeare's verse (an issue we will deal with later in this book). It is difficult to apply one standard set of rules that works for each of the discernible stages of Shakespeare's development. As a result, one really needs to develop a specific system for each stage. What is true of verse work is also true of world building. Situating these plays within such a spectrum begins to answer the question of "which Shakespeare" we might be dealing with; having done this, we can now move on to the more prosaic question of:

Which Text?

Let's return to Richard III who, when we last left him, was deep in the throes of his fifth act. He was, as you may remember, lost in thought, or perhaps looking at his reflection in a mirror. He has just said: "Richard loves Richard." And now we have come to a forked path in the text. We can either choose the **Folio** reading, which was so popular when I first read the play as an undergraduate student, where Richard goes on to resolutely say: "I **am** I." Or we can go with the now more generally accepted **Quarto** version, where Richard says: "I **and** I." This tiny change, as we have seen, has a huge impact on the trajectory of Richard's character arc. How did such a discrepancy come about, and how do we make an informed choice between the two? The problem begins with the several issues surrounding the publication and printing practices of Elizabethan play texts and creates something of a perfect bibliographic storm. The issue, in a nutshell, comes down to the basic fact that we do not have Shakespeare's plays in his own hand to use as a substantive text. This means we must rely on either the Quartos, published in Shakespeare's lifetime, or the First Folio that was published after Shakespeare's death. Many scholars prefer:

The Quartos

As perhaps the closest we can get to Shakespeare's actual authorial intention. The Quartos, as you may remember, are inexpensive pamphlet-style books that are folded twice, therefore making a total of four leaves or eight pages, hence the name Quarto. The Quartos were published during Shakespeare's lifetime and break down into two basic categories: Good Quartos and Bad Quartos. Good Quartos were believed to be based on Shakespeare's actual "foul papers" (i.e. first draft) or "fair copy" (a "cleaned-up" version, by either Shakespeare or a company scribe). Hardin Craig explains in *A New Look at Shakespeare's Quartos* that: "Normal practice in the supplying of plays to the theater brought into existence two texts:

the author's original or so-called 'foul papers' and a fair copy of the same . . . both sorts . . . found their way into the hands of printers."[45] This theory of transmission suggest the least amount of intervention between Shakespeare and the compositor. At most there might be a scribe coming between the two. Like the game of telephone, the fewer participants, the more chances that the message that is whispered from ear to ear will resemble what was first uttered. The Bad Quartos, on the other hand, are much more inexact and are now generally believed to be what are called memorial reconstructions. These are usually the work of an itinerant actor who might have had a bit part in a play, perhaps when it toured the provinces. Mary Maguire, in her book *Shakespearean Suspect Texts,* posits that many of these actors, upon their return to London, would sell their memory of a given play to the first available stationer, who was always looking to turn a quick profit by publishing a popular play, especially since acting companies worked hard to keep such valuable texts to themselves.

If this is so, why should we waste our precious preparatory time on a Bad Quarto when it seems nothing more than a bowdlerized copy of a Shakespeare play? One reason is that these Bad Quartos often possess a wealth of stage directions that are not found in either the Second Quarto or the Folio. This gives us a better/clearer idea of how the play might have initially been staged. In addition, the brevity of these texts may not always be the result of an actor's bad memory, but examples of how the acting company went about cutting Shakespeare for actual performances. Such texts could represent a pared-down version of a play that the company might have done on tour. This can give us a better sense of what audiences outside of London fancied. For these reasons, Bad Quartos still maintain a great deal of helpful performative information. When we combine Good and Bad Quartos, we have roughly twenty-two texts to compare and contrast:

GOOD QUARTOS	BAD QUARTOS
Titus Andronicus (1594)	*Romeo and Juliet* (1597)
Richard II (1597)	*The Taming of the Shrew* (1594)
Richard III (1597)	*Henry VI, Part 2* (1594)
Henry IV, Part I (1598)	*Henry VI, Part 3* (1595)
Love's Labor's Lost (1598)	*Henry V* (1600)
Romeo and Juliet (1599)	*The Merry Wives of Windsor* (1602)
Henry IV, Part 2 (1600)	*Hamlet* (1603)
The Merchant of Venice (1600)	*Pericles* (1608)
A Midsummer Night's Dream (1600)	
Much Ado About Nothing (1600)	
Hamlet (1608)	
King Lear (1608)	
Troilius and Cressida (1609)	
Othello (1622)	

Many scholars favor the Good Quartos of Shakespeare as a more authoritative text than the Folio since these were published in Shakespeare's lifetime and, as the argument goes, were most likely sourced from pages that came directly from Shakespeare's own hand. This does not necessarily mean that what was on those pages is what one might have seen on the stages of the Rose, Globe, or Blackfriars Theatres. Just because the text that constitutes Shakespeare's Quarto is what he might have gone into rehearsal with, it does not necessarily account for all the cuts, amendments, and improvisations (especially by Shakespeare's clowns) that reflect the combined acumen and whims of Shakespeare's acting company. This is where:

The Folio

Comes into the argument. Folio editions, as you may remember, are more expensively bound books printed on larger sheets of paper that have been folded once, making two leaves, or a total of four pages. The First Folio of Shakespeare was printed after his death in 1623 under the supervision of John Heminge and Henry Condell, who were chief shareholders in the King's Men (aka Shakespeare's company). It was printed by Isaac Jaggard. Charlton Hinman, in his two-volume scholarly magnum opus, *The Printing and Proof-Reading of the First Folio of Shakespeare*, tells us, "The printing was by no means a continuous operation ... work on the plays, begun not later than August of 1621, was presently interrupted for a period of more than a year in order to speed the completion of another book."[46] There were a total of six compositors who worked on the book. They are known simply as Compositors A, B, C, D, and E, and 'The Prentice Hand.' I must confess I am fascinated by these six individuals, who spent over a year of their lives painstakingly putting together Shakespeare's First Folio. It seems like a play waiting to be written by Tom Stoppard. All we know about them are their typographical idiosyncrasies, which is what has led to their individuation and ultimate alphabetical identification. For instance, Hinman tells us: "Fortunately Compositor B's preference for 'do' and 'go' and 'heere' (not to mention 'greeue' and 'yong' and 'Traitor') is both so strong and so peculiarly his that there is seldom any difficulty in determining what he set."[47] Whereas poor Compositor D's work "can by no means always be identified with confidence."[48] *But I digress!* Neil Freeman, the editor of *The Applause First Folio in Modern Type*, imagines that the manuscripts for each of the plays that made up the First Folio came from a variety of potential sources: "Some had already been printed. Some came from the playhouse complete with production details. Some had no theatrical input at all, but were handsomely copied out and easy to read. Some were supposedly very messy, complete with first draft scribbles and crossings out."[49]

The volume contains thirty-five plays that are divided into Comedies, Histories, and Tragedies (remember, Romance is a category that was invented by scholars to address the dynamics of Shakespeare's final works). There is also the last-minute addition of *Troilus and Cressida*, which is not mentioned in the initial table of contents. We will have to wait until the Third Folio of 1663 to get a text for Shakespeare's *Pericles*. For some scholars, these texts reflect the final thoughts on Shakespeare's plays that have been forged after they have gone through the crucible of first performances. These scholars argue that the Folio texts bear the markings of an informed series of amendments that seem to be responding to certain issues, often dramaturgical, that improve upon the Quarto versions of the play. Other scholars maintain that it is impossible to tell whether these are changes by Shakespeare, by his company, or both. If both, the question arises: did Shakespeare do this willingly, or under the collective pressure of the company? You see the problem that emerges: one text (the Quarto) may be closer to Shakespeare's intention, but does not necessarily reflect what actually ended up on stage (which may be better reflected by the Folio), and yet those changes may not necessarily align with Shakespeare's authorial vision, who may have bowed to the collective will of his company. So, what is one to do?

Blended Editions

When I was a student the common answer was a blended edition prepared by a noted Shakespearean scholar, who weighed the pros and cons of all the editions and came up with what they felt was the best of all textual worlds. There is nothing necessarily wrong with this approach, although we have entered a period where this sort of editorial intervention has fallen out of favor. It is similar to what happened in the world of early music. When I was a student, early music (the works of Monteverdi or Bach) was performed on modern instruments; now, the current fashion is that early music is played with the actual instruments that would have been employed at the time (i.e., instruments like the viola da gamba). In a similar manner, editors, directors, and actors have moved away from blended texts in favor of either the Quarto or Folio. This final choice between texts is often based on their own theories of which text is closer to Shakespeare's imagined intentions. One of the benefits of such an approach ends up being in the realm of punctuation; which, for many, might seem somewhat inconsequential, but actually has huge repercussions on the experience of a Shakespeare text in performance. Most blended texts that I grew up studying were heavily re-punctuated by modern editors. Punctuation has changed a great deal from Shakespeare's time to our own (we will cover this in more detail in our next chapter). For Shakespeare, punctuation was more for the ear of the audience, as opposed to our modern-day usage which is more for the eye of the reader. One of the big issues with modern blended editions of Shakespeare is that they tend to be overpunctuated, especially when it comes to the use of semicolons, which slow down the rapidity of a given line and ultimately, depending on the preponderance of semicolons, the speed of an entire show. On the other hand, many contemporary editors and directors feel that they want to stay faithful to either the Quarto or Folio punctuation. A significant number of scholars favor the punctuation of the Quarto over the Folio. They argue that the Quarto text has less intermediaries between Shakespeare's intention and what ends up on the printed page. In the case of the Quarto, one imagines the transmission to be pretty straightforward: from Shakespeare's text, through a possible clean copy prepared by a scribe, to the compositor's version. But that punctuation could have come from Shakespeare, the scribes, the compositors, or some combination of all three. With the Folio, we have to factor in the possibility of the acting company's further interventions. Again, we must also seriously consider myriad instances of potential composter error. This can still strike at either the Quarto or Folio level, which is why scholars want to look at all variants (the various Quartos and Folios) to arrive at an informed decision.

Differences From the Quarto to the Folio

Or, From the Infinitesimal to the Consequential

Let us look at two examples of common differences that can be found between the Quarto and the Folio. We'll begin with a small punctuational discrepancy that occurs in the fifth act of *Twelfth Night*. Sir Toby and Sir Andrew have arrived, both beaten and bruised from their altercation with Sebastian, whom they have mistaken for Cesario. They relate the injustice done to them and then, as they begin to exit, Sir Andrew says, "I'll help you, Sir Toby, because we'll be dressed together."[50] The Sir Toby of the Quarto responds:

Quarto

> Will you help? An ass-head and a coxcomb, and a knave, a thin-faced knave, a gull.[51]

The Folio has the same words, but different punctuation. It reads as follows:

Folio

> Will you help an Ass-head, and a coxcomb, & a knave: a thin-faced knave, a gull?[52]

The changes are so slight that they might go completely unnoticed. The Folio has omitted the question mark after "Will you help" and has replaced a comma with a colon between "a knave" and "a thin-faced knave." Now I know what you are thinking: "This feels like, to quote Shakespeare, 'much ado about nothing.'" But for some editors and actors, the ramifications of this shift in punctuation are huge. In the Quarto it is not exactly clear who exactly is the "ass-head/coxcomb/knave/gull." Sir Toby could be referring to himself, or commenting on the continued gullibility of Sir Andrew who, even after all Sir Toby's duping, is still fool enough to want to be his friend. The Folio omits the question mark and makes it clear that, in this instance, the "ass-head/coxcomb/knave/gull" is none other than Sir Toby himself. And so, depending on a whim of one piece of punctuation, we can end the relationship of Sir Toby and Sir Andrew on a note of unity or discord. Who is responsible for the appearance and disappearance of this seemingly innocent question mark? Shakespeare? The scribe? The prompter? The compositor? A member of the acting company who played the role of Sir Toby? It is impossible to know for certain. All we can do is arrive at our own choice based on our informed comparison of the Quarto to the Folio and what we believe to be the arc of Sir Toby and Sir Andrew's relationship. Often these changes seem to suggest that the Folio is a second draft of a given Shakespeare play, signifying a rethinking of the author or the acting company based on the initial performances of the play. This seems to be very much the case when we compare the Quarto of *King Lear* to its Folio version. Here are two versions of Lear's last moments:

Quarto

> And my poor fool is hanged. No, no life.
> Why should a dog, a horse, a rat have life,
> And thou no breath at all? O, thou wilt come no more.
> Never, never, never. Pray you, undo
> This button. Thank you, sir. O,O,O,O![53]

Compare this with the Folio (I have put in bold what has been changed or added):

Folio

> And my poor fool is hanged, No, no, **no** life.
> Why should a dog, a horse, a rat have life,
> And thou no breath at all? **Thou'lt** come no more.
> Never, never, never, **never, never.**
> Pray you, undo this button. Thank you, sir.
> **Do you see this? Look on her, look, her lips,**
> **Look there, look there.**
> **(He dies)**[54]

And so, in the Quarto version, Lear dies with no hope; whereas, in the Folio version he dies believing that Cordelia might still be alive ("Do you see this? Look on her, look, her lips / Look there, look there). I leave it you, dear reader, as to which ending is less nihilistic. I tend to look on the Folio version as actually rather transcendent. I mean, Lear is technically not delusional in this moment. The actress playing Cordelia is not actually dead and so she is indeed breathing. For me, this is an extraordinary moment of meta-theatrics that anticipates the theatre of Pirandello. At the beginning of the play, Kent implores Lear to "See better."[55] By the end of the Folio, Lear is finally doing just what Kent has asked: he is seeing so clearly that he sees beyond the theatrical conceit of this made-up world and has noticed that the actress playing Cordelia is actually alive. It would seem that these changes might be that of an author continuing to revise his work after its initial performances.

There are not only significant additions like this, but also equally significant omissions. Gone in *King Lear* is the mad trial scene where he condemns bits and pieces of furniture which he thinks are his heedless and neglectful daughters. Most editors hate to part with these moments; but for many theatre practitioners, the scene is redundant. We have seen Lear mad in the previous scenes and enough is enough; it is time for Lear to move to the next stage of his character's development. The same is true of another famous Folio omission: Hamlet's Act 4 soliloquy, "How all occasions do inform against me."[56] This entire speech is absent in the Folio. Why? Many argue that it is another example of dramatic redundancy; the audience is tired of seeing yet another soliloquy of Hamlet's indecision and so Shakespeare, the ever-shrewd playmaker, nixes a beautiful piece of writing for the good of the overall drama. Others might argue that the actor Richard Burbage demanded a longer break to ready himself for Act 5. Regardless of the reasoning, the speech is absent from the Folio. The director and actor must weigh the pros and cons of such omissions and decide what is best for their production. Since we are on the subject of *Hamlet*, let's turn our attention to unique textual status of this particular play.

The Three Hamlets

Bad Quarto, Second Quarto, and Folio

It seems somehow appropriate that one of Shakespeare's most intricate plays should also have one of the most complex textual histories. We are the beneficiaries of three very different *Hamlet* texts. These are: the Bad Quarto (1603), the Second Quarto (1604), and the Folio (1623). Let's start by understanding just how bad the Bad Quarto actually is by comparing its version of "To Be or Not to Be" with the version found in the Second Quarto:

BAD QUARTO	SECOND QUARTO
To be, or not to be - aye, there's the point.	To be or not to be – that is the question;
To die, to sleep—is that all? Ay, all.	Whether 'tis nobler in the mind to suffer
No, to sleep, to dream -ay, marry, there it goes,	The slings and arrows of outrageous fortune
For in that dream of death, when we're awaked	Or to take arms against a sea of troubles
And borne before an everlasting judge	And by opposing end them; to die: to sleep
From whence no passenger ever returned-	No more, and by a sleep to say we end
The undiscovered country, at whose sight	The thousand natural shocks
The happy smile and the accursed damned.[57]	That flesh is heir to . . .[58]

Earlier scholars believed the Bad Quarto to be Shakespeare's very first draft of *Hamlet*. But now, most scholars agree (after the pioneering work of W.W. Greg) that this is an example of a memorial text. Since there were no copyright laws at this time, all Shakespeare could do to retaliate was to publish his actual version of *Hamlet* as a way of saving himself the embarrassment of this other bastard edition that was out and about in the world with his name on it. Perhaps this explains why the title page of Shakespeare's Second Quarto reads:

THE
Tragicall Historie of
HAMLET
Prince of Denmarke
By William Shakespeare
Newly imprinted and enlarged to almost as much again
as it was, *according to the true and perfect coppie.*[59]

Favoring the Folio

I suppose, when all is said and done, I gravitate more toward the choices found in the Folio than the Quarto. I believe this preference often divides those who are scholars from those who are practitioners. Practitioners seem to sense in the Folio a myriad of choices and changes that have been born out of the realities of having performed these texts before audiences and the various lessons that have been learned from this. This seems particularly true to me with a play like *King Lear*, where the Quarto feels very much like a first draft of the play, and the Folio a second draft. But the changes found in, say, *Hamlet*, may simply be the company of actors imposing their collective will on poor old Will (or literally over Will's dead body). This certainly feels the case with *Macbeth*, where the draft that we possess in the Folio (the only extant version) may have been specifically shaped for touring. The common denominator for me, in terms of the majority of Folio plays, is that many bear the mark of either Shakespeare or the acting company's final thoughts on the best way of performing these works. This, of course, is very different from reading them, which can always be done at one's leisure. Theatre, being a time-based art, does not have this luxury and is often willing to lose a battle (cut "How all occasions do inform against me") in order to win the war (holding on to the audience's attention).

But What About Richard III?

Given that we'll never know whether a given variant is due to Shakespeare, Burbage, or a compositor error, what's an actor or director to do when faced with deciding whether Richard III says "I am I" or "I and I?" As I said, some forty or so years ago, when I was an innocent undergrad first studying this play, the standard editorial response was "I am I." But, some thirty years later when I was directing a production of *Richard III*, I learned that many editors had changed their minds on this issue. Now the favored variant is "I and I." This grows out of the current editorial wisdom which favors the less obvious choice. Why? These editors argue that Shakespeare is more prone to employ an inventive turn of phrase than the use of a common coinage. To these editors, it makes sense that the compositor saw the line "I and I" and thought, "That careless Shakespeare! He's always in such a rush to finish his plays, he's continually making mistakes like this, he doesn't mean "I and I," he means "I am I." Thank God I'm around to catch these things." This is a good lesson for us all to heed, in our continual desire to "fix" or properly "regulate" Shakespeare. This is true of editors who re-punctuate Shakespeare's plays to make better modern sense, but rob it of its dramatic rapidity. The same is true for editors who attempt to regulate Shakespeare's meter so that it behaves in a "proper" iambic manner. The problem with such an approach is that the power of iambic pentameter is not in its regularity but in the moments it becomes irregular and spirals out of control. *The rule is established so that it can be broken.* In these matters, rather than "fix" Shakespeare, we actually should just let Shakespeare be Shakespeare in all his wonderful and varied strangeness.

EXERCISE #1

I suspect you know what I'm going to ask you to do:

1 Decide where your Shakespeare play falls in terms of James's stages
   of:
   first-born
   twice-born
   sick soul
   rebirth.

   If you are dealing with the later plays, ask yourself which characters
   match which stage.

2 If your play exists in both Quarto and Folio formats, compare the two.
   After considering both, which would you choose? Or would you favor
   your own blending? There is nothing wrong with this third path of
   mixing and matching on your own. Remember: *these plays were
   assembled and reassembled to be performed outdoors, indoors, on
   tour, or at court, and one finds that these texts are amazingly malleable,
   as if this were something in the very DNA of the texts that allows them
   to be tinkered with in such a way.* In this respect, a Shakespeare text is
   a bit like a child's train set: the track can be laid a variety of ways.

Having done this we can move to the next phase of our prep work.

2 "And There is Much Music": Reading the Visible and Invisible Score of Shakespeare

"Words, Words, Words"

As Hamlet says when Polonius asks what it is he is reading. The first thing that strikes many of us about Shakespeare is his use of words: how strange, how beautiful, how lyrical, how very different from our own modern-day usage, and yet somehow the passage of centuries has not stopped us from getting the gist of what Shakespeare has to say. In the sixteenth century, he would have had at his disposal roughly some 150,000 words, and his vocabulary is estimated to have been somewhere in the vicinity of 20,000 to 30,000 words. Compare that to today, when the English language has grown, according to the Oxford English Dictionary, to about 600,000 words, with the average English speaker possessing a vocabulary of 50,000 words. And so, in actuality, we know more words than Shakespeare; if only we knew how to put them together the way he did. We are told that Shakespeare invented somewhere between 1,700 and 2,200 words. About half of these inventions are still deployed today, centuries after they were first coined. Here is a brief list of some of these alleged words:

admirable	half-blooded
barefaced	ill-tempered
catlike	jaded
distasteful	kickie-wickie
epileptic	lack-lustre
foul-mouthed	madcap
green-eyed	never-ending

overblown	useless
pale-faced	vasty
quarrelsome	worn out
rose-cheeked	yelping
sanctimonious	zany
tortive	

My favorite Shakespearean coinage is: sea-change. Many of these words were the result of having fused two already existing words together into new and expanded meanings. It is as if Shakespeare were like H.G. Wells's mad Dr. Moreau; only instead of grafting humans and animals, Shakespeare chose to experiment with the English language, creating a menagerie of lexical hybrids.

Shakespeare-ese

The Battle Between the Latinate and the Anglo-Saxon

Borges would joke that Shakespeare was not only impossible to translate into Spanish, but into English as well. This is "because if we were to translate Shakespeare into an English which is not the English of Shakespeare, a great deal would be lost. There are even sentences of Shakespeare's that only exist if pronounced with those same words, in the same order and with the same melody."[1] Part of this is due to a kind of euphonic battle that is being waged within Shakespeare's language. A war between Latinate and Anglo-Saxon words. Borges singles out the following phrase from *Macbeth* as the perfect example of this lexical skirmish:

> The multitudinous seas incarnadine,
> Making the green, one red.[2]

Borges observes that these two lines manage to mean the same thing twice, the first in splendid Latin and the second in ever-so-succinct Anglo-Saxon. It is here, according to Borges, that Shakespeare reveals his truly profound feeling for the English language, which he believes:

> Is perhaps unique among Western languages in its possession of what might be called a double register. For common words, for the ideas, say of a child, a rustic, a sailor, or a peasant, it has words of Saxon origin, and for intellectual matters it has words derived from Latin. These words are never precisely synonymous, there is always a nuance of differentiation: it is one thing to say, Saxonly, "dark"

and another thing to say "obscure"; one thing to say "brotherhood" and another to say "fraternity"; one thing—especially in poetry which depends on the atmosphere of words—to say Latinly, "unique" and another to say "single."[3]

We can see these shifting of registers in *Much Ado About Nothing*, where Benedick muses on the differences between himself and his young colleague, Claudio:

BENEDICK

I do much wonder that one man, seeing how much another man is a fool when he dedicates his behaviors to love, will, after he hath laughed at such shallow follies in others, become the argument of his own scorn by falling in love; and such a man is Claudio. I have known when there was no music with him but the drum and the fife; and now he rather hear the tabor and the pipe. I have known when he would have walked ten mile afoot to see a good armor; and now he will lie ten nights awake carving the fashion of a new doublet. He was wont to speak plain and to the purpose, like an honest man and a soldier; and now is he turned orthography; his words are a very fantastical banquet – just so many strange dishes.[4]

We can break these changes down into the following two categories: those phrases with a Latinate tendency; and those with a preferred Anglo-Saxon bent:

Anglo-Saxon/Firm	Latinate/Flowery
To see a good armor	Carving the fashion of a new doublet
Plain and to the purpose	Turned orthography
Like an honest man	A very fantastical banquet

The speech comes to life when the actor plays the changes between what Claudio was and what Claudio has become. This is a dynamic that runs throughout the entire canon of Shakespeare's work, and much humor is often rung out of these juxtapositions. My favorite example comes from *Macbeth*:

LENNOX [LATINATE]
    The night has been unruly. Where we lay,
    Our chimneys were blown down, and, as they say,
    Lamentings heard i' th' air, strange scream of
        Death
    And prophesying with accents terrible
    of dire combustion and confused events
    New hatched to th' woeful time: the obscure bird
    Clamored the livelong night. Some say, the earth
    Was feverous and did shake.

MACBETH [ANGLO-SAXON]
'Twas a rough night.[5]

In tandem with this double-voicing, there is also the matter of Shakespeare's:

Metrics

I suspect all of you who are reading this sentence have, at least, some vague recollection of the role of metrics in Shakespeare, perhaps dating back to your days in high school. I have to confess, metrics always felt like math to me and I was never very good at math. But the more I have worked on Shakespeare, the more I have grown to appreciate the metrical aspect of his art. Once you get into the swing of things, it stops being something that you silently beat out in your head and becomes something you just naturally feel, which is the whole point of iambic pentameter. It is supposed to mirror the way we actually speak. An *iamb* is made up of two simple beats (syllables), often transcribed as de-dum, basically one syllable that is unstressed (de) and the other syllable that is stressed (dum). It is usually notated as u = unstressed and / = stress or: u / . This type of notation is often scribbled just above the two iambic syllables and looks like this:

u /
de-dum

Pentameter, as I am sure you remember, means five of those de-dums in a row so that a standard iambic line goes:

u / *u* / *u* / *u* / *u* /
de-dum, de-dum, de-dum, de-dum, de-dum

This should feel natural to us, since the iambic beat mirrors our own heartbeat. You can't get more natural than that. It also turns out that:

u / *u* / *u* / *u* / *u* /
we tend to speak this way for days on end.

This is the basic rhythm of our bodies. So, if an iamb is a heartbeat, then its sister metric, the *trochee*, can be thought of as a heart attack. It goes:

dum-de

This is one syllable that is stressed (dum) followed by a syllable that is unstressed (de). It is usually notated as / = stress and u = unstressed, so that the notation for a trochee would be: / u. This feels terribly wrong to speak. Try it out loud:

/   u   /   u   /   u   /   u   /   u
dum-de, dum-de, dum-de, dum-de, dum-de

Go ahead, don't be shy, it's just you and me, right? If not, wait till later tonight, after your significant other goes to bed, sequester yourself in another room, shut the door, and just try whispering:

dum-de, dum-de, dum-de, dum-de, dum-de.

Doesn't it feel terribly wrong to do? As if you were doing something contrary to nature. The body rebels against it because it goes against the very beat of our heart. The most famous example of a string of trochees is in Act 5 of *King Lear* when Lear enters, carrying the corpse of his daughter Cordelia. He lays her on the ground and howls:

/   u   /   u   /   u   /   u   /   u
Never, never, never, never, never. [6]

And just a few lines after that, Lear expires. He has had both a figurative and a literal heart attack. Now, following on the heels of the iamb and the trochee comes the *pyrrhic*. The pyrrhic is de-de, or unstressed-unstressed. It is notated as:

u u
de-de

Pyrrhics help a line pick up speed; whereas our final metric, *spondee*, slows a line down by its double stress. This is notated as:

/   /
dum-dum

Metrics should ultimately become as simple and second nature as driving a car: an iamb is the speed limit, a pyrrhic speeds you up, a spondee slows you down, and a trochee is a pothole. A Shakespearean line does this naturally. First, by usually establishing an iambic rhythm and then, from there, it might speed up (pyrrhic), slow down (spondee), or trip us up (trochee). The whole point of iambic pentameter is not that it remains regular; but rather, that it becomes *irregular*. We can naturally feel those irregularities when a line wants to move a little faster or slower. Joseph Brodsky, the great poet, once said that iambic pentameter gives us the opportunity to experience the same ten seconds differently each time, line by line.

The beauty of this metrical scheme is in the subtle shifts. Let's look at them in action. These four scanned examples are cribbed from George T. Wright, who, as far as I am concerned, is the last word on all things metrical.[7] Here is his example of a straight-up iamb from *A Midsummer Night's Dream*:

u / u / u / u / u /
Ti-tan-ia wak'd and straight way lov'd an ass

The line is nice and orderly, skipping syllable by syllable to land on its ass. And now, from the same play, here's Wright's example of a trochaic moment:

/ **u** *u* / *u* / / *u* *u* /
met we on hill, in dale, **for-est,** or mead

I love how, in this verse line, it is the encounter and the forest that are both trochaic, throwing the line off-kilter. Isn't that exactly what love and forests do? And, continuing with our metrical tour of *Midsummer*, here is a wonderful pyrrhic moment:

u / **u** **u** u/ u/ u /
My Mist**ress with** a monster is in love.

Can you feel how this verse line picks up speed with these three unstressed beats in a row? Now compare this to one of Shakespeare's most famous (double) spondees, which brings this very line to a dead halt:

u / u/ u / / / / / u
The way to dusty death. **Out, out brief can**dle.

You will also note that this line has eleven beats rather than our usual ten, with the last syllable unstressed rather than stressed. The unstressed "dle" of candle does indeed feel like a candle extinguishing itself, with that one faint whiff of smoke dissipating in the air. Such extra-syllable lines are called feminine endings. We also have enjambed lines when a phrase spills from one verse line to the next. *The Winter's Tale* is rife with such moments of enjambment. Here is one from Leontes:

Go, play, boy, play: thy mother plays and I
Play too; but so disgrac'd a part, whose issue
Will hiss me to my grave: contempt and glamour
Will be my knell. . .[8]

See how these thoughts are incomplete. How, by the end of the verse line, they spill over into the next. This is typical of late Shakespeare. Compare this with the more orderly early Shakespeare; take Romeo, for example:

> But soft! what light through yonder window breaks?
> It is the east and Juliet is the sun!
> Arise fair sun and kill the envious moon
> Who is already sick and pale with grief
> That thou her maid art far more fair than she.[9]

You can immediately see how each verse line holds a self-contained meaning/image/idea. This is the quintessence of early Shakespeare, what we might call poetically curated thought.

When I got out of school, you couldn't show up for the first day of rehearsal without your entire part metrically scanned. Nowadays, during the first week of table work, I am always curious to discover if anyone still scans their parts. Not wanting to embarrass anyone, I wait until a ten-minute break transpires and then I wander around the rehearsal table, glancing at the actors' open scripts. It always amuses me that only actors of my generation still seem to feel compelled to "beat" out their texts in this metrical fashion, and their scripts are pockmarked with page after page of hastily penciled u and / marks floating above Shakespeare's verse line. This is not a judgment of those who do not, just an observation of changing times and practices. When I was finishing school the more "musical" kind of Shakespeare reading was giving way to a more "muscular" approach. Much of this has to do, I believe, with the advent of the Royal Shakespeare Company, which revolutionized the way we spoke and heard Shakespeare in the late twentieth century. Listen to John Gielgud and even Laurence Olivier and then compare them with Ian McKellen or Judi Dench. There is such a sea-change in delivery that if you didn't know the language, you might think these sets of actors were performing two entirely different authors. Is one closer to what Shakespeare might have intended? No one knows, and no one will ever know. Ours is a broken playing tradition. This is the nature of much Western Art. The East learned quicker than us about the necessity of passing down performative culture from generation to generation. I am always somewhat dubious when some Shakespeare practitioner says that they can trace the lineage of a certain approach all the way back to Shakespeare's leading actor, Richard Burbage. To me this is as fantastical as Michael Crichton's *Jurassic Park*, where dinosaurs can be resurrected from the genetic material found in equally ancient mosquitos preserved in amber. Good luck with that. Shakespeare tells us our work should hold a mirror up to nature, and since nature is constantly changing so too should its reflections. In this respect Shakespeare's verse is malleable, able to bend with the times. What is true with Shakespeare's verse is even more so with his:

Punctuation

As we noted in the previous chapter, and it bears repeating here, punctuation in Shakespeare is highly contested. We only have one example of a page of dramatic writing, from the manuscript for the play *Thomas More*, that is generally believed to be in Shakespeare's hand; and in these scant 147 lines there are just three punctuation marks, all periods (full stops). It is certainly much less than one would find in modern editors' editions of his work. At the end of the day, we don't know if the punctuation that comes down to us is that of Shakespeare, a copyist, a compositor, or a company member. G. Blakemore Evans, the editor of *The Riverside Shakespeare*, argues that if the punctuation we find in the Quartos or Folios are not Shakespeare's, "it was at least the work of his contemporaries, men in whom the rhythms and special emphasis of the language are alive and immediately felt."[10] Anthony Graham-White, in his *Punctuation and Its Dramatic Value in Shakespearean Drama*, notes:

> Probably the most striking and consistent difference between the punctuation in the sixteenth and seventeenth-century editions and the modern editions of English and Renaissance plays is that speeches in the former tend to be treated as single units—that is, the only period is often at the end of the speech—while modern editors break up the complex flow into shorter syntactic units and thus not only suggest a different rhythm of delivery to the actor but also inevitably strengthen the connection between some phrases and clauses while severing their connections in other directions.[11]

The result is that modern re-punctuation by many contemporary editors aims to bring out the sense of a passage often at the expense of the original rhythms of the text. What we do know is that punctuation in Shakespeare's time was more for the ear than the eye; for the orator rather than the reader. Walter J. Ong[12] reminds us that Renaissance still favored a grammar of the ear that dates back to the fourth century where:

> These marks were designed primarily to meet the demands of oral reading or for the declamation, and to meet them on a very practical level. They are breath marks in musical scores. It is convenient to place the breath pauses, and consequently the function marks, where they will not interfere with sense . . . so far as I have been able to find, these grammarians *never* refer to the position of a punctuation mark in terms of grammatical structure.[13]

Richard Mulcaster, the author of *The Elementarie* (1582), provides a ranking of punctuation. He begins with the comma, which demands the least breath, followed by the colon, which he suggests requires a half breath, followed by the period, which "warneth us to rest there, and to help our breath at full."[14] All the markings he catalogs "are helps to our breathing, and the distinct utterance of our speech."[15] Daines's *Orthoepia Anglicana* (1640) breaks things down in the following fashion:

> **The Comma** (is used) "only in long sentences, in the most convenient places to make a small pause for the necessity of breathing; or in Rhetoricall speeches . . . to make a kind of Emphasis and deliberation for the greater majesty or state of the Elocution."
>
> **The Semicolon** was not known to the Ancients, but has become what he calls the "pack horse" of long-winded sentences. It is "the time of pause about double that of the Comma generally, which yet is very small."
>
> **The Colon** "is chiefly used in the division of sentences, and exacts half the pause of a Period and half the as much againe" as a Semicolon.
>
> **The Period** "is altogether used at the end of every speech or sentence, as the name itself implies (being derived from the Greek) and signifies conclusion." When we find it at the end of a line (as opposed to falling in the the middle of a line) it is "four times as long as a Colon."[16]

Daines goes on to assign each of these punctuational marks a numeric weight ranging from one (the lightest weight) to four (the heaviest). And so, our comma = 1, semicolon = 2, colon = 3, and period = 4. Daines explains that he borrows this system from his singing master, who:

> Taught me to keep time, by telling from 1 to 4, according to the nature of the time I was to keep, and I found the practice, thereof much ease and certainty to me, till I was perfect in it. The same course I have used to my pupils in their reading, to inure them to the distinction of their pauses, and found it no less successful.[17]

A similar weights and measures exists to this day. I was taught the following:

> **The Period** = full stop
> **The Semicolon** = a half breath
> **The Comma** = a mental blink
> **The Dash** = rush whatever comes after
> **The Parenthesis** = rush what comes between the parenthesis.
> **Colon** = we will talk about in the section on First Folio Techniques.

In this land of weights and measures the period is king.

The Rule of the Period

This was how I was taught to begin to think about Shakespearean verse. The idea being to *play to the period of the sentence.* This is in direct contradiction of the idea of taking a little beat after each verse line. The idea of the rule of the period is that it favors the integrity of the entire thought as opposed to each verse line which contains components of that thought. In this way, it is easier to understand the idea of the sentence by moving as quickly to the period as possible. Imagine the period like a black hole, whose immense gravitation sucks all the words of the sentence into it. Following the rule of the period gives one a kind of instant X-ray of the skeletal structure of the speech, showing us the bones of each thought. Let's look at Romeo's famous balcony speech. Ignore all punctuation and just concentrate on the period. His first two lines (in the Folio version) are pretty easy going:

> He jests at scares that never felt a wound,
> But soft, what light through yonder window breaks?[18]

Two verse lines equals one sentence. Most actors tend to treat the comma after "wound" as though it were a period (full stop), but it is merely a comma (a mental blink). Our exercise immediately points out this difference. It also suggests that the appearance of Juliet comes right on the heels of Romeo's dismissal of his friends, catching him almost by surprise.

Now, let's continue. If you are reading this out loud, which you should, try also not to take a breath until you reach the period. In other words, let nothing get in the way of getting to the end of each sentence. Okay, ready? Set. Go:

> It is the East, and Juliet is the sun,
> Arise, fair sun, and kill the envious moon,
> Who is sick and pale with grief
> That thou her, maid, are far more fair than she,
> Be not her maid, since she is envious;
> Her vestal livery is but sick and green,
> And none but fools do wear it, cast it off:
> It is my lady, O it is my love, O that she knew she were,
> She speaks, yet she says nothing, what of that?[19]

Nine verse lines equals one sentence. Would you play the scene like that? Without any pause? NO! But the exercise begins to show you how the image of Juliet gets Romeo's imagination going. The exercise also reveals a hint of humor, that Juliet does something at the end that stumps him, brings him to a dead halt; had she not, he probably would have kept on going, image upon image, until he dropped. "What of that?" He stops, he ponders, and then . . . are you ready? Here we go again:

Her eye discourses; I will answer it:
I am too bold; 'tis not to me she speaks:
Two of the fairest stars in all the heaven,
Having some business, do entreat her eyes
To twinkle in their spheres till they return.[20]

From nine verse lines to five. Clearly Romeo is revving back up. Many editors turn the first two colons into periods. We will have more to say about colons in a little bit, but for now, please note that by not making them periods we get the feeling of Romeo's soliloquy as more steam of consciousness than poetic speech. Just one thought stumbling into another and another and another, until he comes up with beautiful images of her eyes as stars. He stops here, perhaps, to marvel at his own poetic inspiration. Perhaps he thinks this is his best metaphor yet. This seems to encourage him to keep going. You ready? Okay. Let's dive back in:

What if her eyes were there, they in her head,
The brightness of her cheek would shame those stars
As daylight doth a lamp; her eye in heaven
Would through the airy region stream so bright
That birds would sing and think it were not night:
See how she leans her cheek upon her hand.[21]

Six verse lines till our next stop. Again, please note the colon after "night." Most modern-day editors put a period there, but the colon suggests that he has almost completed his poetic metaphor when Juliet does yet another thing that brings him to a full stop. All she has to do is touch her cheek to make Romeo come to a crashing halt. He concludes, as he began the soliloquy, with two verse lines that equal one full sentence:

Oh, that I were a glove upon that hand,
That I might touch that cheek![22]

Through the rule of the period we begin to get a sense of the larger architectonic shape of the speech itself. We see how Romeo's imagination runs wild with metaphors about Juliet, only stopping when Juliet does something new that provokes yet another new flight of poetic fancy.

This happens again with Juliet uttering her first words in the scene: "Aye me."[23] This provokes a wonderful one-sentence response from Romeo: "She speaks."[24] And then he launches into his next and longest poetic revery:

Oh speak again, bright angel, for thou art
As glorious to this night, being o'er my head,

As is a winged messenger of heaven
Unto the upturned wondering eyes
Of mortals that fall back to gaze on him
When he bestrides the lazy puffing clouds
And sails upon the bosom of the air.[25]

Note that each of these poetic flights grows: the first ("Two of the fairest stars...")
is a mere three verse lines. The second ("What if her eyes...") grows to five verse
lines, and his final poetic burst ("Oh speak again, bright angel ...") is a full seven.
This is the music of Romeo's thought, made more self-evident by playing with the
rule of the period.

Speech Measures

This is a practice that I first encountered in Scott Kaiser's fantastic book, *Mastering
Shakespeare,* which I think is one of the best books for actors on speaking
Shakespearean verse. He describes a speech measure as a parcel of text that
contains one single acting choice. It is a unit of sense in which the actor can play a
thought, feeling, image, or action. Here a word or words become a vessel for the
actor to pour out a single moment of human behavior. Kaiser gives several terrific
examples of speech measures, moving from the most succinct to the most
labyrinthian:

—O
—Banished
—Damned Saint
—He jests at scars that never felt a wound.
—How art thou out of breath when thou hast breath / To say to me thou art
out of breath?[26]

Each of these are, indeed, discrete moments of complete and total actability. They
capture one thought, feeling, action, or image. You can live fully inside each of
these speech measures.

Let's begin with the simplest: O. Sound it out, live within that sounding, sound
it out again, elongate it, find the limits of its potential articulation. You could spend
an entire evening in your shower, tumbling this simple speech measure about. Go
on. You have to try it. Sound it out, along with me:

o
O
O

OO
OOO
OOOOOOOOOOOO

You want to keep tumbling this speech measure until it feels right, until it feels like one of your favorite articles of clothing, something lived in; by doing so, you find the time signature of each speech measure, of how it moves differently from what proceeds and follows it. The exact rate of utterance that feels right for you. In this way, you can arrive at a phrasing of a line like "He jests at scars that never felt a wound." Drive the words of that sentence to "wound" and it suddenly takes on a weight that stops the sentence dead in its tracks. This is the work of speech measures, and it augments the work of the rule of the period. In the ideal verse world, an actor is able to identify all the speech measures in a given speech *and yet keep moving to the end of the period.* It is kind of like patting your head (rule of the period) and rubbing your tummy (speech measures) at the same time. I think the greater the actor, the greater their sensitivity to speech measures. So that if there are, say, forty-five speech measures in a given speech, they are able to play all forty-five *and still observe the rule of the period at the same time.* With this in mind, we can return to the balcony scene of *Romeo and Juliet*, only this time let's follow Juliet and track her potential speech measures.

> Oh Romeo, Romeo, wherefore art thou Romeo?
> Deny thy father and refuse thy name;
> Or, if thou wilt not, be but sworn my love,
> And I'll no longer a Capulet.[27]

I count five potential speech measure in just the first line. They are as follows:

Speech Measure 1: O
Speech Measure 2: Romeo
Speech Measure 3: Romeo
Speech Measure 4: Wherefore art thou
Speech Measure 5: Romeo

Do you have to play all five? No. There is no right or wrong here. This is not like metrics. This is all open to interpretation. One actor might want to play this as three speech measures:

Speech Measure 1: O Romeo
Speech Measure 2: Romeo
Speech Measure 3: Wherefore art thou Romeo

One choice is not more correct. Again, this is the art of interpretation. This is one of the reasons we can see multiple Romeos and Juliets: we want to see how each brings these characters to life. Continuing with Juliet:

> 'Tis but thy name that is my enemy;
> Thou art thyself, though not a Montague.
> What's a "Montague?" It is nor hand, nor foot,
> Nor arm, nor face, nor any other part
> Belonging to a man. Oh, be some other name!
> What's in a name? That which we call a rose
> By any other word would smell so sweet;
> So Romeo would, were he not Romeo called,
> Retain that dear perfection which he owes
> Without title. Romeo, doff they name,
> And for thy name, which is no part of thee,
> Take all myself.[28]

All right. Let's break this down into potential speech measures. Remember there is no right or wrong here, just possible actable moments:

Speech Measure 1:	"'Tis but thy name that is my enemy"
Speech Measure 2:	"Thou art, thyself, though not a Montague"
Speech Measure 3:	"What's a "Montague?""
Speech Measure 4:	"It is nor hand"
Speech Measure 5:	"nor foot"
Speech Measure 6:	"nor arm"
Speech Measure 7:	"nor face"
Speech Measure 8:	"nor any other part/Belonging to a man"
Speech Measure 9:	"Oh"
Speech Measure 10:	"Be some other name!"
Speech Measure 11:	"What's in a name?"
Speech Measure 12:	"That which we call a rose / By any other word would smell as sweet / So Romeo would, were he not Romeo called / Retain that dear perfection which he owes/ Without title."
Speech Measure 13:	"Romeo, doff they name"
Speech Measure 14:	"And for thy name, which is no part of thee"
Speech Measure 15:	"Take all myself.

Now, I may want to revise Speech Measures Four, Five, and Six. Perhaps rethink them as:

Speech Measure 4: "It is nor hand, nor foot, nor arm, nor"
Speech Measure 5: " face"

This, of course, is what rehearsals are for: to find what ultimately works best through a continual process of discovery that can and should continue into performance. The point, at this juncture, is to be on the lookout for discrete and actable speech measures. In terms of preparation, I like to begin looking at a text in terms of the rule of period so that I can get that immediate X-ray of the skeleton of the thoughts. From there, I then want to break things down into discrete speech measures. I forget about the rule of the period and just live in each speech measure until I find the right weight/time signature, what some call "the rate of utterance": how the speech measure moves, slows down, picks up speed, in comparison with other speech measures. This ensures that everything *is not equally measured*. After I have a sense of the speech measures that make up the speech and how I want to play them, then I move back to the rule of the period to make sure that the speech measures do not completely overwhelm the sentence/thought. It is like the old saw of not being able to see the forest for the trees; there is a danger that one cannot see the sentence from the speech measures, if one is not careful. But by melding these two techniques together, one can achieve both specificity (speech measure) and flow (rule of the period). From here, I want to turn our attention to a closer examination of the Folio from the Quarto, based on what has come to be known as:

First Folio Practices

There also seems to be a certain amount of performative information that can be mined from the First Folio text. A close scrutiny of these performative aspects was first introduced in 1948 by Richard Flatter in his *Shakespeare's Producing Hand: A Study of his Marks of Expression to be Found in the First Folio*. Professor Flatter was a scholar of Shakespeare who also translated these works into his mother tongue of German. He also had the singular distinction of being a dramaturg for Max Reinhardt, one of the great German directors of the early twentieth century. This particular background made Flatter a unique figure for his time, someone who had one foot in the academy and the other foot in the actual profession of mounting plays. His book had a great deal to tell the English-speaking world about their Shakespeare; but being printed just after the Second World War, the English-speaking world still wasn't quite ready to listen to a former "enemy" talk about their beloved paragon of the English language. As a result, the work languished in relative obscurity until such recent theatre practitioners as Neil Freeman and Patrick Tucker brought Flatter's observations back to the light of day. The focus of all this collective work is often called the Original Practices approach to acting Shakespeare. It is based on the theory that the First Folio contains not only the final authoritative playing version of Shakespeare's plays (as far as his company was concerned) but also a wealth of performative information that is conveyed through the punctuation and other ignored aspects of the printed text. These theories continue to be hotly contested by many academic scholars who are very cognizant of the printing practices of Shakespeare's time and insist that many of these theories can be written off as either a compositor's whim or simple errors.

To help us begin to understand both sides of this debate, let's take a brief look at one of Hamlet's key speeches as it is laid out in the original Folio and compare it to a modern-day version of the same text. We are in Act 1, Scene 2 of *Hamlet*. Hamlet is alone on stage for the first time, when he turns to us, the audience, and says (in the third revised edition of the Arden Shakespeare based on the Second Quarto):

Modern Version Based on the Quarto

O that this too too sallied flesh would melt,
Thaw and resolve itself into a dew,
Or that the Everlasting had not fixed
His canon 'gainst self-slaughter. O God, God,
How weary, stale, flat and unprofitable
Seem to me all the uses of this world!
Fie on't, ah, fie, 'tis an unweeded garden
That grows to seed, things rank and gross in nature
Possess it merely. That it should come thus:[29]

Let's stop here and see how the Folio version renders these lines. I will make bold the various changes:

Folio

Oh that this too too **solid** Flesh would melt,
Thaw and resolve **it self** into a **D**ew.
Or that the Everlasting had not **fixt**
His Cannon 'gainst Self-slaughter. (*) O God, **O** God!
How weary, stale, flat, and unprofitable
Seemes to me all the uses of this world?
Fie on't, (*) **Oh fie, fie,** 'tis an unweeded Garden
That **growes** to Seed: Things rank, and gross in **N**ature
Possesse it meerely. (*) That it should come **to this:**[30]

Let's review the various discrepancies between these two versions. First, there is the famous difference between **sullied** and **solid**. Many editors gravitate toward the

Folio "solid" because it makes for a clearer antithesis with the desire to dissolve into a dew. Also note the capitalizing of **Flesh** and **Dew** in the Folio. Folio practitioners think that this is not a quirk of composer B (the fellow who typeset this speech) but a shorthand for what the actor should stress. Doing so makes Shakespeare's antithesis stand out for the audience. For a First Folio practitioner, this notion of capitalization as signifying what word to stress would also be true for: **C**annon, **S**elf-slaughter, **G**arden, **S**eeds, and **N**ature. These are the words an actor wants to "hit" so the sense of the line is clear. Next is **itself** vs. **it self**. This is truly a tiny thing, a product of how the modern eye thinks of this word, but for people interested in First Folio practices this is about the ear and hearing the silent space between "it" and "self." Is this how Shakespeare, his company, or the compositor heard/saw this word? We don't know. But the space between "it" and "self" becomes, for First Folio practitioners, an interesting grace note. The same is true for Elizabethan spellings. This is something that is often lost in modern editions of both the Quarto and the Folio. Those who follow First Folio practices want to respect the spellings of such words as **Seemes**, **growes**, **possesse**, **meerely**, all of which slightly alter the weight and duration of the given word. It is another set of grace notes that the First Folio practitioner savors. Editors like G. Blakemore Evans of *The Riverside Shakespeare* also prefer holding on to old spellings because, "Although the forms preserved may in many cases represent scribal or compositional choices rather than Shakespeare's own preferences, such an approach nevertheless suggests the kind of linguistic climate which he wrote and avoids unhistorical and sometimes insensitive leveling that full-scale modernization ... imposes."[31] Then there are the intriguing and much-disputed spaces, here noted by (*). For most scholars this is just an inconsistency of the compositor. For the First Folio practitioner, however, they can further emphasize the full stop of the period (more on this controversial issue later). Now we come to my favorite Folio additions: "O God, **O** God" instead of "O God, God". And "**Oh fie, fie**," rather than "ah, fie." I can't help but think that this comes from Richard Burbage, who played Hamlet. I can hear him insisting, "I don't give a good goddamn how it scans, it plays better this way!"

Another issue for followers of the First Folio is the nature and preponderance of colons which, for them, become another acting tip rather than a mere grammatical tic on the part of Shakespeare or the compositor. Here are two examples taken from the same speech by Hamlet, who is still bemoaning the unbecoming turn of events that have taken him from his father's funeral to his mother's remarriage. We'll pick up where we left off in the Folio version of the speech. I have put brackets ( ) around the colons so that they will stand out more to the eye:

> But two months dead (:) Nay, not so much; not two,
> So excellent a King, that was to this
> Hiperion to a Satyre (:) so loving to my Mother,

That he might not beteene the windes of heaven
Visit her face too roughly. Heaven and Earth
Must I remember (:) why she would hang on him,
As if encrease of Appetite had growne
By what it fed on; and yet within a month?
Let me not think on't (:) Frailty, thy name is woman.[32]

In each instance *the use of a colon seems to mark a fundamental change in thinking.* This can manifest itself as a reversal of thought ("Nay, not so much"), a new thought ("so loving to my mother"), a return to an old thought ("why she would hang on him"), or a sudden conclusion ("Frailty, thy name is woman").

These are not necessarily the punctuational quirks that can be attributed to Compositor B. We can see this happening in other plays that have been set by other compositors. We know this thanks to the extraordinary work of such scholars as Charlton Hinman (*The Printing and Proof-Reading of the First Folio of Shakespeare*). Here is Benedick from the Folio version of *Much Ado About Nothing*, typeset by Compositor C. In this passage, Benedict is contemplating whether he could ever fall in love like his friend Claudio.

One woman is faire, yet I am well (:) another is wise, yet I am well (:) another vertuous, yet I am well (:) but till all graces be in one woman, one woman shall not come in my grace (:) rich shee shall be, that's certaine (:) wise, or Ile never look on her (:) milde, or come not neere me (:) Noble, or not for an Angell (:) of good discourse (:) an excellent Musitian, and her haire shal be what colour it please God, hah! The Prince and Monsieur Love, I will hide me in the Arbor.[33]

As with our example in *Hamlet, each of these colons falls before a new thought occurs.* Here's one final example from the Folio of *King Lear*, typeset by Compositor E. We are in Act 5, Scene 3. Lear has just entered carrying Cordelia in his arms:

Howle, howle, howle (:) Oh you' are men of stones,
Had I your tongues and eyes, I'd use them so,
That Heavens vault should crack (:) She's gone for ever.
I know when one is dead, and when one lives,
She's dead as earth (:) Lend me a Looking-glasse,
If that her breath will mist or staine the stone,
Why then she lives.[34]

Here the colon is less grammatical marker and more musical notation. These colons, for me, are like the Xs on a pirate's map, signifying where the treasure of a new thought can be found.

Now that we've discussed some of the major points of First Folio practice, let's return to the balcony of *Romeo and Juliet* and see what helpful hints the Folio might have for us. I'll highlight all changes and use of colons, and I've added the notation: *(NEW THOUGHT)* to help us remember how these colons function for First Folio practitioners. All right, here we are, once more, with Romeo, beneath Juliet's balcony:

> But soft, what light through yonder window breaks?
> It is the East, and Juliet is the **Sunne,**
> Arise **faire S**un and kill the envious **Moone,**
> Who is already **sicke** and pale with **griefe,**
> That thou her Maid art far more **faire** then she (:) *(NEW THOUGHT)*
> Be not her Maid since she is envious,
> Her Vestal livery is but **sicke** and **greene,**
> And none but **fooles** do **weare** it, cast it off (:) *(NEW THOUGHT)*
> **It is my Lady, O it is my Love, O that she knew she were,**
> She **speakes,** yet she **sayes** nothing, what of that?
> Her eye discourses, I will **answere** it (:) *(NEW THOUGHT)*
> I am too bold 'tis not to me she **speakes** (:) *(NEW THOUGHT)*
> Two of the fairest **starres** in all the Heaven. . .[35]

Take note of the sixteen-beat verse line "It is my Lady, O it is my Love, O that she knew she were." This is most likely a compositor error, but a happy, almost John Cage-like accident that accentuates how the sight of Juliet completely undoes all sense of the regular iambic pentameter in Romeo. It is a mistake I would most definitely want to incorporate into the actual playing of the scene. Suffice to say, there is a lot for the director/actor to process once they get into the weeds of the First Folio. Are these typographical tics or actor tips? *Who knows?* Is it helpful? I must confess, I often find it so. Now, onto:

The Invisible Score of Events and Cores

There is also the invisible score to a Shakespeare text, which is of equal importance. This is not restricted to Shakespeare; it can be found in much of normative Western Theatre. It begins with the Greeks, runs through Shakespeare, and continues onto Chekhov and beyond. This is the score of Events and Cores. The Event is what happens to change a given situation from scene to scene, and the Core is what each of those events reveals (i.e., their subsequent meaning that emerges because of the Event). Think of Events and Cores as two sets of parallel dramatic integers. If we add up all the Events of play, we have its plot; if we add up all the Cores of a play, we have its theme. Say, for example, that you suddenly slapped me in the face. That slap would be the Event. My reaction is the Core. My Core, in this instance, could be to slap you back, to break down and cry, or to wait until you leave and then break down and cry. Each of these potential reactions reveals something particular about me, something that you would not necessarily have known without the Event of the slap. That is what makes the reaction a Core Moment, revealing something that would have remained hidden in my character. Now, you may respond to this analogy, "Well, that's all very well and good, but what does it have to do with the score of a Shakespeare text?" Good question. One of the first things about Events and Cores is that both are tied to our experience of time in the theatre.

Our sense of how time moves in the theatre has very little to do with speed. We can act a play with great speed and it can still feel slow; speed, you see, has a tendency to flatten things out, leading to an overall generalized feeling. In the theatre, what is general or undifferentiated quickly becomes boring and interminable; as a result, we begin to disengage. So, if speed does not move theatrical time along, *what does?* Events. Theatrical time is determined by Events; or, more precisely, the rhythm from one Event to the next. The more Events, the faster theatrical time moves. Two hours of an "eventful play" can whisk by; whereas ninety uneventful minutes can feel like a lifetime. Our sense of time (aka duration) depends on the magnitude of the Event and how that leads us to the next Event. Look at how quickly the sequence of Events drives a play like Shakespeare's *Macbeth*. We move from Macbeth's first encounter with the witches through the murder of King Duncan to Macbeth's own inevitable downfall as though the play itself were an express train. The work is driven onward by the relentlessness flow of Event upon Event, giving audiences little time to breathe. Now, compare this to Beckett's *Happy Days*, which is approximately the same actual running time as *Macbeth* and yet, thanks to the absence of Events, it seems to take twice as long when performed. A world where only Events occurred would be like our modern-day electronic games which are structured from Event to Event with no need for Cores (revelation/reflection) whatsoever. We go from destroying one thing to destroying a bigger thing and so on, and so on. These wall-to-wall Events create an ever-present *present*. Often, when we stop playing such games, we are shocked to learn that *three and a half hours has elapsed!* It seemed to us, we had only been playing for twenty or so minutes. This is the all-consuming spell-like power of Events.

Cores, like Events, have their own rhythm. As a general rule, we play to the Event. Events are like black holes; they draw energy into them, we cannot resist their extraordinary gravitational pull. The Event, like a magnet, pulls the scene ever forward; having done so, it gives way to the Core. A comment one often hears in the theatre is, "Such-and-such actor *earned* that moment." What this means is that the actor *played* to the Event of the scene so that they could take their time with a moment that is meaningful to them, a moment that reveals something about the character or the theme of the play. In other words, they *earned a Core Moment.*

Events are, in some ways, just excuses to get to Cores. Think of an Event as a car and the Core as the destination. You want to get to that destination as soon as you can to savor your time there.

So, if the Event speeds us along, then Cores allow us to slow down, pause, show the impact of the Event. To say that "such and such is a Core Moment" is like a composer saying to a musician, "This is legato." Or, it is like a director explaining to a cameraman that "This moment is a close-up." When one thinks of a Core, one should think: "Slow down/close up."

In other words, how can I make this moment stand out? There are two immediate ways: put air (silence) on either side of the Core and/or bring the Core Moment in closer proximity to the audience (downstage). These are the ways an audience can begin to feel the impact of Cores. Some directors, to insure the maximum clarity of a Core Moment, will not allow any pause in a scene until just before or just after an Event. Events are ultimately less significant than the Cores they produce. Events are mechanical plot points that propel the story forward. They are gunshots, slaps, fainting spells; whereas Cores are the realization or truth that ensues from these moments. The Event is a cause; the Core, the effect. Events have a tendency to be more rigorously defined. Cores are much more open, less rule-bound. Cores are interpretational. Events, which are singular, have the ability to open up a wide array of Cores. It is up to each interpreter to choose what is the most meaningful Core on either side of an Event. In this respect, the Event is constant from production to production (it is the province of the playwright), but the Core can vary (which is the province of each actor/director). Theatrical time is felt time rather than clock time, driven by the power and frequency of Events and Cores as they unfold over the course of the play. Most plays are made up of a sophisticated deployment of both, existing somewhere between *Macbeth* and *Happy Days*.

Theatrical temporality, if anything, is much like water. It can flow or it can be still; it can move at a somewhat sluggish rate, or carry us away with tremendous force; it can swallow us up or drain away. Theatrical time, in short, has its own unique liquidity. Now let's turn our attention to:

The Nature and Magnitude of Events

Events, as I said, are slightly more rule-based than Cores. They grow out of the late work of Stanislavsky and a small circle of his students. An Event must follow a discrete set of conditions to be considered an Event. These conditions are:

1   Events create, as we already noted, clear temporal demarcations, a distinct before and after, thanks to the Event's emergence. For many the birth of Jesus is such an Event, dividing all human history into either "Before Christ" or "After Death."

2 Events create polarity shifts. A polarity shift is a discernible change in tone or energy as a result of the Event's emergence.

3 Events tend be irreversible. Scenes are forever altered by the emergence of the Event. It is difficult for them to return to their earlier polarity.

4 Events engender further Events, creating a chain of happenings.

Events, as we said, are plot-driven. They are things like a slap in a face, a gunshot, an earthquake, a revolution. And they can happen on three different scales of magnitude:

1 **Micro Events** which demarcate the shift in a scene.

2 **Macro Events** which demarcate the shift in an act.

3 **Architectonic Events** which demarcate major storytelling moments of the play.

Let's turn our attention to these three types of Events, beginning with the smallest of these:

Micro Events

Are the discrete (or not so discrete) Events that change the polarity of a scene. They can be as deceptive as a seemingly inconsequential bit of new news, or as blatant as one character shooting another. Here are two Events drawn from *Hamlet*. The first is Act 1, Scene 2, where Horatio visits Hamlet. The scene begins with the two making the Elizabethan equivalent of small talk with such lines as "I am glad to see you well," "The same my lord," "And what make you from Wittenberg, Horatio?"[36] They talk about how "the funeral bak'd meats / did coldly furnish forth the marriage tables."[37] They talk about Hamlet's father: "He was a goodly king."[38] And then, finally, some thirty lines into the scene comes the **Micro Event:**

HORATIO
  "My lord, I think I saw him yesternight.
HAMLET
  Saw who?
HORATIO
  My lord, the King your father.[39]

This is the hinge of the whole scene. Before this moment, Hamlet and Horatio were engaged in small talk; after this revelation, they shift to a very consequential discussion of what has actually transpired, what it might mean, and what must now be done. With the shift in the direction of conversation (inconsequential to consequential) comes a shift in tone (from light to ominous). Finally, the scene can never return to its former state. Having clarified all this, the actors must now work to make this shift manifest in the playing of the scene. One of the simplest ways of arriving at the Event of a scene is to ask, "The scene started here and ended there; how did it get there?" In this case, it is clear that the shift happens with Horatio's revelation. The shift = the Event. It will lead to the next Micro Event of the act: Hamlet's decision to join the night watch and see whether this apparition is indeed the ghost of his father.

Our second example of Micro Events is drawn from Act 3, Scene 1 of *Hamlet*. This is the scene where Hamlet breaks off his relations with Ophelia. He has come to return her letters of love. He at first denies the sentiments of these letters but finally confesses, "I did love you once."[40] But this is no longer the case, as he has now foresworn love, which only breeds sinners like himself (this an Elizabethan version of "No, no, it's me, not you.") And then he implores her to escape this bawdy planet by becoming a nun ("Get thee to a nunnery").[41]

Up until this point, Hamlet is cold, distant, hard. But after his "Get thee to a nunnery" speech, he suddenly goes wild and begins to verbally abuse Ophelia in the most violent fashion. What accounts for this change from cold and distant to hot and bothered? In other words: is there an Event? Many pinpoint this shift happening around Hamlet's question:

HAMLET
    Where's your father?
OPHELIA
    At home, my lord.[42]

There is a playing tradition of adding a noise offstage just before Hamlet speaks this line, to account for the seemingly sudden and out-of-the-blue nature of Hamlet's question. This playing tradition suggests Hamlet's hearing of this noise signals to him that he is being spied on by Ophelia's father Polonius. This forces him to go back to playing "the mad Hamlet" which is his cover. But such an invented Event is not necessary. It is perfectly reasonable that Hamlet might, given the situation he is in, wonder aloud as to what provoked Ophelia to visit him unexpectedly. Perhaps he suddenly suspects this visit has something to do with her father's surveillance of him. The Event of the scene, for me, happens after Hamlet's question. It is Ophelia's lie: "At home, my lord." Ophelia is not a "good actress," she cannot dissemble effectively, and Hamlet sees through her ruse, realizes she is part of her father's trap, feels betrayed, and attacks her. This accounts for the change in Hamlet from cold to hot. This is the Event.

Macro Events

Macro Events deal with a major Event that organizes the actions of an entire act. It is an Event that, by its very nature, *impacts on everyone in the world of the play*. Macro Events can be tricky and are often easily confused between Micro Events of scenes and the larger Architectonic Events of the story proper. Macro Events are collective moments like certain social ceremonies (weddings, funerals), festivities (plays, sporting events) civil procedures (investigations, trails, elections), catastrophes of nature (storms, fires, earthquakes, plagues), or man-made catastrophes (war, insurrection, madness). What all these Events have in common is their ability to have a direct impact on the world of the play; everyone must respond to them, each in their own individualized way. Often each act of a play hubs around one such major Event. Let's look at how these Macro Events map onto the act structure of *Hamlet*:

Act 1: The wedding of Claudius and Gertrude
Act 2: Hamlet's sudden madness
Act 3: Hamlet's play
Act 4: Laertes' insurrection followed by Ophelia's suicide
Act 5: Fencing match between Hamlet and Leartes.

We can begin to see how the collective energy of each act is defined by these Macro Events. The Macro Event creates a certain pressure on the world of the play. This is in opposition to:

Architectonic Events

Which organize the unfolding of the play's major story points as a whole. There are four fundamental Architectonic Events:

1 **The Inciting Event.** This event puts the plot in motion.

2 **The Irrevocable Event**. This event radically changes the world and the very course of the play.

3 **The Penultimate Event.** The second-to-last major event that forces things to their final conclusion.

4 **The Culminating Event.** This event is the terminus for all previous events.

In *Hamlet* these Architectonic Events would be as follows:

1 **Inciting Event:** The night watch keeps seeing the Ghost of Hamlet's father.

2 **Irrevocable Event:** Hamlet meets the Ghost who demands that Hamlet kill Claudius.

3 **Penultimate Event:** Hamlet accidentally kills Polonius and is banished to England.

4 **Culminating Event:** Hamlet returns from banishment and kills Claudius, dying in the process.

Now, let's take a brief tour of Architectonic Events in five of Shakespeare's plays:

The Inciting Event

Romeo and Juliet: Romeo and Juliet fall in love.
Othello: Othello marries Desdemona.
King Lear: Lear steps down from power, divvying up his kingdom to his daughters.
Macbeth: Macbeth is told by the Weird Sisters that he will be king.
The Winter's Tale: Leontes believes that Hermione has been unfaithful to him.

The Irrevocable Event

Romeo and Juliet: Romeo kills Tybalt, leading to his banishment and separation from Juliet.
Othello: Iago insinuates that Desdemona is unfaithful.
King Lear: Feeling betrayed by his daughters, Lear goes mad.
Macbeth: Macbeth and Lady Macbeth murder Duncan to become King and Queen.
The Winter's Tale: Because of Leontes' mad jealously his son dies, his wife (we are led to believe) dies, and his newborn daughter is taken away to be exposed to the harsh elements of nature to die.

The Penultimate Event

Romeo and Juliet: The Friar plots Juliet's false death, believing it will reunite the lovers; the plan backfires.
Othello: Othello is given (false) proof (Desdemona's handkerchief) by Iago, proving in Othello's mind that his wife is unfaithful and this drives him to madness.
King Lear: Lear is reunited with his spurned daughter Cordelia.
Macbeth: Lady Macbeth, driven mad by guilt, dies.
The Winter's Tale: Leontes is reunited with his lost daughter Perdita.

The Culminating Event

Romeo and Juliet: The mutual deaths of Romeo and Juliet.

Othello: Othello, in a fit of jealous madness, murders Desdemona.

King Lear: Cordelia is killed, Lear dies heartbroken.

Macbeth: Macbeth is finally killed by Macduff.

The Winter's Tale: Leontes is reunited with Hermione, who we discover was not dead but in hiding for sixteen years.

These Architectonic Events possess the most dramatic heft. As theatre practitioners, we need to be aware of the weights and measures of all three modalities of Events, whether they are scenes (Micro Events), acts (Macro Events), or the arcs of the play as a whole (Architectonic Events). We ride these events to their end, often hoping against hope that it will not lead to the destination we suspect.

The Rhythmic Nature of Events

Micro and Macro Events draw all energy into them. One wants, in directing/acting terms, to play to the event. The Event is pulling the actors irrevocably toward it. If it is a love scene, the possibility of consummation draws the actors irrevocably toward the Event of their first kiss. If it is a murder scene, the possibility of a killing has a similar driving force. If a character is going to lose his job or become king, the Event of termination or coronation pulls one along to the cusp of its actuality. The rhythm of a play happens by moving from Event to Event to Event. *This is the play's music, determined by the arrangement of events.* When you look at Greek plays you find that Events have a tendency to happen at the center of each scene, giving these plays a kind of balanced, stately feeling. Think of / / a signifying the boundaries of a scene and think of . (a dot) as the event. With this system of notation in place, we can score a Greek play in the following fashion:

$$/./././././/$$

Each Event of a Greek play (particularly those of Sophocles) falls at the center of each scene. The result is a predictable, stately rhythm to the work; whereas, in a Shakespeare play, the events are far less regular. Shakespeare's events happen at radically different points in a given scene, giving it a kind of unstable, more surprising, lifelike feeling. The score of a Shakespeare act might resemble the following:

$$/ ./. / ./. /./ ./. //$$

Where the Event falls in a scene is much like where the stress falls in verse. Suddenly scenes feel like iambic pentameter, where they can shift from the reassuring regularity of iambs to the more unpredictable use of trochees, spondees, or pyrrhics. There is, in short, a kind of scansion that can be applied to the flow of Events. Now let us move to the Event's sibling:

Cores

Events, as we said, demarcate turning points: they change polarities, and shape time; but, perhaps most importantly, they have the ability to bring certain hidden things to light. Things that would otherwise go unseen are made visible by Events. We call such visibility and the meanings they engender Core Moments. If an Event is plot driven, then the Core is thematically inclined. Events traffic in happenings, Cores with their meanings. With Core Moments, we are given insight into the hidden motivations or potentialities of others. Much of this possibility can lay dormant for the lifetime of a character, waiting for a certain Event to make it manifest.

Often, these moments can be a revelation to the characters themselves; Events are what help us move from what Heidegger calls "seeming" to "being." The Core is a moment where this "being" is fleetingly glimpsed. Think of a being as a reclusive deer in the woods. The Event flushes the deer out into the open for us to momentarily catch sight of it. It is the chain of Events that ultimately brings a character into full view.

Cores are not just restricted to the hidden characteristics of individuals; they can also reveal the buried history of entire worlds, those hidden tendencies that are secretly at work just underneath the surface of the play. All of these things, by the pressure of Events, can be forced to reveal themselves. Cores are those moments of revelation.

Events will not only forward a plot, but deepen our understanding of those involved in the ever-unfolding story. We can argue that Events are ultimately mechanical; they are merely plot points constructed to bring forth a variety of Cores which can reveal character, or theme, or both simultaneously. Just as every Shakespeare scene has an Event, every scene has a resulting Core. Events are, by nature, rule-bound; but Cores are much more open to interpretation. Events, which are singular, have the ability to open up a wide variety of Cores. It is up to each interpreter to choose what is the most meaningful Core on either side of an Event.

Cores Growing Out of the Events Of Scenes

I have three favorite Cores that grow out of the scenes with Hamlet, beginning with the first scene between Hamlet and his old friends Rosencrantz and Guildenstern. The Event of the scene is Hamlet's getting them to confess that their arrival is not of their own prompting but by order of Claudius, who has asked them to report on Hamlet's aberrant behavior. Out of the Event of Rosencrantz and Guildenstern's confession comes Hamlet's admission that "I have of late, but wherefore, I know not, lost all my mirth."[43] Here, the whole scene slows to a beautiful halt and floats like the clouds that Polonius and Hamlet will later discuss.

Events and Cores often fall scene to scene like a series of trochees which, as you may remember, we notate as:

/ u
Dum-De

Events and Cores could be transcribed in a somewhat similar fashion:

e   c
Event – Core

I keep a running notation from scene to scene of each Event and Core. This becomes my informal flow chart, reminding me where every Event falls and, more importantly, *the duration of each Core, since each Core has a different length of resonance*. Some are quite brief and others as elongated as the musical line in a Mahler symphony. Here are two examples:

Scene 1   **Scene 2**
(. . . . . e c. . . . .)   (e . . . . . . ccccc . . . . .)

From the point of view of orchestration, I want to drive the scene to the event (notated as **e**) and then I want to pause/dwell during the ensuing core (notated as *c*). The length of the core is notated by the number of *c*s (short = **c**, medium = **ccc**, long = **cccccc**). *This becomes, for me, the score of the scene*. A good example of an elongated Core can be found in the last scene of Act 2 of *Hamlet*. The Event is the arrival of the traveling troupe of players and the Core is the Player King's Speech, the soliloquy of the death of Priam by Pyrrhus (Achilles' son). I would score this Event and Core in the following fashion:

SCENE:
EVENT: **CORE:**
Troupe entrance   **Player King's speech**
(. . . . . . . e . . . . .cccccccccccc. . . . .)

Again, **e** = Micro Event of acting company arrival and **cccc** = the Core of the Player King's speech. I keep a running tab of each scene, notating where the event falls in each scene and the length of the ensuing core until I have notated every scene in the act. This is how I build a score for each act. One drives from event to event and pauses for each core.

My final example is drawn from an observation by Hélène Cixous, who remarks that Shakespeare dramaturgy has such velocity (from Event to Event to Event) that he actually achieves whole scenes which, are in a way, almost entirely Core. In this respect, Shakespeare has created such narrative momentum, he has "earned" a moment's respite where the actor and the audience can catch their breath; where the plot can relax and the theme of the work can get out and stretch its legs. I think it is fine to think of such an entire scene as a Core Moment.

Such an example can be found in Act 5 of *Hamlet*, the famous gravedigger scene, which fits Hélène Cixious' criterion of a Dramatic Caesura Scene.[44] It does not, in any way, advance the plot, but allows us to meditate on the play's central theme of death, giving us one of the most iconic Core Moments in all of theatre: Hamlet, holding the skull of Yorick (the court jester) and musing: "Alas, poor Yorick. I knew him, Horatio. A fellow of infinite jest …"[45] I would notate such a scene in the following manner:

CAESURA SCENE

CORE:	EVENT:	CORE:
Hamlet at the graveside	Discovery of Yorick's skull	"Alas Poor Yorick" soliloquy
(.....ccccccccccccccc.	.............e.	..........ccccccccccccccc.....)

Other Caesura Scenes

Hélène Cixious refers us to the famous scene in *Henry V* where King Henry, in disguise, wanders his camp at night, overhearing his soldiers talk of their king and the coming battle, as another example of a Caesura Scene. I would add to this the drunken porter scene in *Macbeth,* and the extraordinary Act 5 Scene in *Othello* where Desdemona and Emilia are making a bed and small talk, unaware of their impending doom. These scenes exist as temporal islands, safe havens in an otherwise stormy ocean of Events. They are examples of time outside of time. None of these scenes advance the plot, but they do deepen our understanding of the character or theme of the play. These Core Moments of narrative reprieve function just like a caesura in one of Shakespeare's verse lines. It also reminds us, in the case of the scene between Desdemona and Emilia, how a quotidian moment can be as profound (if not more so) as any Event. With the exception of Desdemona's premonition of death, one could not find a more quotidian scene in all of Shakespeare: a bed being made, a lady undressing, gossip about a handsome young man, and the singing of a popular ballad to pass the time. But all of this takes on such profound, poignant significance because we, like Desdemona, intuit her ensuing death. Here, under Shakespeare's genius, small talk becomes Core. As profound and consequential as Hamlet's "To be or not to be," but all the more so because it is so far from such grand philosophic speechifying. It is just two friends talking, passing time, as one readies for bed. But it takes on such profound resonance thanks to its placement. Here, life—simple, unobtrusive, banal life—is made Core.

EXERCISE #2

Scoring the Play/Event Work

Create the following sets of scene division for an act of Shakespeare:

ACT ONE:
(Scene One) (Scene Two) (Scene Three) (Scene Four) (Scene Five)

Now Place an e where each Micro Event (or Events) fall(s) in the unfolding of a given scene. Remember, the event is what changes the fundamental situation of the scene. An example of this type of scoring could be:

(Scene One) (Scene Two) (Scene Three) (Scene Four) (Scene Five)
    e   e   e   e e   e

This, as we said, gives you the rhythm of the scene, since you want to always *play to the Event* (e). As we said earlier, most plays have one Micro Event per scene, but in some playwrights, like Shakespeare, you can find two to three events in a given scene. This gives the scene an **extra rhythmic jolt** (the scenic equivalent of a spondee).

Having done this, now add a **c** where the **core (the effect of the event) falls and its length** (series of small cs). Such a scoring of the text might end up looking something like:

(Scene One)   (Scene Two)   (Scene Three)
   e **c**   e **cc**   e **ccccc**

Remember to think of **core (c)** as: *Close up, slow down.* It is legato/lento in nature (the length of which is notated by the number of **c**s. If this were *Romeo and Juliet,* perhaps the first significant core is when they first meet and the longest core in the first half of the evening might be in the subsequent balcony scene where they shift from attraction to love. **For scoring purposes, we want to know where the event falls in the scene (you play to that) and how long the core is (what you take time to reveal on the other side of the event).**

These larger dynamic shifts lead us from Micro Events to Macro Events which impact on a given act. Let's render Macro Events with a capital E.

For Architectonic Events (the largest possible storytelling points) let's render them with a capitalized and bolded **E**. Cores for these types of events would follow suit with C = Macro Core and **C** = an Architectonic Core. And so the Macro Event of Act One of *Romeo and Juliet* would be their meeting at the dance. This is the inciting event and could be rendered as:

(The Capulet Party Scene)

E   e ccccc

E = is the Macro Event of the Act, the Capulet Party.

e = Micro Event Romeo kisses Juliet.

ccc = the core aftermath of the kiss. They are indeed attracted to one
    another.

The Architectonic Event which changes the world of the act could be the ensuing balcony scene where Romeo and Juliet go from attraction to falling in love. We could score this scene in the following fashion:

(Balcony Scene   )

e c c e   **E Ccccccccc**

e = Micro Event of Romeo seeing Juliet.

c = his core response to seeing Juliet (i.e., filled with wondrous desire).

c = Juliet's core soliloquy, musing on her attraction to Romeo ("what's in a
    name?")

e = the Micro Event of Juliet seeing Romeo and startled by his presence.

E = The **Inciting Architectonic Event:** Romeo and Juliet **FALL IN
    LOVE.**

Ccccccc = **The Architectonic Core** aftermath of this realization, their
    basking in this newfound emotion.

Note that this scene has two Micro Events/Cores *as well as* an Architectonic Event/Core. Also note the juxtaposition the first e c (the event of Romeo seeing Juliet and then the core of his musings) which is followed by the inverted c e (the core of Juliet musing about Romeo followed by the event of seeing him). Again, these shifts in energy give the scene its inner dynamics, similar to moving from a trochee (e c) to an iamb (c e). We want to become sensitive to these shifts in energy within a scene.

Now, if you add up all your events (micro, macro, and architectonic), you will have the basic plot of *Romeo and Juliet.* And if you add up all the cores (micro, macro, and architectonic), you will have the play's central theme(s).

All right, now take an act of the Shakespeare play you are working on and score an entire act.

3 "Wherefore Are These Things Hid?": Pattern Recognition in Shakespeare's Plays

Looking for Patterns

While reading Shakespeare and comparing the Folio and Quarto versions (if there is a Quarto version), I also begin looking for various patterns. These patterns could be in terms of the repetition of certain words, images, actions, situations, and/or subplots. Each can function much like Ariadne's thread, helping us through the interpretational labyrinth of a Shakespeare text. It is rather disconcerting when one realizes just how much patterning is actually at work in Shakespeare. What we first thought was a thread begins to multiply into a fine weave of shimmering associations, a veritable tapestry of varying significations. I'm often asked how conscious I think Shakespeare was about these sorts of things. One often feels, as I've noted earlier, that there is a kind of dream logic at work in these plays. Conscious or unconscious, the fact remains that these patterns are there, creating an aura of meaning. In Shakespeare there is not a precise destination where meaning resides. The work isn't like a pirate map where an X marks the spot of buried treasure. In Shakespeare, the treasure of meaning is dispersed all around us, often right there in plain sight, if only we'd bothered to pay close attention. Therefore, the best we can do is to take in the sights and see what impressions they make on us. Here, meaning is not so much arrived at, but *absorbed*, ever so gradually. That said, we must make our peace with the fact that even with all this work we will never reach the full meaning of these plays. This makes me think of the character of K in Kafka's *The Castle*. The clouds may slowly part and a castle of meaning may be discerned in the distance, but this does not mean we will ever actually reach it, or dwell inside of it. The best we can do is to admire its architecture from a distance. Part of this architecture is the very patterns which make up the bricks and mortar of Shakespeare's plays, including:

Patterning on a Cellular Level;
The Vowels of *Twelfth Night*

Patterning in Shakespeare can begin on an almost cellular level. Take the repetition of certain letters or vowels in *Twelfth Night*. Here, we find so many of the central characters sharing the same essential genetic/lexical material. Let's start with the preponderance of characters whose names possess an O or double O. There are the double Os of:

Orsino
Antonio
Malvolio

Who happen to be the most besotted with love (this is also true of other double O characters like Romeo and Othello). Then there are the single Os:

Viola
Curio
Olivia
Sir Toby

And then notice the prominence of A that runs through this set of characters:

Viola
Olivia
Maria
Fabian
Captain
Sebastian
Andrew Aguecheek

One begins to get a bit dizzy among the repetitions of all these As, Os, and double Os. Not to mention the double Es and Us of Aguecheek. As a result, it is not hard to sympathize with Malvolio when he stumbles upon a seemingly discarded letter and tries to tease out the identity of a figure whose name it is made up of: M.O.A.I. Malvolio's question mirrors our question: what, indeed, should all this "alphabetical position(ing) portend?"[1] Ever so slowly he realizes: "M.O.A.I. This simulation is not as the former. And yet to crush this a little, it would bow to me, for every one of these letters are in my name."[2] What is true for Malvolio is also true, as we have seen, for many characters of the play who, save for the letter M, share the other three vowels, just as we all share the same basic genetic material. In short: *we are made of the same stuff.* This is something that Malvolio simply cannot see. Remember, he later says to Sir Toby and company, "You are not of my Element."[3] But he is. All these characters are made out of the same grammatical stuff. This seeing and not seeing is at the very heart of *Twelfth Night* which, if you remember, is the festival that helps usher in the feast of the Epiphany. The epiphany of Shakespeare's play seems to be, in part, about how we all share the same secret set of divine vowels that both makes us who we are and also links us to one another. Here, the grammatical code of the play seems to intimate a far grander divine code for all of humanity.

Word as Theme, Variation, and Musical Notation

Let's take a simple little word like *bear* in *The Winter's Tale* and follow its development over the course of this mysterious play. When we first begin to hear this word it is in relation to bear as signifying a marking (sign). The word is first sounded by Camillo in Act 1, Scene 2:

> . . . but since
> Nor brass nor stone, nor parchment **bears** not one,
> Let villainy itself forswear't.[4]

At the end of this scene Camillo converts the meaning of the word *bear* from a sign/mark to a kind of mental weight (i.e., burdensome thought):

> . . . if it to be:
> If not, how best to **bear** it.[5]

This dichotomy between bear as sign or weight continues in the next series of appearances by the word:

> If therefore you dare trust my honesty,
> That lies enclosed in this trunk; which you
> Shall **bear** along impawn'd, away tonight.[6]

> Though he does **bear** some signs of me, yet you
> Have too much blood in him.[7]

Bear the boy hence, he shall not come about her"[8]

The centre is not big enough to **bear**
A school-boy's top.[9]

Nor night, nor day, no rest: it is but weakness
To **bear** the matter thus: mere weakness."[10]

This female bastard hence, and that thou **bear** it
To some remote and desert place. . .[11]

But then, at the end of this act, the word takes on a new reference, shifting from mark or weight, to become a ferocious creature. Here we find Antigonus telling the infant that they must now be exposed to nature:

. . . Come poor babe:
Some powerful spirit instructs the kites and ravens
To be thy nurses! Wolves and **bears**, they say,
Casting their savageness aside, have done
Like offices of pity. . .[12]

This, of course, will lead to one of the most famous stage directions in the history of Western Theatre:

Exit pursued by a **bear**.[13]

The next major evolution in the use of the word happens as we move to the sheep-shearing festival of Bohemia in Act 4, Scene 4, where a discussion ensues over two characters singing a song together. The shepherdess Mopsa says:

We can both sing it: if thou'lt **bear** a part, thou Shalt hear; 'tis in three parts.[14]

To which Autolycus, the rogue, slyly responds:

I can **bear** my part; you must know 'tis my occupation: have at it with you.[15]

Now, the word *bear* is moving toward the lexical connotations of "taking something on," "taking part in something," and that "something" is musical or sexual. Here, bearing has shifted from a singular task to a plural affair; first with two people, then three, then (in Act 5, Scene 3) an entire community. It is here that Paulina says to all assembled:

Then, good my lords, **bear** witness to his oath.[16]

This leads us to the final variation in the signification for the word *bear* throughout Act 5 where it takes on its full procreative connotation as in bringing things forth (i.e., bearing fruit). One Lord laments:

That which I shall report will **bear** no credit[17]

And then, finally, Leontes uses the word in its full procreative sense to talk about the life force itself. These are his words on first beholding the supposed statue of his wife Hermione:

... See, my lord,
Would you not deem it breath'd and that those veins
Did verily **bear** blood?[18]

It is at this point that the word seems to have run its full course of potential significations and thus mutates to the word for**bear** that Paulina uses for the remainder of the scene, to keep Leontes from discovering the truth of the statue. And so, if we review the journey of the word *bear*, it begins as a mark or a sign, becomes a physical or mental weight, then a ferocious beast, then a taking part communally or sexually, then an image of procreation itself, and finally a call for patience and consideration.

Now, what can you actually do with this information? Well, you can write a paper on the development of the word *bear* in Shakespeare's *The Winter's Tale*; it could even become a chapter in a scholarly book. But that is not my main concern. For me the shifting meanings of the word *bear* line up with the shifts in tone of the play. The word changes as the mood of the play changes. It becomes a shorthand for comprehending these tonal transformations. The word and its multiple usages become, for me, a kind of musical notion from Shakespeare as the composer of dramatic energies and so:

Bear as weight = Agitato (Acts 1, 2, 3)
Bear as ferocious creature = Furioso (Act 3, Scene 5)
Bear as taking part in = Con Amore (Act 4)
Bear as giving forth/bearing fruit = Dolce (Act 5)
Bear as forbearance = Con Spirito (Act 5)

This is where our work as theatre makers parts with the academy: we name these things not just to gain understanding but to make them felt by an audience. If they do not have an actual material impact on the tone, energy, or rhythm of the play, then such knowledge is merely academic. There is nothing wrong with that; it is just not our job. Theatre is not so much about naming; but rather, making things manifest.

Word Clusters

Scene One of *The Tempest* as a Lexical Invocation

Shakespeare can also put words together in a way that they become a kind of lexical weather. He does this literally and figuratively with the opening of *The Tempest*. I use this first scene as one of the first exercises that I do with my students (never actual professional actors, who, at least in New York, don't seem to have the patience for such things). We assign all the speaking parts to the class and then I ask them, while reading the scene out loud, to circle all the words that are repeated or related, as well as any strange words that stand out to them. The play, as you remember, begins on a ship in the midst of a storm. The ship bears the king, his son, and his entourage. But in the midst of a storm the hierarchy of the world is overturned and suddenly the lowly Boatswain is more important than the King himself; for it is the Boatswain, rather than the Master, whose expertise will see the ship safely through the storm. The scene shows the Master, Boatswain, and the King's entourage all contending with the storm and their fears. I will not replicate the scene here, but share the list of words that are repeated, related, or strange. Here is that list:

1	2	3	4	5	6	7
Boatswain	Cheerly	Pray	Cheerly	Down	Drowned	Prayers
Master	Cheerly	Below	Good	Topmast	Drowning	Drowning
Cheer	Yare	Boatswain	Hearts	Yare	A-hold	Hang'd
Good	Yare	Below	Drowning	Lower	A-hold	We split
Fall	Top sail	Good	Gallows	Lower	All lost	We split
Bestir	Tend	Cares	Good	Drown	All lost	Farewell
Bestir	Boatswain	King	Fate	Sink	To Prayers	Farewell
High	Care	Good	Hanging	Hang	To Prayers	Above
Hearts	Master	Elements	Hanged	Hang	All lost	Ground[19]

And the last word of the scene? None other than: *Death*. Now, once we peruse this list, we begin to discern certain patterns emerging. There is the pattern of status, "Boatswain, Master, King"; there is the pattern of verticality, "high, lower, below, down, top, fall, sink"; two types of death, "drowning and hanging," again vertical in nature. There is religion, "pray, prayers"; feelings of hope and despair, "cheer, cheerly, good, all lost, farewell"; and the extraordinary evocative words "Bestir/Bestir" and "We Split/We Split." The scene becomes a veritable index for the major themes of the play: the issue of power relations (master/servant relationships, or king/subject), the language of verticality which situates the characters between heaven and hell (the island becoming a kind of purgatorial space), allusions such as "lower, lower" and "we sink," give the play the feel of dreams, and the evocative cry of "we split, we split" almost feels pre-Jungian, suggesting a reading of the play where Prospero's psyche is split among Miranda, Ariel, and Caliban; with the play, itself, becoming an attempt at re-unifying these divisions of self.

Again, this is all well and good, you can—as I've said—go on to write an academic paper on this opening scene as an overture to the major themes of the play. But we're not engaged in writing a paper, we are attempting to make an evening of theatre. Because of this, I am much more interested in what these words do to you when you hear them. I want to encourage you to go back to the above list and read the words out loud, column by column, from column one to column seven. Go ahead and speak these words, give them full force, release your inner thespian. You will start to feel the spell-like, incantational quality of these words. Now, the interesting thing about these words is that on their own they are quite innocent, but when combined in this very particular way, they put you in a certain state. This is what Borges means by *the atmosphere of Shakespeare's language*. A kind of hypnosis which is taking you lower and lower into your unconscious. Suddenly words like "fall," "bestir, bestir," "below," "lower, lower," "sink," and "split" are working on your imagination, taking you somewhere deep within yourself. This is the place where Shakespeare's plays, which are made up of these very particular patternings of words, can continue to subliminally work on you. And so, on one level, the surface level of plot, these words are telling the story of a group of men battling the elements of a storm; but on another, deeper level, these same words are evoking a spiritual journey that conjures up images of the fall, death, and rebirth. We are at the heart of what makes Shakespeare uniquely Shakespeare.

Further Word Clusters in *Hamlet*

Much of this, as I've said, can go completely undetected by an audience. But I would insist that it is still secretly working away at you on a subliminal level. Another example of this sort of word clustering can be found in the opening scene of *Hamlet*, where Shakespeare tells us right off the bat what the play is about. It is in the very first line: "Who's there?"[20] Who indeed? And how do we go about knowing someone? Is it through what we hear about them or what we see? Where does truth reside? With the ear or with the eye? Ah, that is the other question of this mysterious play. Look at how Shakespeare sets up a dialectical patterning where the eye seems to be pitted against the ear throughout this opening scene. It becomes a major theme throughout *Hamlet*, his most metatheatrical of plays. Right from the start, we find both senses battling for pride of place. The night watchmen ask one another, obsessively, what they have seen and implore Horatio, the visiting scholar, to speak to the ghost. Let's take a closer look at this dialectical patterning of the scene:

1	2	3	4	5	6
Answer	Speak	Spoke	Watch	Voice	Says
Watch	Appear	Question	Tell	Speak	Sing
Hear	Ears	Speak	Watch	Speak	Say
Say	Seen	See	Whisper	Speak	Talk
Appear'd	Hear	Speak	Image	Speak	Heard
Seen	Illume	Speak	Appear'd	Speak	Look
Sight	Look	Speak	Watch	Show	Watch
Seen	Speak	Answer	Behold	Speak	Seen
Watch	Looks	Look	Illusion	Heard	Speak
Eyes	Mark	Eyes	Sound	Faded[21]	

In the first scene alone there are twenty-one references relating to sight and twenty-six references to hearing. Hamlet will alternate between both senses throughout the entire play as he tries to arrive at some semblance of truth. He will learn of the vulnerabilities of the ear, which can be victim to falsehoods and poison. The ghost tells us that it was through the "porches of my ears" that Claudius poured "the leperous distilment"[22] that killed him. Shakespeare, a master of words, knows how they can play games, cast spells, lie, and ultimately destroy us. This is the susceptibility of the ear; why it must, at times, be balanced by the eye. That is why Hamlet will resort to the ocular when he asks Horatio to use his eyes to see whether or not Claudius reveals his true self while watching the incriminating play-within-a-play. This same juxtaposition between sight and sound returns at the end of the play. Let's look at the last moments of Hamlet's life through to the arrival and final words of Fortinbras:

1	2	3	4	5	6
Look	Noise	See	Tell	Hear	Speak
Mutes	Hear	Cries	Mouth	Hear	Sight
Tell	Voice	Sight	Order	Speak	Speak
Report	Silence	Ears	View	Mouth	Sight
Tell	Sight	Hearing	Speak	Voice	Show[23]

In the end, Hamlet seems to have come to favor the ear over the eye, availing upon Horatio to tell his story once he is dead. This is in opposition to Fortinbras, Hamlet's princely rival, who seems more interested in showing the world Hamlet's dead body rather than staying to hear Horatio's tale of woe. If theatre is the blending of the powers of both eye and ear, it is still the ear that, for Shakespeare, seems to take pride of place.

Image Patterns

Let's return to *The Tempest* to continue our investigation of patterns. I want to look at a particular image that runs throughout the play. The image relates to men and wood; or, to be more clear, men trapped in wood; or, clearer still, men trapped by wood and longing to break free. This brings us back to the top of the play where we find a group of men, in the midst of a storm, trapped on a wooden boat, and fearing for their lives. A sixteenth-century nickname for such sailing ships was "the wooden coffin," since so many vessels found themselves buried at the bottom of the sea. This is what I would call a conjured image rather than a literal textual image, like that of water which is woven into the actual verse of the play where things are buried "five fathoms deep," or people are referred to as "standing water" that is learning how to "flow." These sorts of images are text-based, whereas the image pattern I am trying to tease out is a combination of text and context that evokes the play of further associational images. The next reference to men and wood comes from Prospero, who reminds Ariel of the time when s/he was punished by the witch Sycorax, who:

> . . . in her most unmitigable rage,
> Into a cloven pine; within which rift
> Imprison'd thou didst painfully remain
> A dozen years; within which time she died,
> And left thee there; where thou didst vent thy groans
> As fast as mill-wheels strike.[24]

Here again, we have the image of a figure encased in the actual wood of a tree, like the men trapped in the wooden coffin of their sailing vessel. Prospero continues his recounting:

> What torment I did find thee in; thy groans
> Did make wolves howl, and penetrate the breasts
> Of ever-angry bears: it was a torment
> To lay upon the damn'd, which Sycorax
> Could not again undo: it was mine Art,
> When I arrived and heard thee, that made gape
> The pine, and let thee out.[25]

This story could pass for a description of the scene we just saw on the boat, where we found a whole group of men groaning and howling in such a way that their torment pierced Miranda. These men, like Ariel, were ultimately released from the ship and into the sea, which, in this case, bore them safely to land. And so, with this, we can begin to discern a pattern of men trapped by wood.

This pattern continues in Act 3 with a stage direction that tells us, "Enter Ferdinand, bearing a log."[26] Part of Ferdinand's indentured service to Prospero is to fetch and stack logs. Here, a bit of stage business, like a word, has powerful associational possibilities. To see Ferdinand crossing the stage bearing a massive log might conjure another famous bearer of wood; think of Christ on his path from Gethsemane to Golgotha. Again, man, wood, entrapment, and death are all contained within this image; an image which is later subverted by Prospero when he renounces his ways and promises to "break my staff, / Bury it certain fathoms in the earth."[27] This marks his own liberation/release from the green-eyed monster, revenge. But what about the actor who is playing Prospero? It seems he too seeks liberation. In the end, he steps forward and addresses the audience, gently imploring us to:

> . . . release me from my bands
> With the help of your good hands.[28]

Suddenly we are no longer on an enchanted isle, but returned to the Globe Theatre, also known as "the wooden O." It is here in this theatrical encasement of wood that we are being told that without the use of our "good hands" (i.e., applause) the show cannot end, and our actor cannot go home. For it is this simple gesture that ensures the release of both actor and audience. This is Shakespeare doing his "Shakespeare thing," where he conflates the image of applause and the image of prayer, both of which require us to bring our hands together. Once, as is the case with prayer; multiple times, as is the desired case with theatre. Both of which have the ability to pierce/assault:

> Mercy itself, and frees all faults.
> As you from crimes would pardon'd be,
> Let your indulgence set me free.[29]

In other words, applaud/pray so we can all be released from the wooden theatre and our collective sins. Once again, we are faced with the question that continues to haunt our entire investigation of Shakespeare, how does knowledge of this pattern transcend the usual confines of literary criticism and speak directly to theatrical practice? Certainly this image captures the essential theme of the play: people entrapped (by their destructive behaviors) who are able to break through and reach liberation. They all arrive at the very last word of this play: "free." The question becomes *how to convert this theme into energy.* What does it mean for the actor to be caught, trapped in something that they cannot escape? What does it mean to be finally released? Here, the image pattern can be converted into a kind of Stanislavsky magic "as if" where the actor is asked to imagine Prospero as if he were buried alive in a coffin of revenge, and to imagine what it would feel like to be released from such a situation. Or to imagine you were stumbling under a literal cross you must bear: what would it feel like to have that weight finally lifted? This is the imaginative work that can grow out of an investigation of this particular image pattern. *It turns theme into thermodynamics*; energies that the actors can create and radiate to the audience. The theme/image becomes embodied and this embodiment can be sympathetically felt by an audience. This is our work as theatre makers. *It is the art of conversion. The art of embodiment. And the art of radiation. It is undertaken so that the audience understands the play not just intellectually, but on an intuitively felt level. Theatre becomes the space where we can feel a thought and think a feeling.*

A Plots, B Plots

Another pattern in Shakespeare is that of plotting. Often we will find that there is an A plot and a B plot, the most famous example being *King Lear*, where the plot involving Lear is mirrored in the subplot of Gloucester. A lesser looked at A Plot/B plot would be that of the Leontes storyline in the early part of *The Winter's Tale* and the Autolycus storyline in the latter half of the play. There are also examples of A, B, and C plots like *Much Ado About Nothing*, where we follow three stories: the story of Beatrice and Benedick, the story of Hero and Claudio, and the story of Dogberry. There are even A, B, C, D, E, and F plotted plays like *A Midsummer Night;s Dream*, where the play branches off into five distinct paths: those of Theseus and Hippolyta, Titania and Oberon, the Lovers, the Rude Mechanicals, and Titania and Bottom. One of the ways to understand Shakespeare's meaning is to figure out the common denominator at the center of each of these various plots. This is how one can navigate meaning in Shakespeare. In other words, we are back to the issue of the pattern: what particular pattern emerges when we compare these various plotlines. Let's take a brief look at the patterns in plotting as they unfold in *The Winter's Tale* (Basic A Plot/B Plot), *Much Ado* (A ,B, and C Plots), and *Midsummer* (A, B, C, D, E, and F Plots). We'll begin with the simplest plot patterning in *The Winter's Tale* where we are presented with a basic:

A PLOT	B PLOT
LEONTES' JEALOUSY	AUTOLYCUS' TRICKERY

Unlike the A plot and B Plot of King Lear and Gloucester, there is little that is immediately discernible in the relation between these two characters and their storylines. One is a great king, the other a lowly thief. One is a sovereign lord, the other the lord of misrule. Perhaps that is the first discernible pattern, that both characters "lord" over their parts of the play, Leontes in Sicila and Autolycus in

Bohemia. The next shared trait is their names, each of which conjure up a predatory animal: Leontes, the lion and Autolycus, the wolf. Following this animal imagery further, one could say both prey on innocents: Leontes on his wife, son, and newly born child; Autocylus on the naiveté of the Shepherd and his son. Both are ultimately tamed: Leontes repents for the destruction of his family and Autolycus for taking advantage of others. Leontes is forgiven by his wife and child and Autolycus by the Shepherd and his son. They are both brought back into the fold of the civilized world. This point is driven home late in the fifth act when Autolycus is confronted by five gentlemen, followed by the Shepherd and his son, who are now also gentlemen, and it is they that invite Autolycus to join them. The operative word in this scene (another pattern) is *gentlemen*, which appears some eleven times in quick succession (the scene itself is only some fifty lines in length). The repetition of the word begins to have an incantational quality to it and soon *gentlemen* morphs into *gentle man*, which is literally what Autolycus and Leontes will become. The journey of each story is that from beast (lion/wolf) to gentle man. We are able to understand the implication of the action (aka the unspoken meaning of the play) when we see how the A plot and the B plot align. Once we do the math, the secret point of the play reveals itself to us. We arrive at meaning by triangulating the A and B plot, finding the pattern or common denominators in each story. Now let's move onto the A, B, and C plotlines of *Much Ado*. They are as follows:

A PLOT	B PLOT	C PLOT
Beatrice and Benedick	Hero and Claudio	Dogberry and the Night Watch

Let's take Hero and Claudio out of the mix for a moment and just look at Beatrice, Benedick and Dogsberry. What could the amazingly urbane Beatrice and Benedick have in common with a ridiculous, half-literate fellow like Dogberry? Two things emerge: 1) All three have a high estimation of themselves (as wits); and 2) All three have terribly thin skins and are mortified of being made fun of. Think of the moment where Benedick reveals how hurt he is by Beatrice's estimation of him, "Oh, she misused me past the endurance of a block ... She told me ... that I was the Prince's jester, that I was duller than a great thaw ... She speaks poniards and every word stabs!"[30] Now compare this to Dogberry when he is called an ass. He responds in the same mortified manner as Benedick:

Dost thou suspect my place? Dost thou suspect my years? Oh, that he were here to write me down an ass! I am a wise fellow, and which is more, an officer, and which is more, a householder, and which is more, as pretty a piece of flesh as any is in Messina, and one that knows the law, go to, and a rich fellow enough, go to, and a fellow that hath had losses, and one that hath two gowns and everything handsome about him. Bring him away. Oh that I had been writ down an ass![31]

Now, let's bring Claudio into this orbit, and it becomes clear that he too is afraid of being thought less of, or, in this case, as a cuckold. In all these instances, all four fear how others perceive them. This fear stands in the way of their happiness. In short, the problem for each is not the other, but themselves, *their egos*. This issue is picked up again in *A Midsummer's Night's Dream*, where instead of following three storylines, we are now ask to follow six.

PLOT A	PLOT B	PLOT C	PLOT D	PLOT E	PLOT F
Theseus and Hippolyta	The Lovers	The Rude Mechanicals	Oberon and Titania	Bottom and Titania	Play about Pyramus and Thisbe

Again, the question becomes, what pattern emerges when we compare these disparate narrative paths that run through Shakespeare's wooded comedy? We can begin to discern a pattern with plots A, B, D, E, and F, since they all have to do with lovers falling in and out of love. But what, if anything, does the story of a bunch of men rehearsing a bad play have to with these variations on a theme of love? Is it just that they are rehearsing a play about lovers, or is there some deeper connection that ties all these stories together? Here, as in *Much Ado*, it is the silliest plotline, the one focusing on the Rude Mechanicals, where the secret meaning seems to be hidden. Bottom, like Dogberry, holds the key. The two have a lot in common, with both reduced to being an ass; one figuratively (Dogberry), the other literally (Bottom). I often wonder if they were played by the same actor. If so, it must have been doubly amusing for an Elizabethan audience to see the actor who insisted he wasn't an ass in *Much Ado* become one in *Midsummer*. Be that as it may (or may not be), Bottom's ego is the Rosetta Stone in which to decipher the other plotlines. For it is Bottom's inability to "play well with others" (i.e., rehearsing the play-within-a-play) that signals a similar initial problem with Theseus/Hippolyta, Titania/Oberon, and the young lovers, all of whom seem to want to control the ones they love. Part of the process of the play is watching those who can let go of control (Hippolyta, Titania, and Bottom) and how their relationships flourish as a result. In the end, everyone seems to be harmonious except the lovers, who have not actually gone through the work of the other couples. We are only able to understand all this through observing Shakespeare's patterning of dynamics. This has to do with what I call actional rhymes that run from character to character. In the case of *Much Ado*, the actional rhyme for Beatrice, Benedick, Claudio, and Dogberry, is to "look good" in the eyes of others, no matter what the cost. In the case of *Midsummer*, the actional rhyme between Theseus/Hippolyta, Oberon/Titania, Peter Quince/Bottom, and the young lovers, is "control" (i.e., "who's the boss"). With this in mind, let's turn to two tragedies, *King Lear* and *Hamlet*, and see how this last and least understood form of patterning works.

Actional Rhymes Within Shakespeare's Multiple Plots

In *King Lear*, the actional rhyme of both Lear and Gloucester is neglect. These two fathers favor one child (Cordelia and Edgar respectively) at the expense of their other children (Regan, Goneril, Edmund). This results in engendering an all-pervasive envy that ultimately curdles into malice. We could chart this actional rhyme in the following fashion:

A PLOT

Lear Favors Cordelia and neglects Regan and Goneril.

B PLOT

Gloucester Favors Edgar (his legitimate son) and neglects Edmund (his bastard child).

Which results in the following actional response from their children:

C PLOT

REGAN, GONERIL, EDMUND

Reject and punish their fathers for their lack of being properly cared for.

By understanding the actional rhymes of a play we can begin to tease out the larger issue which is the ultimate implication of the action. The implication of this action of neglect has devastating consequences for Lear and Gloucester's respective families and for the nation as a whole. Later we see that Lear has favored his court at the expense of his people. By following the actional rhymes we are able to begin to discern the overarching authorial intention behind the action. We can discern this in an even more complicated actional rhyming that happens in *Hamlet*, where we find four sons who are all asked to do the will of their fathers:

A PLOT	**B PLOT**	**C PLOT**	**D PLOT**
HAMLET	**LAERTES**	**FORTINBRAS**	**PYRRHUS**
To do the will of his father by killing Claudius.	To do the will of his father by killing Hamlet.	To do the will of his father by regaining the lands his father lost.	To do the will of his father (Achilles) by killing Priam.

Having established this actional pattern we can begin to discern who deviates from the rhyme. In this respect our chart suddenly shifts to:

FORTINBRAS	PYRRHUS	LAERTES	HAMLET
Over the entire course of the play never seems to waver in fulfilling the will of his father.	Pauses for a brief moment before he fulfills the will of his father.	Restrains his desire to fulfill the will of his father to the most opportune time.	Takes the entire play to fulfill the will of his father.

Suddenly the variation in the actional pattern begins to tell us something about the potential implication of the action in *Hamlet*. The pattern raises the question: what are we to make of Hamlet's procrastination? Particularly in light of this actional spectrum between Fortinbras, who never seems to waver in his duty, and Hamlet, who waits until the final moments of the final act to do his father's bidding? How are we to read these two men who are tasked with the same action and yet execute it on such radically different timetables? Suddenly Hamlet's comments to Horatio take on an added significance:

HAMLET

There is special providence in the fall of a sparrow. If it be, 'tis not to come. If it be not to come, it will be now. If it be not now, yet it will come. The readiness is all, since no man of aught he leaves knows what is't to leave betimes.[32]

With the aid of this actional pattern we begin to tease out one possible reading of the play where the concern becomes *one of the readiness necessary to take right action*. The play, based on such a reading, seems to ask: how does someone arrive at the necessary preparedness to act accordingly? This becomes a way of understanding Hamlet's progression through the play, *a journey toward readiness*. The tragedy of this specific journey is perhaps that Hamlet arrives at this ability too late, making the play a cautionary tale for young princes-in-the-making, like the soon-to-be King James. This is, of course, one potential reading of an immensely mysterious play. But it shows how actionality is another key pattern in Shakespeare's dramaturgy.

EXERCISE #3

Pattern Work

Jot down answers to the following questions:

1 What is the pattern of key words in the text?
2 What is the pattern of word clusters that make up the opening and final scene of the play you are working on?

3 What is the pattern of imagery?

4 What is the patterning of embedded subplots?

5 How do these subplots help reveal the major thematics of the play?

6 What is the pattern of actional rhymes that emerges in the play?

7 How can you translate these patterns into meaning, energy, rhythms, and images for your production?

Now: Work with these words and images to evoke, embody, and radiate energy.

4 "Your Actions Are My Dreams": Structure and Shakespeare

Shakespeare and Structure

All of these previous techniques can be immensely helpful in terms of starting to understand the various moving parts of a Shakespeare play. But what about getting a sense of the whole; or, more to the point, how does one shape the work toward a sense of wholeness? This speaks to a larger set of questions: Can we discern a constant to Shakespeare's plays that undergirds it no matter whether we are dealing with Early, Middle, or Late Shakespeare? Something that even transcends whether we are working on a Comedy, History, Tragedy, or Romance? I think we can. Shakespeare's plays move in a very particular way. This ultimately becomes a question of structure.

Now, the sort of structure that I am talking about comes in two sizes: big and small. Structure with a small s is the basic architectonics of the story; it's how Shakespeare goes about building his houses of meaning, how he keeps returning to the same materials over and over again to make them. This is the patterning of the story which holds all those other, smaller, patterns (themes, images, and words). There is also Structure with a big S. Think: the school of structuralism where the focus is on the relationships of contrast between elements in a conceptual system that reflect a deeper pattern which often passes as difference. This form of structure has gotten something of a a bum rap. It was pretty much invented by the French (thanks, Claude Lévi-Strauss) and, as is their wont, was almost immediately discarded a decade or so later (thanks, Jacques Derrida). When it comes to concepts, it seems, the French are like a child with a toy, happy with it until another bright shiny thing comes along. Once that happens, it's goodbye old plaything. Let's retrieve this somewhat discarded concept of structure and play with it for the next few pages.

Some may argue that these issues of structure, both large and small, can be found at work throughout all our storytelling traditions and are not necessarily unique to Shakespeare. Regardless of these finer points, we can discern in Shakespeare's work a distinct set of architectonic tendencies with their own particular dramatic inflections. Let's start with his penchant for telling tales about:

Jealous Lovers, Fallen Rulers and Murderous Usurpers

In the Woods, at War, and Far, Far Away

Here's a question: "What do Shakespeare's jealous lovers, fallen rulers, and murderous usurpers have in common?" Let's start with a quick accounting:

JEALOUS LOVERS	FALLEN RULERS	MURDEROUS USURPERS
Claudio (*Much Ado*)	Duke Senior (*As You Like It*)	Richard III
Oberon (*Midsummer*)	Richard II	Brutus (*Julius Caesar*)
Othello	Henry VI	Hamlet (Yes, Hamlet!)
Posthumus (*Cymbeline*)	King Lear	Regan and Goneril
Leontes (*Winter's Tale*)	Prospero (*Tempest*)	Macbeth

On the surface, you could say there is no seeming similarity whatsoever; but, after a while, you might begin to discern a certain thematic leitmotif of loss. One could argue that each of these characters has lost something essential to them. For the jealous lover, it is the real or perceived loss of the one they loved; for the fallen ruler, it is the loss of their kingdom; for the murdering usurper, it is the temporary or total loss of their sanity. The result, for all, is a de-centering, a casting out from a place of safety and into states and spaces of uncertainty. It is a kind of banishment, a fall from the familiar, as singular and life-altering as the expulsion of Adam and Eve from their Garden of Eden. They have been transported to a new and forbidding outside, from which they now must attempt to survive and make their way. Such a break can be associated with what we have called the irrevocable event. This plunges our characters into "brave new worlds" which they must now navigate to the best of their abilities. Can they survive these new and unfamiliar vistas? Can they come out the other end of it? Will it be for the better or the worse? These are the new questions that besiege us.

Such a passage is not restricted to just jealous lovers, fallen rulers, or murderous usurpers. There are also all those young lovers whose quotidian world can be instantaneously transfigured by eros. One lover after another finds themselves transported from the even keel of the everyday to the completely unruly world of love. The key, in all these instances, is that the Shakespearean character passes from the world as they know it to a new and unfamiliar domain. It can be as real and elemental as the deluged wasteland of King Lear, or as strange and fantastical as the phantoms that now populate Macbeth's once peaceful castle. Madness can become a world unto itself. But let us, for the moment, put aside such imagined landscapes and focus instead on the actual environs that appear and reappear throughout these plays of Shakespeare, which include:

THE WOODS	THE WAR	THE FAR-OFF
As You Like It	*Henry IV, Parts I & II*	*Twelfth Night*
Midsummer Night's Dream	*Henry V*	*The Merchant of Venice*
King Lear	*Henry VI*	*Winter's Tale*
Cymbeline	*Julius Caesar*	*Pericles*
Timon of Athens	*All's Well That Ends Well*	*The Tempest*

Something separates our characters from the world as they know it and plunges them into one of these alternative universes. Again, the same question emerges: is there a common denominator at work, linking these otherwise desperate realities? From an anthropological point of view, one might be inclined to say that each of these spaces are examples of:

The Liminal

Liminality is, for such anthropologists as Arnold Van Gennep and Victor Turner, associated with primitive rites of passage.[1] Such rites accompany every change of place, state, social position, or age. These are moments that are out of time and out of the secular social structure. The liminal phase in such practices becomes a designated space of transition, of becoming; it is the bridge, or in-between place, where one has the opportunity to move from one state or stage to another. What is true in these rites is also true in Shakespeare. Think of the lovers in *Midsummer Night's Dream* who go into the woods and have all their conceptions of love tested; think of the co-conspirators of *Julius Caesar* who bring about a civil war which tests their very ethical resolve and moral fortitude. In both cases, the woods and the civil war become a kind of liminal no-man's land where these characters are tested and transformed.

Another way to conceptualize this would be to think of the liminal phase as big black box. Now imagine a character or group of characters entering into that big black box where something significant happens to them while they are being held inside of it. Now imagine them leaving, forever altered by their experiences inside. The big black box becomes the woods, war, love, madness, a visit to Illyria; all of these are examples of the liminal. During such experiences of liminality, an individual or group passes through an ambiguous moment where none of the traditional norms or rules apply. Turner says it is "betwixt and between the positions assigned and arrayed by law, custom, convention, and ceremony."[2] In many instances this in-between state is an in-between place where the individual or group faces a series of trials and tribulations which they must either individually or collectively overcome." The traditional rites of passage, according to Van Gennep and Turner, can be broken down into three key stages.

1   The **Separation Stage** where an individual or group is detached and isolated from their familiar social surroundings and network.

2   The **Liminal Stage** where, in this new and unfamiliar space, the individual or group goes through a series of trials, tribulations, and transformations. After which, they arrive at:

3   The **Re-Aggregation Stage** where the individual or group is returned and reincorporated back into familiar surroundings and social network. The success of their overcoming the obstacles of the Liminal Stage confers upon them a newfound social status and new and enhanced responsibilities.

Let's turn to a set of Shakespeare plays to see how well they fit within these three conceptual stages that Van Gennep and Turner find in the primitive rites of passage.

Theban Lovers and Roman Countrymen

I would like to look at two plays which couldn't, at least on the surface, be more different from one another: *A Midsummer Night's Dream* and *Julius Caesar*. The first, as we know, is celebrated as a comedy and the second is designated as a tragedy. One deals with a group of young people falling in love, the other with a group of co-conspirators plotting an assassination. If that isn't an example of two radically differing stories, then I don't what is. And yet. Let's take a closer look. When both plays open, the characters of both are very much enmeshed in their respective worlds. In the case of *Midsummer*, this is the world of Athens; in the case of *Caesar*, this is the world of the Roman Republic. Both worlds are defined by a set of laws that rigorously govern and organize their conduct. In the case of the young lovers of *Midsummer*, they want to rail against these laws, which include a father's right to demand his daughter be wed to a husband she may not love; in the case of our co-conspirators in *Caesar*, they are subject to laws that they fear are about to be broken with the elevation of one potentially authoritarian figure as emperor. This leads both groups, lovers and co-conspirators, to act. In the case of

Midsummer, the lovers escape into the woods; in the case of *Julius Caesar*, this leads the co-conspirators to assassinate their rival, plunging Rome into civil war. Let's place both these plays within the first two stages of Van Gennep and Turner's liminal schema, beginning with *Midsummer*:

SEPARATION STAGE	LIMINAL STAGE
The young lovers unable to marry who they wish flee the city of Athens for the nearby woods.	Once in the woods they are plunged into a strange new world where everything is up for grabs and they must re-think who they are as individuals and as couples

We can argue that the same basic structuring happens in *Julius Caesar*:

SEPARATION STAGE	LIMINAL STAGE
The Co-conspirators, unhappy with the ascension of Caesar, assassinate him, plunging Rome into civil war.	This civil war throws them into a strange new world where everything is up for grabs and they must rethink who they are as individuals and as a group.

And so, on a cursory level, these two dissimilar plots do indeed begin fall into place along the lines of Van Gennep and Turner's liminal stage. Where they differ is in outcome. Let's take a deeper dive into what happens in the liminal stage and how this does or does impact on the final stage of re-aggregation. Again, we will start with *Midsummer*:

LIMINAL STAGE	RE-AGGREGATION STAGE
While in the woods the lovers learn about themselves, who they really are and how to then relate better to the one they love.	The lovers, Theseus and Hippolyta, the Rude Mechanicals, Oberon, Titania, and the entire fairy kingdom are all realigned and back in harmony, thanks to having undergone their various ordeals in the woods.

This trajectory is very much the movement of many of Shakespeare's comedies. Here the liminal stage paves the way for certain forms of re-aggregation when our characters return to society. This is due, in part, to two significant aspects of the liminal experience. These are the deployment of what Turner calls ludic recombination and the engendering of communitas. Ludic recombination accounts for the topsy-turvy nature of the liminal stage, where everything is, indeed, turned upside down. Here the hierarchies of a given society are often playfully reversed; think of the fool becoming king for a day (Bottom in *Midsummer*). It can be the place where gender is crossed; think of women dressed as men (Rosalind in *As You Like It*). These reversals break these characters out of their often rigidly defined place in society and realign one another in new and exciting ways, showing that a person can be more than their prescribed position within an often highly stratified social structure. This often leads to a sudden collective upsurge in fellow feeling, which Turner call moments of communitas, and that these moments have to do with "the sense felt by a group of people when their life together takes on a fuller meaning."[3] This can be something as simple as a newfound sense of togetherness. It is what the lovers and, by extension, Theseus, Hippolyta, Oberon, and Titania all experience the next morning after their encounter in the woods. It is perhaps best expressed in Helena's epiphany that the loved one is "my own and not my own."[4] In other words, not an object to be possessed but rather an autonomous companion for life. It is also the feeling the Rude Mechanicals experience upon being reunited; gone are the fears and differences that drove them apart; now they are ready to work together to bring their production of *Pyramus and Thisbe* to fruition. This is the general feeling of Act 4.

Act 5 is another matter. Shakespeare, ever the realist, reminds us of the limits of communitas in this final act. The Rude Mechanicals are indeed able to put on their play, but their newfound unity does not improve the overall quality of their presentation which remains, to quote another Shakespearean character, rather "rough hewn." This is certainly what the male lovers think of the Rude Mechanicals' play, an opinion they have no problem expressing in a series of openly public and deprecating barbs. This, perhaps more than anything else, jangles against the recently experienced communitas of Act 4. The kinder responses of Theseus and Hippolyta and the polite silence of the female lovers suggest that they have indeed grown through their liminal experiences in the woods; but Shakespeare is too enamored of the truth to ever suggest that such transformations are universal. Communitas, in Shakespeare, is hard won and often quickly lost: think of Prospero's speech after his failed masque, on how one's hopes and dreams can so easily dissolve into thin air. But before we can become too troubled by these cracks in the porcelain teacup of communitas, along come the reunited Oberon and Titania with their fairy trains to bless the lovers' nuptial beds. In this glorious moment, all seems momentarily right with the world.

We can also see the engendering of communitas happening in a play like *Henry V*, where the liminal experience of the war in France unites English soldiers from radically different regions and social ranks, melding together into Henry's vision of a new-formed "band of brothers." Such moments of communitas are more common in the comedies, rarer in the histories, and almost nonexistent in the tragedies. This is where a play like *Julius Caesar* begins to differ drastically from Van Gennep and Turner's third stage of re-aggregation. Let's take a closer look:

LIMINAL STAGE	RE-AGGREGATION
The Civil War has become a rude awakening to the co-conspirators of Caesar's assassination. Their certitude over this and subsequent acts is sorely tested and in this harsh new light, they find themselves wanting, guilt-ridden, and ultimately incapable of success.	There is no re-aggregation for these co-conspirators. They are either beaten by their foes, or destroyed by their own mistakes, doubt, and guilt. In the end they are vanquished, dying by their own hand or the hand of their enemy.

Here the liminal state of the civil war has an adverse effect on the co-conspirators, revealing, particularly in Brutus, their hubris, rashness, and inability to see the full repercussions of their initial actions that, inadvertently, bring about the very event that they were hoping to thwart (i.e. Rome's slide from a Republic to an Empire). Where the liminal phase of the woods in *Midsummer* brings about a certain harmonious growth, the liminal phase of civil war in *Julius Caesar* brings about its opposite, further splintering this group of co-conspirators from one another. In the end, their cause, beliefs, and very sense of self are completely shattered. In both instances, it is the liminal stage that accounts for this transformation. In both of these examples, the liminal stage is tangible/concrete. It is a place like the woods, or an event like a civil war.

But, as we indicated earlier, the liminal can also be a state of mind. We can see this happening, more and more, as we move to the mature works of *Hamlet*, *Othello*, *King Lear*, and *Macbeth*. Here in these middle tragedies, the liminal becomes a trick of the mind. What does Hamlet say? "There is nothing either good or bad, but thinking makes it so."[5] Thinking, in these four instances, leads to increasing degrees of madness. The seeds of this can be found in *Hamlet*, they grow in *Othello* and *Lear*, and they reach their full flower with *Macbeth*. It is at this juncture that we find ourselves moving:

From the Liminal to the Imaginary

The Imaginary Order is a term coined by the French psychoanalyst Jacques Lacan. It is a part of his larger theory of what he calls The Three Orders of Subjectivity (the other two orders being those of The Symbolic and The Real).[6] In many ways Lacan's thinking rhymes with aspects of Van Gennep and Turner's Three Stages of Liminality. In this respect, Lacan's thought can help us further articulate what we have been looking at, deepening our understanding of what is happening to one's interior life while moving through Van Gennep and Turner's liminal paradigm. Let's briefly look at Lacan's three orders and then attempt to graph them onto Van

Gennep and Turner's theories. Lacan tells us that we continually move through three basic subjective states.

The Symbolic

These are things we are born into: The Family, The Classroom, The Church, The Work Place, The Courts, The State. Such "institutions" are symbolic in that they give us language and rules so that we can function within them. They usually have a symbolic figure who we are asked to endow with meaning. This figure could be The Father, The Teacher, The Priest, The Boss, The Judge, The Ruler. These systems and the people who represent them have been put in place by a given society to maintain a certain order and maintain the status quo. They end up organizing our lives, giving it meaning, and keeping us in our place whether we like it or not.

The Imaginary

This is the way that each of us internalizes The Symbolic Order, how reality (that aggregate of all our Symbolic Systems) gets re-scripted by our imagination. The residue of this processing is all part of what becomes our personal Imaginary Order. *It is how we interpret the Symbolic for ourselves* and leads to a variety of imaginative projections. For instance, one may have a problem with one's father and then project this animosity onto all authority figures. Such projections onto reality are emanating from the realm of our Imaginary. It can actually change the way we see and interpret the world around us (for better or worse).

The Real

This exists outside the man-made structures of the Symbolic and the fantasy life of our Imaginary. In actuality, the Symbolic and the Imaginary often spend a great deal of psychic and cultural energy attempting to block out the Real. The Real is that which we do not have language for, it marks the moment where our language breaks down. Lacan tells us that the real is that which resists symbolization. The Real is impossible to imagine. Think Death. But there are other moments like wonder that defy our ability to put what we profoundly experience into words and call into question our basic existence.

Perhaps you can begin to see how Lacan's three orders of subjectivity might inform and further flesh out Van Gennep and Turner's thinking. For instance, we can begin to sense that what **The Separation Phase** removes us from is basically Lacan's notion of the **Symbolic Order**. Lacan also helps deepen our understanding of how **The Liminal Phase** can activate our **Imaginary** wishes and fears which have most likely been kept dormant under the pressure of the **Symbolic**. Time spent within the **Liminal** can allow our **Imaginary** to potentially run rampant. Finally, the intertwining of these theories can help us understand how a return to the **Symbolic Order**, after this foray into the **Liminal/Imaginary**, can show up The Symbolic for what it is: a somewhat flimsy man-made affair. As a result of this, we can catch a glimpse of **The Real** which lurks just beyond the boundaries of **The Symbolic Order**. Now I know what you're thinking:

This is All Very Well and Good

But What Does Any of it Have to Do With Shakespeare???

A lot, actually. Imagine, if you will, the movement of a Shakespeare play as being a liminal journey from **The Symbolic**, through **The Imaginary**, and arriving, in the end, at a glimpse of **The Real**. One of the first things one notices when one starts thinking this way is that almost all of Shakespeare's plays begin in:

The Symbolic

This is the world of courts and kingdoms with certain rules and values that a Shakespearean character must adhere to; sometimes willingly, other times grudgingly. Either way, a certain order and status quo reigns. The Court of Athens in *Midsummer* or the world of the Roman Republic in *Julius Caesar* before Caesar's assassination would be examples of such Symbolic Structures. At some point, no earlier than the end of Acts 1 or 2, something happens, what we call the Irrevocable Event, which thrusts these characters out of the realm of the Symbolic and plunges them into:

The Imaginary

This could be the lovers' retreat into the woods, in *Midsummer*; or, in *Julius Caesar*, the assassination of Caesar, which initiates an all-out civil war. The Symbolic Order—with its rules, norms, laws, and pre-imposed hierarchies—gives way to the Liminal/Imaginary traversals of a character or group. In the case of *Midsummer* it is the Imaginary dreams of the Lovers, and in *Julius Caesar* it is the Imaginary nightmares of the ensuing civil war. **This forever alters the world around them, bending it to their overripe imaginations, until the world itself becomes an extension of their secret desires or worst fears.** Such Imaginary transformations can be the result of falling in love (*Romeo and Juliet*), jealousy (*Othello*), the murder of a monarch (*Macbeth*), or the onset of senile dementia (*Lear*). **There's something almost proto-expressionistic about this, where nothing remains untouched by the central character's mental disposition.** It creates its own psychic liminality that, like weather, transforms an otherwise known landscape, affecting everyone in its wake.

The Real

The force released by the Imaginary can be such that it causes a series of ensuing fissures in the fortress-like structure of the Symbolic order which was initially built to keep The Real away. Now, The Real begins to stream through the ever-multiplying cracks until, in the end, it suffuses the world, overpowering both the Symbolic and the Imaginary. Which, in the case of the middle tragedies, is often made manifest with the arrival of death. I should say now that these orders do not need to be thought of as so strictly regulated. One order may dominate a significant portion of the play, but this does not preclude glimpses of the other two orders. Slavoj Žižek notes that The Real often reveals itself discreetly, like a monster in a horror film. At the beginning of the film, you might get a glimpse of the monster's shadow; then, a little later, perhaps the monster's claw; then the monster's torso; and, finally, in the end, the entire monster (who always looks disappointingly like a man in a rubber monster suit). This is how The Real can reveal itself in pockets throughout a Shakespeare play before it asserts itself in the final moments of the fifth act.

Perhaps my favorite Shakespearean Real happens at the end of *Antony and Cleopatra*. Cleopatra, upon learning of Antony's death, decides to die herself. But Cleopatra cannot just die a common death by knife or rope. No. Cleopatra, being Cleopatra, must die by something more inspired. Something that will liven up the dull and dusty books of history that are yet to be written. If Cleopatra is to take her life, it must be by poisonous snakes. Now there is a grand endgame, befitting so magnificent a queen. But the reality of the snakes is another matter. First there is the business of procuring the proper snakes from a local snake charmer who, rather than pass on any last sagacious advice, makes a series of crude double entendres that evoke groans rather than laughs. Then there is the snake itself, which misses its cue to bite Cleopatra's breast. She must hit it on its head to get it to do its deadly job. And then, finally, once Cleopatra is indeed dead, her Chambermaid must readjust Cleopatra's crown, which is now terribly askew and makes her look more like a drunken fool than a majestic queen.

With these three orders and their sequencing clearly in our mind's eye, we can now see how these stages manifest themselves in the middle tragedies of Shakespeare. In these four plays, the Imaginary/Liminal phase has more to do with the mental states of its four protagonists. For Hamlet the Imaginary phase is marked by his feigning madness (to the point where we begin to wonder, after the death of Polonius, whether Hamlet might indeed be insane). This disperses with his return in Act 5 where he begins to encounter intimations of The Real. The same is true for Othello, Lear, and Macbeth, each of whose Imaginary/Liminal phases is marked by a descent into the real madness of Lear, the pathological jealousy of Othello, and the mounting paranoia of Macbeth. These descents into madness begin to dissipate in the fifth acts of these plays as the characters begin to encounter the return of The Real. Let's take a look:

Hamlet

THE SYMBOLIC	THE IMAGINARY	THE REAL
ACT 1	**ACT 1, SCENE 4**	**ACT 5**
CLAUDIUS' COURT	HAMLET'S ENCOUNTER WITH THE GHOST OF HIS FATHER	HAMLET COMES FACE TO FACE WITH DEATH
	This begins the Imaginary/ Liminal Phase that runs through Acts 2, 3, and 4. Which is the length of Hamlet's feigned madness.	First with the skull of Yorick. Then the funeral of Ophelia. Finally the death of Hamlet himself.

Othello

THE SYMBOLIC	THE IMAGINARY	THE REAL
ACTS 1–3	**ACT 3, SCENE 2**	**ACT 5**
OTHELLO'S MILITARY EXPLOITS	IAGO'S INTIMATION THAT DESDEMONA HAS BEEN UNFAITHFUL TO OTHELLO	DESDEMONA'S DEATH
	This marks the beginning of the Imaginary/Liminal Phase of the play, from the onset of Othello's madness which runs through the remainder of Act 3 all the way to mid Act 5.	In which Othello finally "wakes" from his jealous delusion.

King Lear

THE SYMBOLIC	THE IMAGINARY	THE REAL
ACTS 1–3	**ACT 3, SCENE 2**	**ACT 5**
THE COURT OF KING LEAR AND SUBSEQUENT COURTS OF REGAN AND GONERIL	THE STORM AND LEAR'S DESCENT INTO MADNESS	THE DEATH OF CORDELIA
	This marks the beginning of the Imaginary/Liminal Phase of the play which runs from the remainder of Act 3, through Act 4, and into Act 5.	Lear "Sees Better."

It is interesting to note that *Macbeth* opens with what would seem to be an immediate leap to the Imaginary with the introduction of the three weird sisters. This is unique to Shakespeare's plays, as even Hamlet begins with the establishment of the symbolic changing of the night watch before the Ghost of Hamlet's father appears. I always wonder if opening with the three weird sisters is the product of a later revision by Thomas Middleton (who clearly revised the play for later performances). By the time Middleton is reworking *Macbeth*, witches have become all the rage on the Elizabethan stage. I can imagine the company saying, "Tom, can we start the play with more of a bang, and move those witches right to the top?" Suffice to say, this one play differs from the usual Shakespearean opening move of The Symbolic. But after this initial variation, the play quickly falls back into the structural patterning that we have seen dominating the other middle tragedies.

All four of these middle tragedies also resolutely move away from Turner's notion of re-aggregation. What emerges in its stead is the intrusion of Lacan's Real, which puts everything under a stark and unforgiving light. The survivors of the worlds of *Macbeth* and *King Lear* make speeches that evoke the hope of re-aggregation, but they cannot help but ring hollow in our ears, especially when spoken over all the dead bodies that now litter the stage, outnumbering those few who remain standing. The comedies (such as *Much Ado About Nothing*, *As You Like It*, and *Twelfth Night*) fare better in this respect, although there is always one character left who refuses to harmonize with the others, whether that is Don John, Jaques, or Malvolio. We have to wait until the final Romances for Van Gennep and Turner's notion of re-aggregation to return. This also marks the shift from Lacan's Real to its variation, which we are calling the Wondrous. The Real, which has shown itself as death, now returns in the guise of the Wondrous. Remember that the Real, for Lacan, is what escapes language. The tragedies explore the negative valence of The Real; the Romances, its more numinous aspects.

With this in mind, let's turn our attention to Shakespeare's last plays and see how these final works vary from their predecessors. One of the first things that we discover is that they are a not as evenly proportioned as the early plays, which usually allow for an act or so of the Symbolic before we are plunged into the Imaginary. In the Romances, the Symbolic Order is quickly touched upon. In the case of *The Winter's Tale* and *The Tempest*, there is one brief scene before we are plunged into the Imaginary. Let's take a quick look

The Winter's Tale

THE SYMBOLIC	THE IMAGINARY	THE WONDROUS
ACT 1	ACT 1, SCENE 2	ACT 5
THE COURT OF LEONTES	LEONTES' DESCENT INTO JEALOUSY AND MADNESS	LEONTES REUNITED
	This happens almost immediately, plunging us into the Imaginary/Imaginal Phase of the Play from the remaining Acts 2 and 3, which take place in Sicilia, and Act 4 in Bohemia.	First with Perdita. Then with Hermione. Both of whom turn out to be alive, as though they were brought back from the dead.

The Tempest

THE SYMBOLIC	THE IMAGINARY	THE WONDROUS
ACT 1	ACT 1, SCENE 2	ACT 5
THE SHIP	THE ISLAND	PROSPERO'S FORGIVENESS
Undone by the storm that shipwecks all.	This constitutes the Imaginary/ Liminal Phase of the play that runs from Acts 1, 2, 3 and 4, and into Act 5.	

And so, as these breakdowns reveal, the shift and time spent in the Imaginary/ Liminal phase is at its most pronounced in the Romances, with the conversion of The Real to The Wondrous, which suffuses the last moments of these plays much in the same manner as The Real had done in Shakespeare's earlier works. With these exceptions, this schematic mapping can account for most of Shakespeare's Comedies, Tragedies, Histories, and Romances. This is how they tend to move. The opening Symbolic Stage establishes the social order of the play, then the Imaginary Stage follows the desires or fears (dream or nightmare) of a central character (Hamlet, Othello, Lear, Macbeth, Richard II) or group (the lovers of *Midsummer*, the conspirators of *Julius Caesar*). This Stage/movement has an almost proto-expressionist feel to it, where what the main character (or characters) think or feel begins to color the world around them. The Symbolic Order shows how the world dominates the character(s); whereas the Imaginary Stage reverses this dynamic. Throughout these two stages, we are also getting glimpses of the Real or Wondrous, which grow in frequency as we move through the play until they completely dominate much of the fifth acts of these plays. This is the basic unfolding of a

Shakespeare story. With this in mind, we can now look at how this mapping can help us in the actual realization of the production in the acting and design choices.

Making This Mapping Manifest in Production

And now, we must convert the Symbolic, Imaginary, Real, and Wondrous into energies and images. As we have noted, the Symbolic is usually the court of some monarch; it is an ordered world, one with rules and regulations that maintain the status quo. This can be reflected in the order/symmetry of the actual physical environment, where balance and proportion tend to reign. It is a world where one's comportment is equally regimented.

The Imaginary begins, as we've noted, when The Symbolic is negated or broken, plunging us from order to chaos (the in-between/liminal world). Think about the ordered architecture of Athens versus the less controlled and chaotic world of the woods. Such transformations not only impact on the world but also on the characters' comportment, which shifts as the world shifts; in this case, from a certain restraint and rigidity to a freer, more unabated way of being. Shakespeare, the master of antithesis, is working with one of the biggest possible antitheses when he is moving from the Symbolic to the Imaginary, and so we have the opportunity to celebrate such an antithesis in big, bold scenic gestures. Does the world descend into the darkness from Duncan's death? Is it only restored after Malcolm's victory and the restoration of his father's kingdom? The shift from the Symbolic to the Imaginary allows to also exploit the proto-expressionist possibilities where the central character's descent into madness (Hamlet, Othello, Lear, and Macbeth, to name but a few) can alter the world itself. Here we can take the impulse of throwing the world of *Macbeth* into perpetual darkness further stylistically; perhaps the walls begin to bleed, turning the entire stage blood red for the remainder of the play. Perhaps the behavior of those of Macbeth's court begins to take on his own heightened paranoid behavior; what if they all comport themselves like souls in some forgotten circle in Dante's Inferno. The shift into The Imaginary is an invitation to the director to stretch their imaginations toward the heightened, the poetic, the surreal. If the world of the play goes through an Imaginary phase, why not the very design and behavior of the acting company?

Throughout the phases of the Symbolic and the Imaginary we are getting glimpses of the Real which functions like Žižek's monster, ever so slowly revealing more and more of itself as we move deeper and deeper into the play, until the Real reigns supreme in the final moments of the fifth act. How does one image or stage the Real? What does the Real mean to you? Is this an encounter that changes the nature and temperature of the performers? Is it allowing more "air" into the act, more space for silence? Is it made manifest by playing the final moments in the unforgiving bright, surgical white light of Brecht? Is it another opportunity to pull the rug out from under the audience? The same is true with the wondrous: how does this energy suddenly suffuse the final moments of one of Shakespeare's Romances? Is it a change in the "time signature" of these moments? Is it a certain kind of stillness? Simplicity? Perhaps an unadorned kind of playing, a way of being that just is and basks in this is-ness.

This allows a director to begin to think of a Shakespeare play in large, sweeping gestures, like the movements in a symphony. That there is a "look" to each movement as well as a unique time signature that differentiates the Symbolic from the Imaginary, and from the Imaginary to the Real or Wondrous. These are the orchestral questions that face the director, actors, and designers as they move through the Symbolic, Imaginary, Real, and Wondrous potentialities of a Shakespeare play.

EXERCISE #4

Shaping the Play Using Lacan's Three Orders

The Event Work of the previous chapter essentially scores the play; it helps us understand how the play moves, allowing us to sense the play's ever-subtle shifting rhythms. The next phase of work is to move from scoring to shaping. What is the difference? If scoring gives us the *tempo* of the work, shaping begins to organize these dynamics into a larger structural *tonalities* that function like movements in a dramatic symphony. It is at this juncture that we turn to our marriage of Victor Turner (the Liminal) and Jacques Lacan (the Imaginary), organizing the play with this unfolding. With this in mind, can you take a Shakespeare play and break it into Lacan's clearly delineated three orders. Remember that within each dominant Order we can receive ripples/intimations of the other two orders. Chart this out in the following fashion:

THE SYMBOLIC   **THE IMAGINARY**   **THE REAL**
or

THE SYMBOLIC   **THE IMAGINARY**   **THE WONDROUS**

Now, underneath each heading describe in as vivid detail as possible the nature of each order As it makes itself manifest in Shakespeare's unfolding of the story. If you were working on *A Midsummer Night's Dream*, we would want a thick description of Athens as the Symbolic movement of the play versus the woods, which would be the liminal transition into the Imaginary movement. Finally, how would you want to describe the last moments of the play? Is the fairies' blessing at the end an example of the Wondrous?

Having described each of these three movements in great detail, now extract the most descriptive language for each of the orders and make a list. If this were *A Midsummer Night's Dream*, you might end up with the something like the following:

THE SYMBOLIC	THE IMAGINARY	THE WONDROUS
Ordered	Chaotic	Ephemeral
Symmetrical	Irregular	Elliptical
Architectural	Natural	Otherworldly
Straight lines	Zig-Zagged	Circular
Formal	Wild	Harmonious
Mannered	Free	Precise
Stately	Erratic	Hypnotic

With this in mind, answer the following questions:

1. How does one speak in such a world?
2. How does one move?
3. How does one feel?

And most importantly:

4. *How does this* **change** *as we move from one Order to the next?*

It is all about playing these changes. Make sure these dynamics are made manifest in all aspects of the production in terms of the plays visual, aural, and kinetic life.

5 "Stand and Unfold Yourself": Revelation of Character in the Works of Shakespeare

The Challenge

I think one of the biggest challenges for an actor of Shakespeare is in creating a discernible character arc. This is always an issue, but it is compounded by the demands of a Shakespearean text. There is so much to attend to and so little time. First, there's the language: understanding everything you're saying, making sure it is clear, making sure it is grounded, making sure you memorize it, that you can vocally sustain it. This alone can eat up an entire rehearsal process. Then there's the basic moment-to-moment work, blocking, stage combats or jigs, songs, the lack of run-throughs, that hideous costume that just doesn't feel right. So, is it any wonder that when you first step in front of an audience you have all these bits and pieces but they still have not coalesced into a sense of the whole? This is compounded by the mysterious nature of the character you are working on, which often seems to willfully defy immediate interpretation. There is some fundamental mystery or question that you can't seem to answer.

Hamlet begins with a question: "Who's there?"[1] Who indeed. This simple interrogative could be applied to every character we meet in that play. Who is the Ghost? Claudius? Gertrude? Ophelia, her father, and, most famously, Hamlet himself? Hamlet guards his mystery tenaciously; look at the moment deep in Act 3 where he taunts his friend Guildenstern, encouraging him to make music from a simple pipe. Guildenstern demurs; he does not "know the stops." This elicits the following famous attack from Hamlet:

Why look you now how unworthy a thing you make of me: you would play upon me! You would seem to know my stops, you would pluck out the heart of my mystery, you would sound me from my lowest note to the top of my compass; and there is much music, excellent voice, in this little organ. Yet cannot you make it speak. 'Sblood! Do you think I am easier to be played on than a pipe? Call me what instrument you will, though you fret me, you cannot play upon me.[2]

And so we are left with questions. Questions like: Why does Hamlet procrastinate? Why do Romeo and Juliet rush into marriage? Why does Iago want to drive Othello into a jealous rage? Why does Lear divvy up his kingdom? Each of Shakespeare's plays has a very simple, fundamental question that is actually very hard to answer. Don't look to Shakespeare's characters for answers. Othello will ask Iago why "hath thou ensnared my soul and body?"[3] Iago's reply to his former commander is sharp and to the point: "Demand me nothing. What you know, you know. From this time forth I never will speak a word."[4] Shylock tells the court that is adjudicating his case, "You'll ask me why I rather choose to have / A weight of carrion flesh than to receive / Three thousand ducats. I'll not answer that, / But say it is my humor. Is't answered?"[5] Each play and character challenges us to arrive at our own unique answer, knowing full well that all answers are provisional, with a life expectancy that is only as long as that production's interpretation. We're back to our "bottom-less" problem. So what do we do? Let's start with the very concept of character.

Character as a Journey of Mask, Face, Soul

Character is a vertical affair. We are a geology of selves. There is an ur-self as infant, then child, adolescent, young adult, mature individual, etc. At a certain point, a pattern of being emerges and dominates the others. In this respect, a person is like modern-day Rome: beneath him are older Romes, one atop another. The other, older selves support the current iteration of self. The French critic Alfred Simon breaks down the revelation of character into three distinct phases of Mask, Face, Soul. Each phase is built vertically, one atop the other, giving us the archeology of self. Simon says, "The Mask conceals the face, but in turn the face conceals the soul, and the soul conceals itself. The universe of theatre, like the theatre of life, then becomes a vast play of masks which the contemplator cannot accept as such. He must rip away these disguises."[6] Let us break this down to make sure we understand the terms that go into how character is revealed

Mask

This is what we show the world. It is our public persona which we share with strangers and acquittances in an array of social situations (e.g., the workplace). It is usually crafted in relationship with our occupations and engenders certain desired responses from others (e.g., respect, fear, confidence, belief, etc.)

Face

This is what we show those closest to us, those who we trust (wives, children, relatives, close friends). These are the people with whom we can share our more vulnerable side. In this safe remove from the world at large, the audience is granted access to this other, often contradictory self. The shift from mask to face is often comic.

Soul

This is the most secretive side of ourselves, a side we keep from even those closest to us. It is a trace of our earliest most vulnerable sense of self. The shift from face to soul is often tragic in nature.

In short: the mask is how we would like the world to see us, the face is how we really are, and the soul is usually something about a part of us that we have long forgotten or would like to forget. Let's look at two quick examples (one comic, the other tragic) of this type of revelation of character.

MALVOLIO	CLEOPATRA
MASK	**MASK**
Imperious. A figure of solemnity and authority. "Do you make an alehouse of my lady's house?" and "Is there no respect of place, persons, nor time in you?"[7]	A Queen. Resplendent. Powerful. Completely Autonomous. We're told her own person beggars description and she would out-Venus Venus. Theatrical to her very core.
FACE	**FACE**
A man full of a rather overwrought fantasy life. "To be Count Malvolio."[8] He is easily gullible and giddy in love, like a schoolboy. Eager to do anything to win his lady's love. Even go about in yellow stockings.	A lover. Antony rules her unruly heart. "Give me drink . . . that I might sleep out this great gap of time my Antony is away." Her servant warns, "You think of him too much."[11] She loves to play at love. It is sport for her.

SOUL

Vulnerable. Fragile. Permeable. Thin skinned. "Never has a man been thus abused."[9] "Made the most notorious geck and gull that e'er invention played upon."[10]

SOUL

A poet. Behind her power, sense of theatrics, and relish in the games of eros, there is a true poet of love. She dies to be with her Antony. "I am fire and air. My other elements I give to baser life."[12]

In most plays we find that characters move through all three of these modalities of self. When we first meet them, they are often showing us their mask, then as the play progresses we see more and more of their face, and by the final act the mask and face have dropped like veils and we catch sight of their true soul. This does not mean that such revelations are locked into such a rigid schematic unfolding. In almost every given scene we can see how characters move from mask, to face, to soul, and back again. In these instances, what we are often given are glimpses of the face and soul which will grow in length as the play continues to unfold. But the movement between these three modalities of self—whether in the course of a scene, or over the long unfolding of a play—is the way in which dramatic characters tend to reveal themselves; adjusting from one phase of being to the other, depending on the circumstances.

It is usually much easier to arrive at a character's mask and face than it is its soul. In this respect, the soul of a character is very much like Lacan's notion of the real. The real, as you may remember from our previous chapter, is that which escapes our language. This makes sense since the soul would be, in this sort of schema, the oldest, most primordial part of ourselves which begins in infancy, before the acquisition of language. Therefore, it is often a set of inchoate sensations that mark us before we have language to understand or name what we feel. Eventually the face and mask grow out of the soul, often to protect it. This is not so different from Lacan's three orders of subjectivity where the symbolic and the imaginary are hard at work to combat or at least mediate the discomfort that comes from the inchoate nature of the real. In this respect, we can actually graph Lacan's three orders of subjectivity onto with Simon's three modalities of self. The result would be:

THE MASK	THE FACE	THE SOUL
THE SYMBOLIC	THE IMAGINARY	THE REAL

Now the soul can become so well protected, so buried beneath us, that we lose touch with it, often to the point where we are no longer aware of its existence. This makes things all the more disruptive when the soul returns to us, usually in moments of crises that triggered these earliest formative sensations. Suddenly, we have no language for what we are experiencing, except for a palpable feeling that we have been in this situation before; we sense a rhyme between our "now" and a long-lost "then." But bringing this into words is a challenge in real life and even in the life of fictive characters. Finding a language for the soul is therefore a tricky hermeneutic procedure. Let's return to Hamlet and take up his challenge to see if we can pluck out the secret heart of his mystery.

Back to Hamlet

It is a relatively straightforward affair to discern the Mask and Face of Hamlet. When he is in most scenes, he shows his mask; when he is sharing a soliloquy or speaking with Horatio, he shows his face. What's the initial difference?

MASK	FACE
(shown in Court)	(shown to us and to Horatio)
Sharp, quick, cutting, nimble, dexterous, witty, satiric, antic, mercurial, obstreperous, hot, sure-footed, in control even when pretending to be out of control, the consummate performer, not afraid to make a scene.	Moody, melancholic, sullen, lost, emotionally tempest-tossed, in over his head, riven with self-doubt, suffering from low self-esteem, blocked, incapable of taking actual action. Afraid. And yet incapable of explaining why.

What accounts for this radical division which pulls at Hamlet to the point that we worry that the center of his very sanity will not hold? Might it have something to do with his soul? And if so, how? If the soul is forged in childhood, do we have any clues about what Hamlet was like as a child? We actually have to wait until the beginning of the fifth act to get a glimpse of Hamlet's earliest days. It is when the Gravedigger shows him the skull of Yorick, the court jester. Hamlet famously tells Horatio:

HAMLET

Alas, poor Yorick! I knew him, Horatio, a fellow of infinite jest, of most excellent fancy. He hath borne me on his back a thousand times, and now, how abhorred in my imagination it is! My gorge rises at it. Here hung those lips that I have kissed I know not how oft. Where be your gibes now – your gambols, your songs, your flashes of merriment that were wont to set the table on a roar? Not one now to mock your own grinning? Quite chopfallen? Now get you to my lady's chamber and tell her, let her paint an inch thick, to this favor she must come. Make her laugh at that.[13]

This is an extraordinary little speech, especially when we realize Hamlet shares no such warm and personal memories about his own father. Whenever he refers to his father, it is in mythic terms. His father is a "Hyperion," or "Jove" himself. There are no images of his "dad" carrying him on his back, or of Hamlet kissing him again and again with love and affection. Even when Hamlet meets the ghost, it is as if he were speaking to a distant acquaintance rather than his father. In this moment, one realizes that *Yorick was more a father figure to Hamlet than his own father*. No wonder Hamlet models so much of his behavior on Yorick's antic disposition. Suddenly, in retrospect, all of Hamlet's previous interactions seem to be a variation on the theme of Yorick, with Hamlet providing his own repertory of gibes, gambols, songs, flashes of merriment, and especially mockery (remember that *Amleth* means fool). This is how Hamlet models himself: *as a jester rather than a warrior like his father.*

But if all this is indeed true, why is he so upset with his mother for so quickly transferring her affections from his father to Claudius? Doesn't this show his deep love for his father? Does it? Perhaps. Or perhaps it is Hamlet, not his mother, who "doth protest too much." Perhaps his anger stems from his mother showing what he himself is afraid to show: a deep-seated ambivalence toward his father. Perhaps this is what is blocking him. Perhaps Hamlet hesitates to do the will of his father because he's never felt anything for the man who goes by this name. Perhaps Hamlet had no real relationship because this parental figure was always away at war. One can imagine Old Hamlet coming home, like Hector, still wearing his armored helmet, and scaring the infant in his arms who does not recognize him. Does young Hamlet stop crying, even after Old Hamlet removes his helmet? Or is he still frightened by the image of his father? Did he run, in tears, from his father, into his chamber to hide? Did Yorick find him there, wipe away young Hamlet's tears, make him laugh? Have we finally reached the soul of this young prince? Does his father, the warrior, equal death? Does Hamlet's being scared of his father mean he is scared of death? Is he, in fulfilling his father's will, coming to terms with his father, which means *coming to terms with death?* Also known as that "undiscovered country, from whose bourn / No traveller returns, puzzles the will."[14]

And so, in my reading, Hamlet's soul is that of a frightened child who develops the mask of his role model, Yorick, to protect himself. He rejects the brute force of his warrior father and defends his subsequent self with the wit and infinite jests taught to him by his secret paternal surrogate. But this willful affinity toward Yorick cannot completely stave off the complicated feelings surrounding Hamlet's relationship with his true father. It is a blockage which comes to the fore whenever Hamlet is alone with us or Horatio. In these moments, Hamlet can remove his over-confident mask and show us his conflicted face. The play, in this reading, sees Hamlet as having to overcome the fear of his real father. This also means overcoming his fear of death since the two, father and finitude, have become irrevocably fused in his unconscious.

Now, is this *the* answer to contents of Hamlet's soul? No. It is merely *an* answer, one among many. And this "many" stretches into infinity. Unlike Hamlet's mask or face, the soul of this character is much, much harder to grasp. The mask and the face of Hamlet are very much there on the page for all to see. Not so with Hamlet's soul. This is why, from production to production, there is very little variance in these first two modalities of the Hamlet's self. But the soul of Hamlet is another matter. It remains far more elusive and continually open to conjecture. It is buried deep within the text, waiting for each actor and director to do their best to excavate it. This is why we, as an audience, keep coming back to *Hamlet*, to see what potential riches the actor and director have dug up. Perhaps, in such instances, the ineffable soul of Hamlet is fulfilled (or is it replaced) by the ineffable soul of the actor. In this way, Hamlet becomes the ultimate vessel to hold a multitude of souls.

Having looked at how the mask, face, and soul function in the making of a Shakespearean character, let us now turn our attention to how these modalities of self are phased/sequenced over the course of a given play. A journey that takes us:

From Seeming to Being

Mask, Face, Soul in *Richard II*

When we first meet Richard, we meet his imperial mask. It is a work of regal art: cold, distant, otherworldly, godlike. It is present in such pronouncements as:

RICHARD II
> We are amazed, and thus long have we stood
> To watch the fearful bending of thy knee,
> Because we thought ourself thy lawful king;
> And if we be, how dare thy joints forget
> To pay their awful duty to our presence?
> If we are not, show us the hand of God
> That hath dismissed us from our stewardship;
> For well we know no hand of blood or bone
> Can gripe the sacred handle of our scepter,
> Unless he do profane, steal, or usurp.
> And though you think that all, as you have done,
> Have torn their souls by turning them from us,
> And we are barren and bereft of friends,
> Yet know: my Master, God omnipotent,
> Is mustering in His clouds our behalf
> Armies of pestilence, and they shall strike
> Your children yet unborn and unbegot
> That lift your vassal hands against my head
> And threat the glory of my precious crown.[15]

But behind this imperious mask of detached sovereignty, there is a royal face that is shown to only his inner circle, a face that engenders complicity between the King and his intimates, letting them in on his secret thoughts. Where his mask is somewhat stern, his face reveals a lighter, more sardonic and "naughty" or "wicked" cast of mind. When he learns that his Uncle Gaunt is ill, he jokes with his inner circle of courtiers:

> RICHARD II
> Now put it, God, in the physician's mind
> To help him to his grave immediately!
> The lining of his coffers shall make coats
> To deck our soldiers for these Irish wars.
> Come, gentlemen, let's all go visit him.
> Pray heaven we may make haste, and come too late.[16]

The same antic disposition is found when Richard learns of Gaunt's actual death. He begins in his royal mask: "The ripest fruit first falls, and so doth he / His time is spent, our pilgrimage must be."[17] And then, immediately on the heels of this, he shows his face: "So much for that. Now for our Irish wars."[18]

But, believe it or not, there is a poetic soul lurking in this seemingly detached and idle king. We catch our first sustained glimpse of it when Richard returns from Ireland. At first it is hard to tell whether this is part of his mask or intimations of something deeper. Let's listen in:

> RICHARD II   I weep for joy
> To stand upon my kingdom once again.
> Dear earth, I do salute thee with my hand,
> Though rebels wound thee with their horses' hooves.
> As long-parted mother with her child
> Plays fondly with her tears and smiles in meeting,
> So weeping, smiling, greet I thee, my earth,
> And do thee favor with my royal hands.[19]

Perhaps this is part of Richard's mask, but it betrays a complicated knowledge of his even more complicated feelings. After this, we see his familiar self-interested face, invoking the land to rise up against his foes. This is the Richard we've come to know. But when Richard learns a little later of his massive defeat, this other Richard, the part we will associate with his soul, returns for its first major visitation. It is the sad soul of a poet and leads to one of Shakespeare's most famous speeches:

> RICHARD II
> Let's talk of graves, of worms, and epitaphs,

Make dust our paper, and with rainy eyes
Write sorrow on the bosom of the earth.[20]

And after he explains how no king is able to escape death, he concludes this famous
soliloquy with:

RICHARD II

Cover your heads, and mock not flesh and blood
With solemn reverence. Throw away respect,
Tradition, form, and ceremonious duty,
For you have but mistook me all this while.
I live with bread like you, feel want,
Taste grief, need friends. Subjected thus,
How can you say to me I am a king?[21]

This is Richard's truest self, the self he hides from everyone, including himself. In the
past, when it gurgled up, he banished it just as he banished Bolingbroke. Such humble
sentiments did not help him rule. They only got in the way. And so they were
submerged. But over the remainder of the play he becomes reacquainted with this
secret self until it becomes his new persona. We will see Richard grappling with this
emergent self after he has been completely defeated and is brought before Bolingbroke
to hand over his crown. Richard enters the court, and tells all assembled:

RICHARD II

(begins perhaps with this new, humbler persona)
Alack, why am I sent for to a king,
Before I have shook off the regal thoughts
Wherewith I reigned? I hardly yet have learned
To insinuate, flatter, bow, and bend my knee.
Give sorrow leave awhile to tutor me
To this submission.
(But the old catty and callow Richard cannot help but return)
                Yet I well remember
The favors of these men: were they not mine?
Did they not sometime cry, "All hail!" to me?
So Judas did to Christ, but He in twelve
Found truth in all but one; I, in twelve thousand, none.
(And now, suddenly he has found his regal mask again)
God save the King! Will no man say, "Amen"?
Am I both priest and clerk? Well, then, "Amen."
God save the King, although I be not he;
And yet Amen, if heaven do think him me.[22]

And so, throughout this remarkable scene, Richard's three selves—his mask, face, and newly regained soul—will battle for pride of place in Richard's new relationship with the world. Mask and face, which he has known for so long, are not easily cast off; they will fight for their place at the table of Richard's consciousness until the very end. But slowly, scene by scene, soliloquy by remaining soliloquy Richard's newly regained soul will grow and share itself with Richard and those who encounter him. Listen to it speak, through Richard, to his long-suffering wife:

RICHARD II

> Join not with grief, fair woman, do not so,
> To make my end too sudden. Learn, good soul,
> To think our former state a happy dream,
> From which awaked, the truth of what we are
> Shows us but this. I am sworn brother, sweet,
> To grim Necessity, and he and I
> Will keep a league till death. Hie thee to France
> And cloister thee in some religious house.
> Our holy lives must win a new world's crown,
> Which our profane hours here have stricken down.[23]

In Richard's final scene we find him, monklike, in deep meditation. He tells us, "I have been studying how to compare / This prison where I live to the world."[24] One thinks he has arrived at his new soul-sated self. He hears music, but then his old self returns to criticize: "Ha, ha, keep time. How sour sweet music is / When time is broke and no proportion kept."[25] The music "mads" him to the point where he becomes the petulant king again and cries out, "let it sound no more!"[26] But, in the end, when the music stops, his soul soothes and subdues the last vestiges of his regal mask. He blesses the off-stage player, "For 'tis a sign of love, and love to Richard / Is a strange broach in this all-hating world."[27] Between the old Richard who is quick to criticize and the new Richard who gives his blessing, the soul of Richard, that has been ever so gently schooling him, thinks these thoughts for Richard to share with us:

RICHARD II

> And here have I the daintiness of ear
> To hear time broke in a disordered string,
> But for concord of my state of time
> Had not ear to hear my true time broke.
> I wasted time, and now doth Time waste me.[28]

This is Richard's soul speaking, a soul that has returned and assumed its rightful place in Richard's consciousness. In this case, it has not only been revealed over the course of the play, but allowed to grow. What we have witnessed is something of a

Shakespearean chrysalis. Now, if we had to graph this journey of Richard, it might look something like this:

Richard II

ACT 1	ACT 2	ACT 3	ACT 4	ACT 5
MASK	FACE	SOUL	MASK	SOUL
(King)	(Wit)	(Poet)	FACE	
			SOUL	
with glimpse of face	emerges more and is shared with moments of mask	emerges for the first time in relation to mask and face	all **BATTLE** for dominance	wins

With the emergence of the soul in Act 3, we will watch its subsequent ascendence. Richard's soul rises as his status falls. The dramatic events of the play reactivate this primordial part of himself. The soul, in this case, can become a medicinal balm for the character; or, as we will see in other Shakespearean plays, the soul can just as easily be or become poisoned. Here, we have reached:

Shakespeare's Secret Garden of the Soul

In Shakespeare's work, souls are secret gardens that are either cultivated or left to rot, blooming or decaying over the course of a given play's unfolding depending upon how they are tended. Within the deep interior of these characters, we find their very selves to be like the infant rind that Friar Laurence is contemplating when we first meet him in *Romeo and Juliet*. As you may remember, our gentle Friar tells us:

FRIAR LAURENCE
  Within the infant rind of this weak flower
  Poison hath residence and medicine power:
  For this, being smelled, with that part cheers each part;
  Being tasted, stays all the sense with the heart.
  Two opposed kings encamp them still
  In man as well as herbs—grace and rude will—
  And where the worser is predominant,
  Full soon the canker death eats up that plant.[29]

The question at the heart of many Shakespeare plays is which opposed king will reign in the very soul of the character: the medicinal one? Or its secret sharer, poison? In the case of *Richard II* we see that it is the secret poet/priest in Richard that comes to the fore like medicine in attempt to cure his griefs. But not so for other rulers such as Macbeth or Richard III, both of whom cultivate that which is poisonous in them until it poisons not only their kingdoms but their very selves. Both are ultimately driven mad by allowing this dark part of themselves full dominion over their souls. Macbeth, who gains his crown through a series of murders that multiply out of control, tells us, in the end that:

MACBETH
    I have lived long enough. My way of life
    Is fall'n into the sere, the yellow leaf,
    And that which should accompany old age,
    As honor, love, obedience, troops of friends,
    I must not look to have, but in their stead
    Curses, not loud but deep, mouth-honor, breath,
    Which the poor heart would fain deny and dare not.[30]

His soul is now a garden gone to seed, leaving him barren. It is only a short step from this sentiment to Macbeth's ultimate image of futility: a tale told by an idiot, full of sound and fury, signifying nothing. At this point, all that is left for these characters is to end it all. This is the only way to stop the pain of their poisoned soul. And so, in much of Shakespeare, when the mask and face fall away, we are left with a soul that favors one of these two opposing monarchs, with the play allowing us to see which is victorious. Let us take a brief look at the act-by-act poisoning of Macbeth's soul.

Shakespeare's Poisoned Souls

Or, Macbeth as Case Study

Macbeth's mask is that of warrior. This becomes clear in the description of his prowess on the battlefield where it is reported that

    . . . brave Macbeth (well he deserves that name)
    Disdaining Fortune, with his brandish'd steel,
    Which smoked with bloody execution
    Like Valour's minion, carved out his passage,
    Till he faced the slave;
    Which never shook hands nor bade farewell to him,
    Till he unseated him from the nave to the chops,
    And fix'd his head upon our battlements.[31]

In addition to this, Macbeth presents himself as a loyal warrior who knows his place; listen to him address the King:

MACBETH
> The service and loyalty I owe,
> In doing it, pays itself. Your Highness' part
> Is to receive our duties: and our duties
> Are to your throne and state, children and servants;
> Which do but what they should, by doing everything
> Safe toward your love and honor.[32]

Beneath this is the face of a contemplator, a way of being which is often at odds with his warrior mask. In these moments we could easily mistake Macbeth as being more a *worrier* than a *warrior*. In many ways, he is not all that different from Hamlet or Brutus in his private musings. We see it straight away in his first soliloquy to us, when he learns that the witches' prophecy of his becoming the Thane of Cawdor is true, leading Macbeth to wonder if the witches' second prophecy, that he will be king, might also come to pass. Let's listen in on how he parses all this out:

MACBETH
> ... This supernatural soliciting
> Cannot be ill; cannot be good:
> If ill, why hath it given me earnest of success,
> Commencing in a truth? I am Thane of Cawdor:
> If good, why do I yield to that suggestion
> Whose horrid image doth unfix my hair,
> And make my seated heart knock at my ribs,
> Against the use of nature? Present fears
> Are less than horrible imaginings.[33]

This is the same deeply reflective fellow who later, after saying he will take the King's life, has second thoughts:

MACBETH
> If it were done, when 'tis done, then 'twere well
> It were done quickly: if the assassination
> Could trammel up the consequence, and catch
> With surcease success; that but this blow
> Might be the be-all and end-all—here,
> But here, upon this bank and shoal of time,
> We'd jump the life to come.—But in these cases,
> We still have judgement here; that we but teach
> Bloody instructions, which, being taught, return

To plague the inventor: this even-handed Justice
Commends th' ingredient of our poisoned chalice
To our own lips.[34]

And here, like Hamlet, that other reflective fellow, his conscience gives him just
pause. But beneath this contemplative disposition is Macbeth's soul, which tires of
the continual stalemate between warrior and thinker, and yearns for advancement.
This overachieving soul makes its first appearance when the King lavishes
advancement upon his son, bestowing upon him the title of Prince of Cumberland.
This news pricks Macbeth to the core, as he tells us:

MACBETH
The Prince of Cumberland!—That is a step
On which I must fall down, or else, overleap,
For in my way it lies. Stars, hide your fires!
Let not light see my black and deep desires;
The eye wink at the hand; yet let that be,
Which the eye fears, when it is done, to see.[35]

This is the poisonous part of Macbeth's soul, the part he will listen to more and more
until it reigns supreme. This mixes with paranoia ("Our fears in Banquo / Stick
deep"[36]) which begins to infect Macbeth-the-thinker and all his subsequent thoughts:

MACBETH
We have scorch'd the snake, not killed it:
She'll close and be herself; whilst our poor malice
Remains in danger of her former tooth.[37]

Lady Macbeth tells him, "You must leave this."[38] And here—in Acts 3 and 4—Mask,
Face, and Soul all battle for dominion over Macbeth . Lady Macbeth implores him
to put on his mask: "sleek over your rugged looks / Be bright and jovial among
your guests tonight."[39] And Macbeth promises, "So shall I, Love; and so, I pray, be
you ... make our faces vizards to our hearts / Disguising what they are."[40] But he
cannot, and on the heels of this confesses, "full of scorpions is my mind, dear
wife."[41] But there is also some remnant of his good and well-intentioned Face
which refuses to make Lady Macbeth complicit with the murders that will follow.
She attempts to uncover this:

LADY MACBETH
What's to be done?
MACBETH
Be innocent of the knowledge, dearest chuck,
Till thou applaud the deed.[42]

There is a part of Macbeth that wants to protect Lady Macbeth from undue pain or worry. As his poisoned soul takes root, his care for his wife will be the last vestige of his once-human face. It is the only humanity we witness in Act 5. It is here that, when he learns of his wife's mental decline, he pleads with the doctor:

MACBETH
  Canst thou not minister to the mind diseased,
  Pluck from the memory a rooted sorrow,
  Raze out the written troubles of the brain,
  And with some sweet oblivious antidote
  Cleanse the stuff'd bosom of the perilous stuff
  Which weighs upon the heart?[43]

This will be the last moment of care on Macbeth's part. From this point on, the poison has completely overtaken him, leaving him to muse: "I 'gin to be aweary of the sun / And wish th' estate o' th' world were now undone / —Ring the alarm bell! —Blow, wind! Come, wrack! At least we'll die with harness on our back."[44]

  And so, if we were to chart this journey of Macbeth's from Mask to Face to Soul, it might look something along the lines of this:

Macbeth

ACT 1	ACT 2	ACT 3	ACT 4	ACT 5
		Dominated by:		
MASK	**FACE**	**SOUL**	**SOUL**	**SICK SOUL**
(The Warrior)	(The Worrier)	(Striver)	(Striver)	(Dominates)
		With simultaneous moments of:		
FACE	**MASK**	**NEW MASK**	**NEW FACE**	**OLD FACE**
(The Worrier;	(Warrior;	(King)	(Paranoia	(Ghost of
With	worthy;		grows into:)	his former
Thoughts not	vassal)			self in
that far from				relation to
us; a loving				his now
husband)				sickly wife)
		As well as fleeting intimations of:		
SOUL	**SOUL**	**FACE**	**SICK SOUL**	**SICK SOUL**
(Striver)	(Striver)	(Worry turns	(Emerges)	(Completely
		to paranoia)		overtakes
				him)

In both this and our previous *Richard II* chart, we tend to see the central characters moving in a linear fashion from Mask, through Face, and eventually to the final destination of their Soul (whether medicinal or poisoned). In the final phase, it is the Soul which becomes ascendent and tends to dominate the remainder of the play. In both charts there is a clear moment where all three modalities of self battle for ascendency. In *Macbeth* this battle begins in Act 3; in *Richard II* it reaches its zenith in Act 4. The more the character relies on his or her soul, the more powerful it becomes, until it stands forth as the primary feature of the character. Again, this progression mirrors Heidegger's observation that tragedy moves from seeming to being. Or, in our terminology: from mask to soul.

EXERCISE #5

Developing the Arc of Characters: Mask/Face/Soul

Take a look at each scene from a particular character's vantage point. Designate what is the predominant mode of being is your character primarily showing their

Mask?
Face?
Or Soul?

Now designate moments in the scene where your character shifts Modalities of Being. Mark these shifts from Mask to Face to Soul clearly. There is rarely a scene where a character is all mask, face or soul. Characters tend to move back and forth between mask and face with tiny glimmers of their soul (as we move into Acts 4 and especially 5, we have more a chance of catching sight of a character's soul). Delineate these moments. Mark them alongside the text so that a pattern begins to emerge, say, for the sake of argument:

Act 1, Scene 1: Mask
              M
              M
              M
              M

M

M

*F*ace

F

F

Mask

M

M

M

M

M

Face

F

F

Soul

Mask

M

M

Soul

Now:

give each Modality of Being a different:

Color

Intonation (lyric, blunt)

Quality (light/heavy)

So that I can **see**, **hear**, and **feel** the difference in Being. I must be able to palpably sense these shifts in modality. **Remember**: Always play the **difference**.

Now that we have gathered all this information (which Shakespeare, which text, how it's scored, what patterns emerge, and trajectories unfold), we can move to our next phase of work: interpretation.

PART TWO

"What Means This, My Lord?": Toward a Fourfold Reading of Shakespeare

INTRODUCTION
Standing in the Textual Garden of Forking Paths

Having amassed all this information, two essential questions emerge, both at odds with one another. The first being, "How do we organize this material into an interpretation?" The second countering, "Given all this information, do we even need an interpretation?" This is often followed with a third and even more emphatic question that goes something like, "Can't we just perform the score of the text as the previous chapters have laid out and call it a day?"

Let's put aside question one, for the moment, and delve into questions two and three. We could rephrase these two questions even more bluntly: "Why do we need to bother ourselves with overlaying an interpretation? *Can't the text speak for itself?*" Perhaps the best answer to this question is yet another question: "Yes, *Hamlet* can speak for itself, but *which Hamlet are we talking about?*" The late, great critic Jan Kott reminds us that there are a multitude of Hamlets within *Hamlet*; by his count there is:

1 Hamlet as dialectic over force versus morality.

2 Hamlet as a study in theory versus practice.

3 Hamlet as meditation on the ultimate purpose of life.

4 Hamlet as love tragedy.

5 Hamlet as family drama.

6 Hamlet as political analysis.

7 Hamlet as eschatological treatise.

8 Hamlet as metaphysical conundrum.

9 Hamlet as psychological case study.

10 And, finally, Hamlet as a really good potboiler.

Kott concludes, "One can select at will. But one must know what one selects, and why."[1] In short, the story of *Hamlet* functions in a variety of different registers. As an audience member I have always found it helpful when a director foregrounds one register and then lets the others function like associational echoes throughout the unfolding of the play. In this respect, interpretation is also about *emphasis*. I think this is very much the way we naturally read any text. We all have our own highly particularized way of looking at the world and we bring this same unique vantage point to the texts we read. For instance, some of us are political by nature, while others are more spiritually inclined and view the world through these lenses. We should trust and celebrate these different ways of seeing and share them with others who look at the world differently. In this way we, as a culture, begin to gain a 360-degree view of the texts that are truly meaningful to us as a community of readers, expanding ourselves and the text at the exact same time. It is a testament to certain works of art that they can absorb so many points of view, bequeathing to us an ever-expanding vision of the human condition. Such are the works of Shakespeare, which welcome these diverse views and widens our horizons in the process.

This brings us back to Shakespeare and the question of bottomlessness. What further complicates all this is that the way in which these stories can be told can yield even further meanings. And so, not only are we trying to figure out *which Hamlet* to tell; but also, *what that telling can reveal*.

The Fourfold Nature of Certain Texts, Including Those of Shakespeare

Stories come to us in varying degrees of legibility. They can be direct, indirect, or, often, both simultaneously. Such polysemy of meaning is the province of what is often referred to as open texts. I would consider the work of Shakespeare an important part of this tradition of storytelling. Other such open works would be the Bible, Homer, The Mahābhārata, Dante, Kafka, Joyce, and Woolf (to name just a few). These are writings that can be read and appreciated in a variety of different ways, gaining in significance with each approach that is applied. The first interpreters to develop systems for dealing with such open texts were the leaders of the three Abrahamic faiths: rabbis, priests, and imams, who began to craft a series of discrete methods of interpretations that could be applied to sacred works without ever threatening to close the door on other future readings. These systems, developed during different historical timeframes, became known as the Fourfold Method. I have found such an approach helpful in relationship with Shakespeare. This is not to argue, in any way, that Shakespeare is a kind of scripture; just that his work has the same open multiplicity of meaning that is often found in such sacred texts. Perhaps this affinity for openness grows out of Shakespeare's own deep familiarity with the Bible. I leave such speculation to the scholars. All I know is that such an approach has been immensely helpful in unpacking the potential meanings in a given Shakespeare play.

So just what is this fourfold method and how does it work? Let's take a very quick look at each tradition and how they break a given text into four potential interpretations. This begins with a literal reading, then moves to an allegorical interpretation, then to what could be called a comparative reading with other texts/passages/times, and finally ending with a highly anagogical reading which seeks out the highest/deepest and most hidden (think mystical) meaning of the text. We can see this shared approach more clearly when we place these traditions side by side:

JEWISH TRADITION	CHRISTIAN TRADITION	ISLAMIC TRADITION
Peshat (plain reading)	Literal sense	*Zahir* (outer meaning)
Remez (allegorical)	Allegorical sense	*Batin* (inner meaning)
Derash (homiletic)	Moral sense	*Hadd* (moral meaning)
Sod (mystical)	Anagogical sense	*Matla/Muttala* (mystical)

Let's focus, for a moment, on the approach of the Jewish tradition, to better understand the sequencing of these four kinds of interpretations. The Rabbis thought of the text as a kind of heavenly paradise, with each interpretational approach like a rung on the ladder of understanding. The reader must work their way up, rung by rung, until they reached the paradise of the text. These rungs/ interpretative strategies are:

> Peshat
> Remez
> Derash
> Sod

If you take the first letter of each interpretational approach and put them together you get the Hebrew word PRDS which, indeed, means Paradise. In a way, the Christian and Islamic tradition are equally ladder-like, moving upward in interpretational complexity with each approach/rung. In this respect the plain/ literal/outward meaning is thought of as the most immediately discernible and the anagogical/hidden/mystical meaning being the most difficult to tease out. This does not mean that a higher rung is more important than a lower rung of meaning; each rung is interdependent on its predecessor in order to reach the full meaning of a given text.

Now, how would we go about adapting these categories into a secular reading of Shakespeare? The first two categories strike me as pretty straightforward and immediately applicable to any literary text. Our first category would become a Plain Reading which focuses on the literal meaning of a story. Our second category would an Allegorical Reading, which focuses on the hidden meaning that lurks just behind the story. The third category (homiletic or moral) develops its meaning through a kind of cross-referencing of passages, often employing one passage to explain another. We will call this approach an Analogical Reading, which compares the story to other like-stories. The final reading is the most radical/mystically inclined of the four modalities of interpretation. Regardless of the exegete's faith, this becomes the most esoteric and rarified of understandings, meant for only a select few. Such an approach always puts me in mind of the avant-garde. Elaine Pagels, the great scholar of gnosticism, searching for a way to describe the mystical impulse, likened it to artists who would experiment with their respective art forms, since both the mystic and the abstract artist rely on similar non-rational, non-literal, free-associational approaches.[2] We will designate this final category as an Abstract Reading, since it relies on such a non-rational approach to interpreting a given text. The result is the following (secular) fourfold method which includes:

- A Plain Reading
- An Allegorical Reading
- An Analogic Reading
- An Abstract Reading

The following chapters in this section will examine each of these types of readings and apply them to *Hamlet*. Again, it is important to note that we should not privilege any one reading over another. Each approach is of equal value and absolutely necessary for a full understanding of the text at hand. There is often a feeling for those who are starting out that they want to skip steps to get to what they perceive as the more dynamic forms of interpretation. All three traditions would frown upon such interpretational impatience and insist that one cannot arrive at a truly inspired abstract reading without doing the essential groundwork of a plain reading. I have found that working on each of these phases makes it actually easier to reach a truly radical reading of Shakespeare. That said, let's begin with what constitutes the dynamics of a plain reading and see how it can help lead to a better understanding of such a strange and exotic text as *Hamlet*.

6 "To Sing a Song That Old Was Sung": Plain Readings

The great and impossible goal of a plain reading is to get as close to what the original production of a play would have meant for those first initial audiences. It is a truly quixotic quest which puts me in mind of Borges' fictional Pierre Menard, who dreamed of reading everything about Cervantes and his time so that he could re-create, word for word, the novel *Don Quixote* without ever actually reading it. This is how Borges describes this mad venture: Menard must work to "know Spanish well, to re-embrace the Catholic faith, to fight against Moors and Turks, to forget European history between 1602 and 1918, and to *be* Miguel de Cervantes."[1] Even Pierre himself confesses, "To compose *Don Quixote* at the beginning of the seventeenth century was a reasonable, necessary and perhaps inevitable undertaking; at the beginning of the twentieth century it is almost impossible."[2] And yet, through such deep imaginative research, Borges tells us Menard is able to re-create *Don Quixote*! The dream of a plain reading is to transform all of us into an army of Pierre Menards, dedicated readers who know the world which created the text so well that we could re-create the work ourselves. The Sufis have a wonderful term for this type of exegesis; they call it *Ta'wil*, which means to return or lead back; it is the restoring of one to their origins, bringing them back to the place they call home. Such a return is the true and original meaning of the text. We have already done some of the heavy lifting required by a Plain Reading with our examination of such textual matters as the nature of quartos vs. folios, meter, punctuation, and etymology. But what other kinds of question might we need to ask ourselves to bring us into a closer orbit with Shakespeare's original audience? Here are a few questions that immediately come to mind:

1 What were the original sources for *Hamlet*?

2 How does *Hamlet* relate to the popular Revenge Drama of its time?

3 What was going on politically at this moment?

4 What was the Elizabethan understanding of melancholy?

When we unpack each question, we find ourselves closer to a Menard-like understanding of how that initial production might have been received. This is particularly helpful with a play like *Hamlet* that has, in many ways, been forcibly kidnapped by Goethe and his fellow German Romantics. It is they that have bequeathed to us the image of a sensitive, sad prince in an inky cloak, who goes about the stage sighing insufferably with his hand perpetually stuck to his brow. Part of the necessity of a plain reading is often to break through earlier misreadings that have hijacked a given play. Let's see how an examination of these questions might help dispel some of the Romantic mist that obscures an Elizabethan understanding of this play and character. What follows is an immensely condensed look at each of these possible categories of research. Such work, in and of itself, could become its own book; be that as it may, here are four sketches for such an investigation:

Sources for *Hamlet*

The primary source for Shakespeare's *Hamlet* is from Saxo Grammaticus' *History of the Danes* (circa 1200). This is where we first encounter the story of Amleth. Let's begin with a parsing of our central character's name which means "an imbecile or weak person." Its Nordic linguistic siblings include the Norwegian *amblod* (fool) and the Swedish *amblodhe* (one who is not in his right mind). Some lexicographers believe the name derives its meaning from the story itself, becoming a common noun; whether this is true or not, we will never know. Suffice to say, Amleth does indeed behave as his name suggests, or at least pretends that name and self are one and the same. He does so to protect himself from his uncle Feng, who killed Amleth's father and married his mother Gerutha. Saxo tells us that Amleth believed:

> He might make his uncle suspicious if he behaved intelligently. So he feigned madness and pretended that his mind had been damaged. With this cunning he not only concealed his cleverness but also guarded his life. Every day he sat on the ground at his mother's hearth, unkempt and listless, and tossed dirt upon himself. With his soiled face and his skin smeared with putrid slime, he looked like a grotesque madman. Whenever he spoke, he spoke like a fool, and whatever he did he did with utter foolishness. Why should I say more? You would not have called him a man at all but an absurd monster due to a derangement of fate.[3]

While sitting on his mother's hearth he obsessively makes wooden crooks out of sticks which he hardens in a fire and fastens together with opposing hooks to make a kind of immense net. When asked what he was doing, he would say forging spears to avenge his father's, death which elicited much laughter from all those who encountered him. Amleth bides his time and maintains his madman's persona throughout a series of tests which include:

1 The King's Men take Amleth into the woods to see how he will respond to the charms of a young and unaccompanied woman. He merely talks of storms.

2 The King's Men hide themselves in the queen's chamber to overhear the private conversing of mother and son. Amleth kills one of the spies, chops up the spy's remains and feeds it to the neighboring swine.

3 The King's Men escort Amleth to a foreign land where he is to be murdered. Amleth secretly rewrites their letters so that the foreign monarch executes his escorts rather than Amleth.

4 Amleth wins over the king of this foreign land, marries the king's daughter, and returns to his homeland where he discovers his uncle holding a funeral celebration in Amleth's honor.

In the midst of this very ceremony, Amleth appears covered in filth. Horror gives way to merriment as everyone celebrates Amleth's escape from death. Amleth plies everyone with more and more liquor until they are so drunk that they fall to the floor, making the hall their bedroom. This is how Saxo describes what happens next:

> Amleth saw that they were in a fit state for his trap and judged that the time to carry out his plan had come. In a fold of his clothing he put the sticks he had once fashioned and ... cut away the supports of the hangings his mother had made, which covered the inside of the hall, so that they fell to the ground. He placed them upon the sleeping men, and with the crooks he bound them together so skillfully and tightly that none of the men who lay beneath was able to rise, however powerfully they tried. After this he set fire to the building. The flames grew and spread until they covered the entire hall, consuming it and bringing to death all the men inside, whether they were deep in sleep or trying in vain to get up.[4]

So much for Goethe and the Romantics' sad little prince. The point of inspiration for Shakespeare is a terrifically barbaric tale that fits right into the Elizabethan's fascination with (ever popular):

The Revenge Genre

Even the most cursory glance at the Elizabethan genre of Revenge Tragedy reveals a series of dramatic tropes which run throughout these plays: the appearance of a ghost, feigned madness, plays-within-plays, and fifth acts where many of the principal players are killed. All of these elements can be found in Thomas Kyd's *The Spanish Tragedy* (1587), which is generally held as the play responsible for launching this popular Elizabethan genre. Let's quickly compare the similarities between Kyd's play and Shakespeare's *Hamlet*:

THE SPANISH TRAGEDY	HAMLET
Play opens with the ghost of Andrea and the figure of Revenge.	Play opens with the ghost of Hamlet's father.
Hieronimo seeks revenge for the murder of his son.	Hamlet seeks revenge for the murder of his father.
Hieronimo's grief drives him to the brink of madness.	Hamlet first feigns madness and almost becomes mad himself.
Hieronimo hesitates, waiting for more proof.	Hamlet hesitates, not sure if the ghost is his father or a devil.
Bel Imperia, learning of the death of her lover (Hieronimo's son), goes mad and ultimately commits suicide. suicide.	Ophelia learning of the death of her father, goes mad and ultimately commits suicide.
Hieronimo, in order to enact his revenge, puts on a play for the court entitled *Soliman and Perseda*. He replaces the fake daggers with real ones, which leads to the death of his son's murderers.	Hamlet puts on a play for the court entitled *The Murder of Gonzago*, in order to "catch the conscience of the king."[5]
At the end, all the central characters are dead, including Hieronimo.	At the end, all the central characters are dead, including Hamlet.

Kyd, we are told, would go on to pen his own version of *Hamlet* in 1588 or 1589. No version of this play survives. The only line that has come down to us is from the Ghost who was supposed to have cried out, "Hamlet, revenge." The play became another audience pleaser, so much so that writer Thomas Nashe jokes that even a lawyer's clerk could, "if you entreat him fair in a frosty morning … afford you whole Hamlets…". This would lead to further revenge plays such as Shakespeare's own *Hamlet* and John Marston's *Antonio's Revenge*. In the case of these last two plays, there has been much scholarly argument as to which came first, Shakespeare's or Marston's. Editor W. Reavley Gair argues that there are no conclusive grounds on which to establish the precedence of either Marston's play or Shakespeare's and notes: "Shakespeare and Marston were working at the same time and in competition on a revenge play, neither able to see what the other was doing, each with an eye on the old Hamlet play."[6] Be that as it may, Marston's *Antonio's Revenge* has the ghost of Antonio's father beseeching his son to revenge his death, which his son finally does in the midst of a court masque. Here is the opening of Marston's play, which could very easily be put in the mouths of either of Shakespeare's two night watchmen:

> 'Tis yet dead night; yet the earth is clutch'd
> In the dull leaden hand of snoring sleep;
> No breath disturbs the quiet air,
> No spirit moves upon the breast of earth,
> Save howling dogs, night crows, and screeching owls.
> Save meagre ghosts, Piero, and black thoughts.[7]

And here, one cannot resist sharing this Hamlet-like echo from his Elizabethan doppelgänger, Antonio. It is a speech given on his way to an encounter with the ghost of his dead father:

> Graves, vaults, and tombs, groan not to bear my weight,
> Cold flesh, bleak trunks, wrapped in your half-rot shrouds,
> I press you softly with a tender foot
> Most honored sepulchre, vouchsafe a wretch
> Leave to weep o'er thee. Tomb, I'll not be long
> Ere I creep in thee, and with bloodless lips
> Kiss my cold father's cheek. I pray thee, grave,
> Provide soft mount to wrap my carcass in.
> Thou royal spirit of Andrugio,
> Where'er thou hover'st, airy intellect,
> I heave up tapers to thee—view thy son —
> In celebration of due obsequies.[8]

And so an Elizabethan audience would have come to *Hamlet* with certain expectations as to how a revenge tragedy moved and sounded. All of this would have been born out of seeing Kyd's *Spanish Tragedy*, an *Ur-Hamlet*, and plays like *Antonio's Revenge*. It would be similar to our going to an action movie and wondering about what witty one-liner our hero is going to make after shooting the villain, or how the filmmaker is going to make the obligatory car chase different from all the others we've seen over the years. The Elizabethans had a name for such a creative act: they called it a "lively turning." Jonathan

Bate explains that a lively turning was the art of copiousness, learned in school, where every student was expected to take "a proverb, a phrase, a historical incident, a story, or an ancient myth and turn it on the anvil of your inventiveness," giving new life to an old work.[9] And so the audience would have arrived to a given play curious to see how Shakespeare was going to "turn it." Certainly, Hamlet is a new model for a revenge figure (a kind of thinking man's revenger) and yet, although he may be different, the world he is operating in would have been very familiar to an Elizabethan audience. We, of course, are most interested in *when* Shakespeare seems to depart from these genre expectations. Part of our work, as plain readers, becomes a matter of noting what, in this case, Shakespeare recycles and what he reinvents.

Political/Historical Context

There are several external/historical concerns that seem to haunt *Hamlet*. There is the question of who will succeed Queen Elizabeth (aka the virgin queen), the fear of a resulting and protracted civil war to decide this, as well as the ever-imminent threat of invasion by the Spanish that could happen at any moment. The result of these immediate pressures is a kind of low-level anxiety on the part of every Elizabethan audience member who could relate to the following exchange that occurs in the middle of the first scene of *Hamlet*:

MARCELLUS
   ... tell me that knows
   Why this same strict and most observant watch
   So nightly toils the subject of the land,
   And why the daily cost of brazen cannon
   And foreign mart for implements of war,
   Why such impress of shipwrights, whose sore task
   Does not divide the Sunday from the week.
   What might be toward this sweaty haste
   Doth make the night joint laborer with the day?
   Who is't that can inform me?
HORATIO   That can I.
   At least the whisper goes so.[10]

And Horatio goes on to explain that all this fevered activity is in preparation for what is believed to be the impending invasion by Fortinbras of Norway. All one would have to do is strike out the words "Fortinbras of Norway" and replace them with "Philip of Spain" and this could pass for a conversation between any two audience members who were attending a performance of *Hamlet. They would have seen similar preparatory activity as they made their way to the Globe Theatre.*

In addition to this, there is the uncertainty surrounding the curious figure of James I and how he would reign. Carl Schmitt, the infamous German jurist and controversial political thinker, brings these issues to the fore in his intriguing book *Hamlet or Hecuba: The Intrusion of the Time into the Play.* These intrusions of time are, for Schmitt, threefold. The first is what he calls the taboo surrounding the guilt of the queen, which he writes:

> concerns Mary Queen of Scots. Her husband, Henry Lord Darnley, the father of (soon to be King) James, was brutally murdered in February of 1566 by the Earl of Bothwell. In May of the same year, 1566, Mary Stuart married this very Earl of Bothwell, the murderer of her husband. This was hardly three months after the murder . . . The question of the extent to which Mary Stuart was involved in the murder of her husband, perhaps even to the point of having instigated it herself, has remained unresolved and disputed to the present day.[11]

This leads to the second "intrusion of time." Schmitt calls this "the Hamletization of the hero,"[12] which is based on none other than King James himself, whose immediate circumstances mirror those of Hamlet. Schmitt believes that this accounts for Hamlet's character deviating from the traditional avenger to a more considered intellectual, basing such a refined temperament on that of King James, who, Schmitt notes, "was a great reader and writer of books, a friend of sharp-witted speech and ingenious formulations, a famous writer and debater in an age of theological controversy and dispute."[13] Schmitt reminds us that James was the author of *Daemonologie,* which grapples with the issues of ghostly apparitions and further explains Hamlet's fear that the ghost of his father might indeed be a devil from hell. And so, "the philosophizing and theologizing" King James becomes a key model for Hamlet and "the entire conflict of his age, a century of divided belief and religious civil war."[14]

But James is not the only model for Hamlet. This accounts for the third intrusion of time. Schmitt also cites the strong influence of the figure and fate of the rebellious Earl of Essex. This emerges in the second part of the play, where the revenge drama recedes and a new conflict between Hamlet and King Claudius emerges. We can see this in the famous scene where Hamlet bursts into Gertrude's bedchamber. It would be hard for an Elizabethan audience to see this scene and not think of the similar story of Essex breaking into Queen Elizabeth's chamber in a mad attempt to reverse his fortunes. The image of Essex would have also weighed heavily on the last scene of the play, where Hamlet dies. Horatio's "Good night sweet prince / And flights of angels sing thee to thy rest"[15] is uncomfortably close to Essex's last words on the scaffold where he reportedly said, "And when my soul and body shall part, send thy blessed angels to be near unto me which may convey it to the joys of heaven."[16] Schmitt writes, "The details of Essex's imprisonment and execution were all the more present, and the group to which Shakespeare belonged was deeply shocked by them. Thus the features of the character and fate of the Earl of Essex wove themselves into the image otherwise determined by James."[17] And so an Essex–Hamlet is grafted onto a James–Hamlet in the Elizabethan audience's mind. Schmitt goes onto explain: "This is not unnatural because such stage plays form a kind of dream-frame (*Traumrahmen*) as Egon Vietta has noted. Just as people and realities merge with each other in a dream, images and figures, events and situations are interwoven in a dream-like way on stage."[18]

So, whether intended or not, Shakespeare introduces us to a fictional land on the eve of invasion and puts forth young prince Hamlet as its potential savior. This character, consciously or unconsciously, careens between two types of representative leaders: the rash and impetuous Essex or the more considered, intellectual, and cautious James. This bipolar aspect also seems to manifest itself in Hamlet's so-called psychological disposition of:

Elizabethan Melancholy

When we hear the word melancholy today, we basically think "sad" and call it a day; but for the Elizabethans, melancholy was a much broader condition. Look, for example, at Robert Burton and his encyclopedic *The Anatomy of Melancholy* (1621). It will take Burton some 162 pages before he is willing to proffer a proper definition of melancholy. First he must "anatomize the body and soul of man."[19] And so he walks us through the theories of the four humors, of which melancholy is one. Finally he tells us the name is imposed from the matter, a disease dominated by an overflow of black choler. Whether this is the cause or the effect, Burton sidesteps and moves onto a catalog of previous definitions, ranging from the early stirrings of antiquity to height of the Renaissance itself, including:

Fracastorius: "Melancholy, whom abundance of that same depraved Black Choler hath so disaffected, that they **become mad** then, and dote in most things, or in all, belonging to election, will, or other manifest operations of understanding."

Melanelius: "A bad and peevish disease, which **makes men degenerate into beasts.**"

Galen: "A privation or **infection** of the middle cell of the head."

Hercules de Saxonia: "A **depravation** of the principal function."

Holyabbas: "A **commotion of the mind.**"

Aretaeus: "A **perpetual anguish** of the soul, fastened on one thing."[20]

From here, Burton moves to the understandings of what he calls "the common sort" who define this strange mental ailment as "A kind of dotage without fever, having for his ordinary companions, fear and sadness, without any apparent occasion." Or: "Fantasy of the brain." Or: "Anguish of the mind." He concludes this section of the definition of melancholy with the words of Laurentius, who interprets melancholy as "when some principle facultie of the mind, as imagination or reason is corrupted, as all Melancholy persons have."[21] Burton, himself, seems to believe that fear and sorrow are central to the condition but confesses the variety and confused mixture of symptoms makes it difficult to discern this with any "certainty or distinction," since "seldom two men shall be like affected."[22] By being freed of the conception of melancholy as mere sadness, we are able to begin to see more clearly the actual dynamics of Hamlet's behavior which might strike a modern viewer as more bipolar than what we associate with our present-day understanding of melancholy. One minute Hamlet is committed to the idea that "The play's the thing / Wherein I'll catch the conscience of the King,"[23] and in the very next scene we find him pondering the famous question of "To be or not to be,"[24] and concluding, "Thus conscience does make cowards of us all / And thus the native hue of resolution / Is sicklied o'er with a pale cast of thought / and enterprises of pitch and moment / with regard their currents turn awry / And lose the name of action."[25]

A similar sort of contradictory behavior can be found a few scenes later where we find Hamlet a step away from reaching his goal and murdering Claudius. At this juncture, he pauses and goes through a theologically nuanced argument as to whether he can murder Claudius while the man is praying and decides this is not the right moment; and yet, a scene later, he hears a sound and, without a moment's hesitation or contemplation, rashly attacks the figure hiding behind an arras, only to discover he has murdered Polonius rather than Claudius. This is the same person who will give a beautifully considered Stoic speech about death ("Alas, poor Yorick")[26] and then moments later will jump into the open grave of Ophelia and wildly proclaim that he feels more for her loss than her own brother Laertes, exclaiming with a strange and competitive petulance, "I loved Ophelia—forty thousand brothers / Could not with all their quantity of love / Make up my sum. What wilt thou do for her?"[27] How do we account for these radical shifts from overly considered to overly rash? It seems that Hamlet should heed the advice he gives the actors and apply it to himself. It is here, before they are about to perform the play-within-a-play, that Hamlet embarks on the following critique:

in the ... whirlwind of your passion, you must acquire and beget a temperance that may give smoothness. O, it offends me to the soul to hear a robustious periwig-pated fellow tear a passion to tatters, to very rags, to split the ears of the groundlings, who for the most part are capable of nothing but inexplicable dumb-shows and noise. I would have such a fellow whipped ... Pray you avoid it.[28]

But right on the heels of this, Hamlet warns of the other extreme: "Be not too tame neither, but let your own discretion be your tutor."[29] And then he famously begins to speak about the balance ("Suit the action to the word, the word to the action"[30]), a subject he will bring up again in the very same scene when he explains why he so admires his friend Horatio:

> For thou hast been
> As one in suffering all that suffers nothing —
> A man that Fortune's buffets and rewards
> Hast ta'en with equal thanks. And blest are those
> Whose blood and judgement are so well co-mingl'd
> That they are not a pipe for Fortune's finger
> To sound what stop she please.[31]

It is this balance that Hamlet seems to lack and which he spends the entire play attempting to achieve. In the end, as we quoted before, he will tell us:

> There is special providence in the fall of a sparrow. If it be now, 'tis not to come. If it be not to come, it will be now. If it be not now, yet it will come. The readiness is all.[32]

Such a sentiment as "the readiness is all" would no doubt make sense to a certain segment of Shakespeare's audience who were being raised to be a new kind of hero: the scholar/warrior (aka the Renaissance courtier). For them such an adage would be seen as part of the education of a Renaissance prince, and the play itself as a kind of dramatic tutelage for the newly crowned King James.

Plain Reading Conclusions

Having quickly surveyed these Plain Reading issues, certain aspects of the text come into focus:

1 The source material suggests that *Hamlet* belongs very much to the aesthetic zip code of Revenge Tragedy and the play itself borrows many of the tropes of this genre. In this respect, the Elizabethan *Hamlet* would have been closer to these works than the more rarified Hamlet of Goethe and the Romantics. We can also add the textual work we have done in preceding chapters which points to a radical shift in Hamlet's use of language, which suggests a less refined and more direct and unpredictable manner of expression in our young prince.

2   The historical/political context of the work suggests that *Hamlet* is a reflection of the anxieties of an uncertain time. It is inhabited by a new generation of young men who have been educated in the ways of Renaissance Humanism and yet are still expected to, when needed, follow in the barbaric footsteps of their forefathers as warriors and defenders of their nation. It is a world caught between two role models: those of the rash Essex and the more cautious James.

3   Hamlet's melancholic struggle becomes a metaphor for the struggle of this new generation of young scholar/warriors who must find the right balance between both aspects of their being so that they are indeed ready for the philosophical, political, and militaristic challenges that await them.

If nothing else, a plain reading allows us to call into question the Romantic reading of *Hamlet* that has so dominated our thinking, allowing us a glimpse into how that initial Elizabethan audience might have understood the play. It also creates a strong foundation for us to begin to apply allegorical, analogic, and abstract readings. Let's now move to the next rung of the interpretational ladder.

EXERCISE #6

Well, you know what I am going to ask, right? **Now**: Do a Plain Reading of the Shakespeare play that you are working on, answer the following questions along the way:

Plain Reading Questions

1   What is the source material that the play is based on?
    What does Shakespeare add or subtract to the source material?
    Why do you think he makes these changes?

2   What other contemporary plays/genre might have inspired Shakespeare's writing of the play? How does Shakespeare partake and depart from genre expectations of his audience?

3   Where does this play sit within Shakespeare's own canon of work?
    What themes does it share with the plays that come immediately before and after it?
    What does it seem like Shakespeare is trying to work out?

4   What is happening historically at this moment of the play's composition?

What events/dynamics might be inspiring Shakespeare's writing?

7 "You Speak a Language That I Understand Not": Allegorical Readings

The word allegory hails from *allegoria*, which is derived from *allegorien* (to speak otherwise than one seems to speak). This tiny word is made up of the following three lexical integers: *allos* (different), *agoreuein* (speech), and *agora* (public space). Put them all together and you get the rather literal and ungainly translation: "to speak otherwise in the marketplace." A more succinct distillation of meaning would be something like "other-speak." Here, the words one hears are still familiar, like those you would find in the public square, only now they are being used for other, often secret, ends. To the average ear such words go by unnoticed, but to the initiated, their true meaning is understood. It is a kind of coded speech, and once one understands it, the true meaning snaps into focus. What began in the marketplace of Athens eventually finds a home in literature. Allegory really begins its career in the Hellenistic age and reaches its apotheosis in the medieval period with works like *The Divine Comedy* and *The Romance of the Rose*, so it was still a somewhat dynamic form of expression when Shakespeare was coming of age. Although allegory has fallen out of favor in our modern times, we can still find it alive and well in such popular works as George Orwell's *Animal Farm* or C.S. Lewis's *The Lion, The Witch and the Wardrobe*. Another less overt example would be Tennessee Williams' *A Streetcar Named Desire*, where the relationship of Blanche and Stanley can be read as an allegorical battle between the civilized (Blanche) and the philistine (Stanley). One could argue that most stories can be read as either intentional or unintentional allegories. These allegorical readings can be political, psychological, spiritual, etc.

If that is the case, how would we begin to think of *Hamlet* in allegorical terms? One way would be to examine the differences between the trajectories of Hamlet and Fortinbras. What does it mean that Hamlet takes the entire play to finally take action, whereas Fortinbras never seems to waver in his mission and ultimately succeeds? Or perhaps, put another way, what does Hamlet's death and Fortinbras' arrival mean? Over the next several pages I would like to share two allegorical readings: one which is mystical in nature and the other which is political. I present these two specific readings not because I necessarily agree with either (actually, both, to my mind, have huge interpretive blind spots); but rather, to show how this deeply mysterious play can engender two such radically divergent readings. We will begin with an allegorical interpretation put forward by Martin Lings from his book *The Sacred Art of Shakespeare*.

Hamlet as Religious Allegory

Lings, as the title of his book suggests, sees Hamlet's journey as a spiritual quest, one in which our prince has been tasked by the ghost of his father to restore the fallen world of Denmark, returning it back to its pre-Edenic existence by killing the serpent Claudius. Lings tells us,

> The Ghost's revelation to the Prince is, as regards its allegorical meaning, like a puzzle with a few missing pieces which it is not difficult for us to supply in light of those pieces which we are given—the garden with its fruit trees, the serpent, the guilty woman, whose guilt has something mysteriously unfathomable about it. The *Genesis* narrative is undoubtedly here.[1]

Lings reminds us that this Garden imagery begins in Hamlet's first soliloquy where he exclaims, "Fie on't! Oh fie! 'Tis an unweeded garden / That grows to seed; things rank and gross in nature / Possess it merely."[2] And so, Hamlet, according to Lings, is our heavenly gardener; or, more specifically, a Christ-like figure of redemption. Lings goes on to explain:

> In accordance with worldwide tradition it could be said that to regain what was lost at the Fall is to become once more in all fullness a priest-king, which is what man was created to be, king because he was placed at the center of this early state to be there the vicegerent of God, priest because his centrality has also a vertical aspect, that being mediator between heaven and earth. This definition is relevant to many of Shakespeare's greater plays, and it is nearly always the priestly dimension which most needs to be developed and perfected. At the outset of *Hamlet*, however, the Prince is more priest than king. Not that he has not already also a wealth of royalty in his nature, but it falls short of the fullness in one direction, and his growth to adequacy in that respect is the main theme of the drama.[3]

And so, for Lings, Hamlet slowly moves from priest (reflective) to king (active agent) over the course of the play. This is Hamlet's journey: to blend the priest and king into one unified self who can take "right action" and eliminate Claudius, who is evil incarnate. Hamlet achieves this in the final scene of the final act and dies in the process. Lings reads Fortinbras as an angel sent from God to guide the spirit of Hamlet to his new heavenly abode. He hears Fortinbras' last lines as a veiled nod to Hamlet's ascension to heaven. If we were to graph this reading, it would look something like this:

OLD HAMLET	CLAUDIUS	HAMLET	FORTINBRAS
Represents **Adam**. His Court: The Garden of Eden.	Represents **Serpent** in the garden. Initiates the Fall.	Represents potential **Spiritual Redeemer** of this fallen world by wrestling with the snake. **HE SUCCEEDS**	Represents an **Angel** sent by God to guide a worthy Hamlet to his new abode in Heaven

Now let's compare this reading with an overtly political interpretation of the play based on a reading by Bertolt Brecht.

Hamlet as Political Allegory

In the following gloss, I am very much indebted to Paul Walsh's masterful essay on "Brecht's Dialectical Appropriation of Classic Texts"[4] and Margot Heinemann's equally insightful *How Brecht Read Shakespeare*.[5] For Brecht, *Hamlet* has been read primarily in a psychological rather than historical manner. He sees Hamlet caught between the old feudal world as represented by Old Hamlet and the new world of the Renaissance Humanism that Hamlet is being exposed to as a student in Wittenberg. Brecht writes:

> What a work this Hamlet is! The interest in it, lasting over centuries, probably arose from the fact that a new type, fully developed, stands out as totally estranged in a medieval environment that has remained almost entirely unmodified. The scream of revenge, ennobled by the Greek tragedians, then ruled out by Christianity, in the drama of Hamlet is still loud enough, reproduced with enough infectious power to make the new doubting, testing, planning appear estranging.[6]

By this point Brecht knows the play well; he had adapted it in 1931 for broadcast with Radio Berlin. He begins his adaptation with a prologue drawn from Horatio's last lines to Fortinbras, where he tells him that Hamlet's story is "Of carnal, bloody, and unnatural acts / Of accidental judgements, casual slaughters, of deaths put on by cunning, and forc'd cause."[7] The impetus behind this transposition is twofold: first, to remind a modern audience that the Elizabethan theatre was "Drama for Cannibals," a world which reveled in bloodshed and revenge; and second, that this is very much Hamlet's world which is steeped in a barbaric feudal society. Brecht would later write:

> Hamlet is quite simply an idealist who collides with the real world and gets knocked off course, an idealist who becomes a cynic. To act or not act is not the question, but whether to be silent or not silent, to condone or not condone.[8]

But, for Brecht, Hamlet's quest is a failure. He is born ahead of his time and the world he is trying to change is too entrenched in its violent ways to be transformed. The turning point for Hamlet, in Brecht's interpretation, comes late in the fourth act when Hamlet witnesses his princely doppelgänger, Fortinbras marching toward Denmark. It is here that he sees a young person like himself subscribing to the old feudal ways and succeeding. Here he somewhat cynically/competitively notes: "Witness this army of such mass and charge / Led by a delicate and tender prince / Whose spirit with divine ambition puff'd /Makes mouths at the invisible event / Exposing what is mortal and unsure / To fortune, death, and danger dare. . ."[9] From this observation Hamlet concludes, "Rightly to be great / Is not to stir without great argument / But greatly to find quarrel in a straw / when honour's at the stake," and concludes, "O, from this time forth / My thoughts be bloody or be nothing worth."[10] Brecht himself poetized this moment in a sonnet of his own where he writes: "Fortinbras and all the fools he's found / Marching off to battle for that patch of ground / At that this too, too solid flesh sees red. / He feels he's hesitated long enough. / It's time to turn to bloody deeds instead."[11] Brecht later writes that Hamlet is "Faced with irrational practices, his reason is utterly impractical. He falls a tragic victim to the discrepancy between reasoning and such action."[12] And with this, Hamlet says goodbye to the ways of Renaissance Humanism and embraces old feudal hierarchy's barbarism. His project, in short, becomes a failure. This is the tragedy of a man born too soon, into a world still incapable of converting to his vision. A graph of such a reading would look something like the following:

OLD HAMLET	CLAUDIUS	HAMLET	FORTINBRAS
Represents the old barbaric feudal system.	Represents a cross between the old barbaric way and a new Renaissance Machiavelli.	Represents the new Renaissance humanist, but is unable to change the barbaric world.	Represents a complete and total return to the barbaric, worse than the reign of Claudius or Old Hamlet.
		HE FAILS	

And so we have the same story with two radically different interpretations. Every dramatic integer of the story is given its exact opposite valence from one interpretation to the next. In Lings, Hamlet succeeds; in Brecht, Hamlet fails. In Lings, Old Hamlet is Adam; in Brecht, Old Hamlet becomes a barbaric feudal lord, and so on and so on. This sort of variance of interpretation is, of course, not unheard of in literary criticism; but it once again reminds us of the intensely polyvalent aspects of *Hamlet* and other Shakespeare plays.

So, having looked at such allegorical readings, now what do we do? Do we choose one, OR come up with our own? And, regardless of what reading we ultimately decide upon, how does the resulting allegory manifest itself in an actual production? Isn't an allegory supposed to be a secret anyway? I suppose the simplest answer is that an allegorical reading is more a matter of emphasis than actualization. In other words, if one gravitates toward a religious reading of *Hamlet*, this does not mean that Claudius must wear a red tie to signal his being in league with "the devil." But it may mean that the actor playing Claudius might fancy himself a force of negation, intent on oppressing the world he now lords over. The actor may read Milton's *Paradise Lost* and fashion Claudius's internal life after Milton's Satan (one of the greatest characters of all Western Literature), and may listen to the music of Berlioz's *Symphonie fantastique* for inspiration. The audience can be haunted by the ghosts of the actor's preparatory work. This is what the Ancient Greeks called *enérgeia*, an unseen but nevertheless felt force that is released by the actions of another. It is at this level, or frequency, that allegory functions best. As a result, the audience finds themselves deciphering a series of intimations that are found throughout a given production. A certain allegorical calculus ensues, where the audience tallies up the subtle signage of a character's energy or comportment. The key is, once the audience is able to discern such subtleties, they can start to see how all these characters and actions might be placed along a particular spectrum of signification. How much a director or actor wants to point this up is ultimately a matter of taste and degree; but, at the bare minimum, the audience should leave the production with an intimation of these secret forces. So much so, that they are compelled to continue to tease them out, long after the performance has become nothing more than a memory.

Now, what if you don't want to hide the play's secret intent but would rather make it blatantly manifest? Ah, well, then you have moved from the realm of allegory to the realm of analog.

EXERCISE #7

Provide an Allegorical Reading of Your Text

Can the play you are working on be thought of in terms of an allegory.
Could it be:

a. Political?

b. Spiritual?

c. Psychoanalytic?

d. Feminist?

e. Post-colonial?

Develop three of the above and choose one. Ask yourself why that choice.

8 "A Natural Perspective That is and is Not": Analogical Readings

If an allegory whispers, an analog shouts; if an allegory hides, an analog exposes. The analog's entire purpose is to make the secret underpinnings of a story as clear as they can be. It often does this by comparison. This is how it was first utilized in biblical interpretation, where one passage would be explained by another passage. An analog can be particularly useful in Shakespeare to help a modern audience understand certain things that an Elizabethan audience would inherently get without any aid.

For instance, an Elizabethan audience would understand the fundamental difference between the Greeks and the Trojans in Shakespeare's *Troilus and Cressida*. To us, the Greeks and Trojans might just seem to be two opposing forces in different headgear. To a discerning Elizabethan, the Trojans were thought of as a people steeped in tradition, culture, and wisdom; whereas the Greeks would have been viewed as a bunch of scrappy upstarts, rude and unruly. How does one help a modern audience understand this distinction? Well, one of the simplest ways is through an analog. A director friend of mine has always wanted to update *Troilus and Cressida* to the Dakota War of 1862 with the Sioux Nation as the Trojans and the Greeks as the US Calvary. Such a re-imagining places us firmly within the zip code of an analog.

Or take a play like *Antony and Cleopatra* which, for its initial Elizabethan audience, would have been read as a thinly disguised allegory regarding the opposing forces at work during Shakespeare's time. Here the Egyptians represent the last gasp of a Renaissance humanist stance and the Romans (through Augustus Caesar) represent the emerging Puritan impulse that is coursing through post-Elizabethan society. One of the ways to make this clear is to turn the allegory into an analog, as Vanessa Redgrave did in her production of *Antony and Cleopatra* where the Egyptians were dressed like Elizabethans (with her as Queen Elizabeth and Antony as Sir Walter Raleigh) and the Romans (Caesar and his sister) as Puritans. In both instances, the analogic desire is to help the audience see the play as an Elizabethan audience would have understood it.

Other analogs attempt to collapse the distance between Shakespeare's time and our own by modernizing the plays and their settings. In such cases, the Athens of *Timon of Athens* becomes Wall Street; *The Merry Wives of Windsor* is suddenly set in a trailer park, with Budweiser beer cans and lots of buckets of fried chicken; and in a recent production of *Julius Caesar*, Caesar becomes none other than Donald Trump. Other analogs can be based on intertextuality, where a play like *King Lear* can be treated like Beckett's *Endgame* or *Macbeth* like an Alfred Hitchcock film. Perhaps the most straightforward analog is just to update a Shakespeare play to our own contemporary moment. One such example is:

Michael Almereyda's Modern-Day *Hamlet*

One of my favorite analogs is this film version of *Hamlet* with Ethan Hawke. Here, the country of Denmark becomes a corporation (the Denmark Corporation, to be exact). Hamlet's father was the CEO and his uncle has taken over the family's multinational business. Hamlet himself is a young, disaffected Generation X youth who does his famous "To be or not to be" speech as he wanders the Action aisle of a Blockbuster video rental store. Other inventive analogic revisionings include:

- Fortinbras' victories are corporate takeovers; his army, a team of lawyers.
- While Hamlet muses, his television shows images of Hollywood heroes.
- Ophelia is made to wear a wire during her scene with Hamlet.
- The Mousetrap Play becomes a video montage made by Hamlet.
- Ophelia drowns herself in a fountain rather than in a lake.
- Hamlet learns of Fortinbras' successes from a flight attendant en route to England.
- Osric is a fax machine that extends an invitation to the duel.
- The final killings are done with handguns rather than rapiers.[1]

But my favorite analog moment comes during Hamlet's "Get thee to a nunnery" speech. Ophelia arrives home and turns on her voice message machine to hear the following from Hamlet:

If thou dost marry, I'll give this plague for a dowry: be thou as chaste as ice, as pure as snow, thou shalt not escape calumny. Get thee to a nunnery. Farewell.[2]

Then we hear the phone receiver slam down. There is a **beep** and then Hamlet's voice returns on the answering machine for another, new message:

> I say we will have no more marriages. Those that are married already—all but one—shall live. The rest shall keep as they are. To a nunnery go![3]

This is followed by another resounding slamming of the phone receiver and another **beep**. I love this bit of analogical business because it captures our modern-day penchant for giving free rein to our emotions through technological devices like answering machines, perfectly capturing Hamlet's "and another thing" kind of rant. I suppose that if this were done today, it would have to be a series of emails, social media posts or text messages, one on the heels of the other, replete with a series of emojis at the end. We can imagine Hamlet madly typing away on the screen of his phone or at a keyboard. The joy of an analog is in connecting all the potential analogical dots. The audience, getting a sense of what the analog is, begins to play along with the conceptual conceit, asking themselves, "What are they going to do when they get to X?"

Another of my favorite examples of this sort of creative analogical thinking happens during Baz Luhrmann's film version of *Romeo + Juliet*. It is the moment that Friar Laurence learns that the letter he sent to Romeo was never received. The mishap is due to an error on the part of the postal carrier. We see an image of the culprit, which looks suspiciously like a FedEx van but with the company logo "Post Haste" emblazoned across the side of the vehicle.[4]

As you can see, there is great fun to be had with analogs. In many ways, we have Jan Kott to thank for this. His seminal *Shakespeare Our Contemporary* helped to turn the world on to this approach; although, when I spoke to Kott late in his life, he was somewhat taken aback by how this sort of thinking had so overwhelmed what passes as stagings of Shakespeare. It would ultimately lead him to write one of his late great works, *The Bottom Translation*, which argues that it is next to impossible for a modern audience to ever fully comprehend Shakespeare and his classical references.[5] This is a beautiful book that sadly has not gained the attention of Kott's earlier epoch-making writing on Shakespeare. Some people will argue that analogs "dumb down" Shakespeare, or make Shakespeare a tad too reductive. And yet New York theatre critics seem to love such an interpretative gambit. Perhaps this is due to the fact that in an analog the director has done all the work for the critic, sparing them from any heavy lifting when it comes to the interpretation of the play. Other artists like the director Peter Sellars will argue that any other approach is inherently dishonest since all we ever really know is our own time, so we might as well be upfront about it. At the end of the day, there are good analogs and not-so-good analogs. It is entirely dependent on the creativity of the team that has decided to go down this path. When one adheres to the rigors of the analog, the results can be truly inspired and illuminating. Regardless of the results, the key takeaway in all of these cases is that such juxtapositions are what helps an audience understand either the original intention of Shakespeare or what the director unequivocally thinks about the world of the play.

The Kurosawa Gambit

Some of the most fascinating Shakespearean analogs have been created by the legendary Japanese filmmaker Akira Kurosawa. He has transposed both *Macbeth* and *King Lear* from pagan England to Japan's medieval period. This is a world rife with rival warlords vying for power. The juxtaposition makes startling sense not only for Kurosawa's Japanese audiences, but for western audiences as well. Suddenly we can see the more feudal-like ethos that permeates these two plays. One lesser-known Shakespearean analog of Kurosawa is his 1960 film *The Bad Sleep Well*, which is generally acknowledged as a modern-dress "riff" on *Hamlet*. Michael Almereyda, the director of the Ethan Hawke *Hamlet*, acknowledges it as a major influence on his own film version, writing:

> Kurosawa maintained a loose grip on his Shakespearean source material, applying *Hamlet* as an echo chamber and a funhouse mirror rather than a detailed contour map, All the same, with medieval Denmark transposed to a post-World War II Tokyo, the *Hamlet* parallels in *The Bad Sleep Well* are unmistakable.[6]

In this modern rethinking of Shakespeare's play, Hamlet becomes Nishi (Toshiro Mifune), a minor functionary in a large construction corporation. We will learn that his father was driven to "suicide" in order to preserve his superiors' reputations. Nishi gains access to this upper echelon of executives by marrying the Ophelia-like daughter of Iwabuchi, who is the head of the corporation. From here, Nishi slowly exacts his revenge on each of his father's superiors.[7] Almereyda notes:

> Shakespeare's tragedy gets outrageously reimagined in the shadows and half-light of classic film-noir ... Then, inspired by Hamlet's ghost dad, the director gets maximum mileage out of Nishi's ploy to haunt his father's killers ... the film's most Hamlet-like aspect lies in the way images of waste and ruin invade the visual scheme. Kurosawa conjures an alternate reality—a blasted munitions factory nestled in a rubble-strewn landscape, vivid vestiges of World War II—where Nishi hides out with his Horatio-like pal. These baroque ruins, radiating romantic desolation like the sites of Caspar David Friedrich paintings, undercut any wishful claims for Japan's new-found

prosperity and wholeness. The ruins also register as manifestations of the characters' broken inner lives.[8]

Here we see how style, in this case film noir, becomes part of the over-arching analogic approach to Shakespeare's *Hamlet*. Kurosawa deploys this with effortless cinematic aplomb. In his more famous versions *of Macbeth* (*Throne of Blood*) and *King Lear* (*Ran*), Kurosawa will trade this analogic stylization for an analogic periodization, famously transmuting Shakespeare's Elizabethan age to Japan's feudal period.

Theatre practitioners like Ariane Mnouchkine would borrow such an approach for her inspired stagings of *Richard II* and *Henry IV* (1981), setting them within a similarly Eastern-inflected world; her argument being that this style of presentation brought the plays closer to their mythic origins. Mnouchkine, contra Almereyda, explains her decision to look to the ancient East as opposed to the contemporary West to unlock Shakespeare:

> We took Asian theaters, Japanese theater (Noh, Kabuki), but also Balinese theater, Kathakali, etc. Secondly, the choice of ritual: the play itself as ritual. Shakespeare is not our contemporary and shouldn't be treated as such. He is far from us as our own profoundest depths are far from us ... Now it's true that there is also the necessity of offering images of the ritual and chivalric universe of *Richard II*, and for me, such images are much more vibrant in certain Japanese novels and films than they are in *Thierry la Fronde* or certain engravings of the *Très Riches Heures du Duc de Berry*. Given that Japan left its Middle Ages much later than we did, the closest Middle Ages we have are probably Japanese.[9]

Now, for some, this sort of analog can feel like a form of cultural appropriation. This was something that was not so problematic in the early eighties when these productions were created. But, even then, Mnouchkine was sensitive to this critique and explains that the juxtaposition (what we are calling analog) should not be taken literally, but as an evocation that is trying to use the East to get at what Mnouchkine believes transcends any singular culture. One could argue that Mnouchkine's larger goal is using an Eastern analog as a bridge to get to a certain theatrical abstraction. She states:

> What interests me in Asian theatre is that actors are creators of metaphors. Their art consists of showing passions, recounting the interiority of human beings ... the actors' aim is to open up human beings, like a pomegranate. Not to display their guts, but to depict what is internal and transform it into signs, shapes, movements, rhythms.[10]

Ah, now we have indeed moved beyond analog and begun to enter our next modality of understanding: abstraction.

EXERCISE #8

Provide an Analogical Reading of Your Text

a. What would be a modern/contemporary analog for your play?

b. What would be another historical analog for your play (say, American Civil War)?

c. What would be a genre analog (say, like a gangster movie)?

d. What would be another authorial analog (like a Beckett play or a Faulkner novel)?

9 "Is Not This Strange?": Abstract Readings

When we use the word abstraction in art, what exactly do we mean? When we use the word as a noun it signifies that which is a part (or the most important part) of something larger. When we use the word as a verb it means to withdraw, remove, or take away. So, in representational painting we might abstract just color, line, texture, or geometry and focus on that. This is what twentieth-century artists like Rothko, Pollock, and Mondrian did. When you rip something out of representation you lose context; without context these abstracted fragments float in terms of their meaning and have an opportunity to re-evoke in new and exciting ways. Ultimately, we must provide our own context around the abstracted element. We must collaborate in the re-making of meaning. It is asking more of us, to be more than just a receiver, to become something of a co-author of the work at hand.

Now, what is abstraction in theatre? Story is to theatre what representation is to painting. If you remove the story, what are you left with? Characters, images, emotions, and actions. This begins the abstraction of theatre. Plot is a powerful force: the idea of what comes next is so intoxicating to us humans that it can background so many other aspects when experiencing a story. So, once plot is removed, it puts us in an intriguing situation. Gone is our sense of event, directionality, and context. We now feel unmoored, we float in a sea of ambiguity. The sociologist Zygmunt Bauman tells us, "We can tolerate a certain degree of ambiguity . . . not knowing can be titillating (think mystery novel) but beyond a certain point if it remains unsolved for too long, it become disorienting."[1] Marcel Duchamp calls this interval between knowing and not knowing "the delay," because immediate meaning is being deferred or suspended. In most of our adult life there is little "delay." The role of language and culture has reduced the delay of meaning to a bare minimum. Everything in our current Western culture is immediate, downloadable, and instantaneously gratifying , especially in its direct meaning (think movies, advertisements, politics). So it is very hard to live in the land of delay, especially the delay of the avant-garde. But there is a power in delay, of doing the work to break through a cloud of unknowing. Richard Foreman, the great experimental theatre artist, calls these breakthroughs "pops that go off in our brain" and reminds us of how satisfying they can be. Why? Because you have had to work at them. Other disciplines—philosophy and mysticism—traffic in a similar delay toward meaning and suggest that there are other powerful paths toward understanding. In a way, this forces us to return to our childlike intuitions, where we pursued meaning without the aid of language. All those non-verbal ways of understanding (an intonation, the look of something) are less obvious to us, but can be instrumental in leading to alternate modalities of understanding, returning us to a more primordial (pre-linguistic/rational) way of making meaning.

In this section we will look at two examples of abstracting *Hamlet*, one from the Italian provocateur Romeo Castellucci and the other from the late great Russian director, Yuri Lyubimov. Both abstract *Hamlet* in their own unique way, abandoning Shakespeare's basic plot to focus on other dynamics which speak to these artists and their times. Let's begin with:

Amleto

Romeo Castellucci and his Sociètas Raffaello Sanzio theatre company first presented their production of *Amleto* at the Wiener Festwochen in 1992. The piece itself, unlike much of Castellucci's later work, was a solo performance for the actor Paolo Tonti. In the program for the production we are told that Tonti is playing Horatio. This would immediately suggest that the performance we are seeing follows Hamlet's injunction to Horatio to tell his story. The space in which Horatio will tell Hamlet's tale also reflects another moment where Hamlet refers to "the thousand natural shocks that the flesh is heir to."[2] This is made quite literal by a stage which has become a veritable jungle of dangling electrical wires and a stage floor littered with all manner of car batteries. Even more nerve-racking is the fact that Paolo Tonti's Hamlet/Horatio stumbles about this stage, seemingly incapable of controlling the various spasms of his body, thereby leaving him in imminent danger of electrocution. Rather than worry about the catastrophic consequences of his body in relation to this electrified space, he remains fixated on series of words, actions, and situations which he compulsively repeats. These riffs include:

1 Hamlet with his father, represented by a filthy old stuffed toy bear that he seems to fear and tremble before. Then there is:

2 Hamlet and Horatio, who is represented by a toy parrot that repeats whatever Hamlet says, including the recurrent phrase, "My name is... My name is..."

3 Hamlet and Ophelia, who is a talking doll that Hamlet feds spoonfuls of his saliva and responds in a cooing, infantile voice.

4 Hamlet and Gertrude, represented by a large stuffed kangaroo whom Hamlet viciously interrogates.

5 Hamlet and Death. At the end of which Hamlet cowers in a cupboard and refuses to come out for a final bow.[3]

Along the way, this Hamlet takes a gun and shoots blanks at the audience, urinates in his pants, and quotes a smattering of lines from Shakespeare and Saxo Grammaticus. Now, what makes this fit our criterion for an abstraction? I think this lies in Castellucci's desire to focus solely on Hamlet and investigate his anti-social behavior. In doing so, he moves Hamlet from a sixteenth-century melancholic to a twentieth-century young man who seems to be struggling with autism. The move is instructive. It was Jean Baudrillard who first put forth the notion that each age manifests its own collective pathology as a kind of metaphor for the zeitgeist of a particular time and place. In the sixteenth century this collective pathology/ metaphor was melancholy; for the nineteenth century the pathology/metaphor became hysteria; for Baudrillard's time, it was schizophrenia. Castellucci seems to be saying that we have entered the age of the autistic. In this case, to ask Jan Kott's famous question, "What book is Hamlet reading?" Castellucci answer is, "*The Empty Fortress: Infantile Autism and the Birth of the Self* by Bruno Bettelheim." In this much-disputed book, autism is equated with the author's experiences of the German concentration camps. This work became instrumental in Castellucci's conception of his production. We can suddenly see how his Hamlet's behaviors match many of the traits articulated on such web pages as the Autism Awareness Centre:

Insistence on sameness; resistance to change
Repeating words or phrases in place of normal, responsive language
Laughing, crying, showing distress for reasons not apparent to others
Prefers to be alone; aloof manner
Tantrums
Difficulty in mixing with others
May not want to cuddle or be cuddled
Little or no eye contact
Unresponsive to normal teaching methods
Sustained odd play
Inappropriate attachments to objects
Apparent over-sensitivity or under-sensitivity to pain
No real fears of danger
Noticeable physical over-activity or extreme under-activity
Uneven gross/fine motor skills
Not responsive to verbal cues; acts as if deaf although hearing tests in normal range.[4]

Here we have an example of what Susan Sontag called Illness as Metaphor. If autism is indeed the collective metaphor for the zeitgeist of the twentieth/twenty-first century, what does that mean? That Hamlet, who represents us, is more a condition than a character.? A person who is overwhelmed by the world at large? One of the current theories regarding the cause of autism is that it is the result of a profound hyper-sensitivity to outside stimulus. This theory was put forth by Henry Markram, Tania Rinaldi, and Kamila Markram in a 2007 paper entitled "The intense world syndrome—an alternative hypothesis for autism."[5] In this article, the Markrams and Rinaldi postulate that those who are autistic actually have a propensity to feel too much, a hyper-responsivity that manifests itself in enhanced stress responses which lead the subject to seek a profound withdrawal from the world around them. Could we be suffering from a minor variation of such hyper-emotional overload? A condition that is forcing us to retreat from our feelings for one another and the world? This becomes Castellucci's point of departure for his abstract re-investigating of *Hamlet*.

All Together Now

But does a director have to conform to one of these four modalities of interpretation? Is he or she forever stuck with choosing either a plain, allegorical, analogical, or abstract reading? Can't one mix and match? Combine one or two? Or all four? Certainly. Such an approach is perhaps best celebrated in contemporary German or Eastern European Theatre. This is certainly true of the Romanian theatre directors I watched when I was coming of age. Giants like Lucian Pintilie, Liviu Ciulei, and Andre Şerban. There is an old theatre joke about these giants of Romanian theatre; it goes like this: "Question: How many Romanian directors does it take to change a lightbulb? Answer: Does it have to be a lightbulb?" This pretty much sums up the Romanian school of theatre making. Why limit oneself to one form of illumination when there are infinite possibilities? Why restrict yourself to just one modality of meaning? Why not go for all four and, while you're at it, show the world a fifth way as well! This is, of course, not restricted to the Romanians, and perhaps one of the greatest twentieth-century iconoclasts of this impulse was the Russian director Yuri Lyubimov and his seminal production of:

A Very Russian *Hamlet*

Lyubimov's *Hamlet* grows out of a very shrewd plain reading that gleefully mixes moments of allegory, analog, and abstraction. Its allegorical underpinnings were relatively loud and clear to its initial Soviet audience circa 1970. Elsinore is, allegorically, none other than the Soviet Union; but its Hamlet steps out from the protective shadows of allegory and into the harsh light of analog thanks to a stroke of casting. You see, this Hamlet was performed by protest poet/singer/counterculture heartthrob Vladimir Vysotsky. This would be the Western equivalent of casting a young Bob Dylan as Hamlet for an American production, or John Lennon for an English version. Even with Vysotsky dressed in a kind of timeless garb that could reflect the past or the future, the audience could not shake the very present-tense implications of having this outspoken radical Russian "rock star" essaying the role of Shakespeare's noble prince.

Where Lyubimov begins to venture from allegory/analog to abstraction is in the jettisoning of much of Shakespeare's plot and setting the ensuing montage of brief episodes within a kind of theatrical no-man's-land. We are far from the grand battlements of Elsinore and clearly in some seedy, run-down theatre with its whitewashed back wall fully exposed. Leaning against it are a variety of swords, shields, and implements of torture. As our eye moves downstage, we discover an open grave dug in real dirt. Lyubimov's production begins with Hamlet seated by this grave, guitar in hand, performing Pasternak's once-banned poems which have been set to music. He speaks of the silence of the grave, of those who suffer in silence, and ends with a promise to tear down the wall of silence that separates us from true freedom and enlightenment. However, this "wall" turns out to be much more formidable than our Hamlet has anticipated. It reveals itself shortly after this introduction. It is a huge, mobile, and coarsely woven hemp curtain that is activated by an elaborate aluminum tracking system. It will become the central iconic and enigmatic presence in the play, its only rival being Hamlet himself. Spencer Golub writes in his essay, "Between the curtain and the grave," that this element seemed to possess both stage managerial and symbolic functions which:

> not only unfolded the play, but, to an extent, created it . . . The *Hamlet* curtain was conceived to provide an Elizabethan-like continuous flow across an an empty stage (designer Borovsky's idea) and to impersonate objects and locales which would otherwise have to be built and shifted—[this curtain became] solid walls, tapestries, a shawl and a swing, (etc.).[6]

As the play progresses, it becomes clear that this curtain is a central character in this Hamlet's drama, following him from scene to scene. Like an actor, it ends up playing multiple roles throughout the evening. One moment it reflects the wind; another moment it is part of the cloak of the ghost; another moment it is like a matador's cape, luring Hamlet to Ophelia's room; another moment it is Winston Churchill's "iron curtain," framing Fortinbras' advancing army.

With each intervention of the curtain, the question of what the curtain represents becomes louder and louder. Is the curtain the state? A representation of Hamlet's troubled mind? A kind of mousetrap of its own? Death? Fate? *God*?

Here we are in the presence of abstraction's delight in trafficking with symbols. Unlike a mimetic representation, the symbol in an abstraction tends to resist stabilizing into a single graspable meaning. It suggests there is a more-ness to certain symbols. Usually all one has to do with a symbol is find whatever its missing signification might be, bring that back to the symbol, and the symbol will settle down and behave itself, finally making sense. Without such a discovery, the symbol will continue to radiate, taunting our consciousness to make sense of it. Meaning happens when we find the symbol's missing half or context. The symbolic process is the imaginative putting-it-all-together; that interim between the sign's ambiguity and its resolution into complete meaning. Midway through our experiencing of Hamlet's curtain, we might be inclined to think of it as being an overdetermined symbol. This was a term coined by Freud to explain how certain symbols found in dreams are non-reducible; they simply mean too much. But as we move deeper and deeper into the play, it is harder and harder not to think of the curtain as ultimately some abstract representation of Fate itself. Golub writes, "It pushed Hamlet like Fate toward the womb-like grave, where the guilty and the just end and where it first encountered him."[7] At this point it is hard not to conclude that the curtain is "God and Hamlet's and his world's fate, defined in and by time, space, and nature, and the veil of silence drawn before irrational truth and deathless mystery."[8] The curtain ultimately becomes a funeral shroud for Hamlet and even, at the end of the play, has its own literal curtain call, bowing along with the actors.

And so, Lyubimov gets to have his theatrical cake and eat it too, mixing our four interpretative modalities to his heart's content. Each choice clearly grows out of a very well-considered plain reading of Shakespeare's play. The timeless trappings of the production elicited a kind of allegorical cat-and-mouse-game with the Soviet censors, who could not prove that Lyubimov's rendering of Shakespeare's Denmark was actually Brezhnev's Soviet Union in disguise. Impatient with allegory's coyness, Lyubimov makes a bold analogical move of casting the outspoken countercultural Vladimir Vysotsky as Hamlet, thereby rooting this otherwise timeless tale in a sly associational Soviet present. But then, he turns his energy toward abstraction with his poetic use of the red curtain as a symbol that steals the spotlight from Vysotsky and returns the play to its deepest and most metaphysical roots and energies. The result is a truly multifaceted masterpiece that keeps metamorphosing before the audience's eyes.

In Conclusion

Again, it is important to stress that I do not favor one interpretative approach over another, but use each, as the rabbis of old used to say, as a rung in the ladder that will eventually lead me to the paradise of the text. A large part of my preparation for Shakespeare is to look at the text from the vantage point of these four readings. By the time I enter the rehearsal room I want to know the plain, allegorical, analogical, and abstract readings of the play that I am about to mount; by doing so, I have gained a 360-degree understanding of the text.

Now does this mean that I have to choose one of these as my ultimate approach to the production that I am doing? Not necessarily; although I would argue that when you see a production of Shakespeare (or many classic and modern texts) you are usually getting one of these four modalities as the major interpretative impulse. If you go to the Globe Theatre in England, you will most likely be seeing a plain reading; if you see the late work of Peter Brook, you are basically experiencing an allegory; if you go to see many of the productions at the New York Shakespeare Festival, or at the Royal Shakespeare Company, you will be seeing a variety of analogs; and if you go to Schaubühne Theatre in Berlin, chances are you are going to see an abstraction, or all four modalities at play/war with one another.

EXERCISE #9

Answer the following questions in terms of an Abstract Reading:

a. What central aspect of the play might you want to rip out of the fabric of the story to explore on its own?

b. Would want to explore one character?

c. A situation?

d. A theme?

e. A series of images?

f. What other texts and images might you use in opposition or support?

g. Would there be any text at all?

h. The great avant-garde filmmaker Godard used to say, "I believe in a beginning, middle, and end; just not necessarily in that order." Is there another order to tell this story? What would that re-ordering potentially mean?

EXERCISE #10

Can you build a production employing all four modalities of interpretation? Try it.

PART THREE

"Come, Give Us a Taste of Your Quality": Practical Matters

10 "What Say You?": Finding the Rhyme between Shakespeare, Yourself, and Your Time

Shifting Gears

In these final chapters I want to move from studying and interpreting the text to the beginning phases of realizing it. Our discussion is no longer just between ourselves and the play; now, it wants to open up to include conversations with dramaturgs, designers, and actors who will help make and people Shakespeare's world. This can often be a rather abrupt transition. We are moving away from the rather rarefied rhetoric of critical analysis and into the wonderful rough-and-tumble world of design meetings, auditions, and the first day of rehearsal. With this shift in focus comes a shift in diction. I hope you won't mind if I put aside my somewhat professorial figures of speech and return to my colloquial roots as a journeyman director.

The tone of these last pages is an attempt to capture, as best I can, the way I try to communicate with collaborators on a day-to-day basis. This is a looser, freer, and more rangy way of speaking; it is the language of the rehearsal room, and, in many ways, it's my native tongue. It was much later in life that I learned the language of the classroom and the boardroom. The first twenty years of my life were spent innocently swapping ideas with actors, designers, and producers as we made our way, day by day, through a given play.

In this final section of the book we will look at the last three crucial phases of preparation:

1   Shaping the text

2   Working with designers

3   Dealing with auditions

But before we plunge into this last and crucial phase, I just want to take a moment to acknowledge the strange liminal space that we now occupy. It exists between our listening to Shakespeare and listening to our collaborators. During this brief interim, we want to make sure that we are also listening to ourselves. Before moving forward with our colleagues, we need to sense how the text is settling within us, how we are processing it for ourselves. This is a crucial phase in the conception of the production and it often gets truncated as we slide into meetings, auditions, and rehearsals.

From Interpretation to Personalization

My favorite moment in *The Wizard of Oz* is toward the end. The Great Oz is bellowing away at Dorothy and her friends and, suddenly, a red curtain accidentally opens, revealing a rather ridiculous fellow madly pulling a set of levers and twisting a series of dials. Oz famously intones: "Pay no attention to the man behind the curtain." As an artist, I enjoy remaining behind the curtain unseen, hiding behind another person's story. For an interpretative artist it is all about the story; but, in order to make the story meaningful, you have to figure out how the story relates directly to you. In many ways, the story you tell ends up being an allegory about yourself. It is one of the great paradoxes of art that the more you personalize the story—making it specific to yourself—the more universal it becomes for an audience.

And so, after you've done all this work, after you've figured out which text and what patterns, you still have to ask yourself one final and essential question: *why does any of this matter to you?* If you can't come up with a deeply personal answer, then I'm not sure the production will work its magic on an audience; or, at least it won't if I'm at the helm. I have found that my most impactful productions have been the ones where the story made a deep, initial impact on me. This becomes the final part of the preparation process: I must personalize the story. I rarely share any of this with my collaborators; this is my own private work. It is a period where I have to translate Shakespeare's story into my story. It is a kind of reverse alchemy, where I convert Shakespeare's golden dramatic narrative into the base metal of my life's narrative. Such a process transforms the text from the realm of the abstract to the world of the concrete.

Does this conversion have to be literal? Story-point by story-point? Not necessarily, but something in the story should rhyme with you, touch some part of your core self. I remember when I read *Timon of Athens*; the very first image that came to me was of my father. He was a traveling salesman who spent most of his life in a four-door Lincoln Continental sedan criss-crossing the country selling his wares. He wore flashy suits, smoked enormous cigars, and seemed the epitome of success. One day, when I was nine or so, while we were driving through the city, we passed a homeless person on the street. My father turned to me and said, "Do you see that fellow over there? I'm just a day away from being that guy." That was perhaps the most terrifying sentence I heard during my entire childhood. How could my father, with his grand Lincoln Continental, his fancy suits, and his Havana cigars, be a day away from poverty? After that, the ground beneath my feet was never solid again. I was convinced there was a crack that was going to open up and swallow me whole. Throughout the rehearsals of *Timon*, all I had to do was access that memory, and Timon's terrifying trajectory made immediate sense to me. This work does not have to be tied to a memory, however. It can be a fantasy. I was shocked by how easy it was to sympathize with Richard III and his gleeful dispatching of his foes. All I had to do was replace those soon-to-be-toppled historical figures with a theatre critic from the *New York Times* or a certain Board President and I was as giddy a sociopath as Richard, *if not more so!* Did I share any of this with anyone? No. Especially not my Board President. This becomes my secret work for bringing a text to life.

But why is this important? Isn't there a danger that I will somehow degrade Shakespeare's great work by bringing it down to my ridiculous quotidian level? Perhaps, but there is an equal danger that the characters and the situations might remain abstractions if I don't do this work. A character, even a character as rounded as those of Shakespeare, is an idea, and remains an idea until you connect with it on a personal level; whether that character is you or someone you know. A lot of times this can help actors with their relationships to one another. For instance, why do the courtiers let Leontes behave so badly in the first three acts of *The Winter's Tale?* You could say, "Well, he can do whatever he damn well pleases, he's the king." But a king, at least for Americans, is an abstraction. You could say, "All right, think of Leontes as a president." But a president is, in its own way, still somewhat fantastical, unless you have day-to-day contact with one. It's far better to find a real-life corollary, someone you know who is powerful. How do they wield their power? Why do you let them wield power over you? Even kings and presidents, who do have power, must use tactics like charm or (my personal favorite) withholding love in order to keep their inner circle in line. Who do you know who is powerful? Who has power over you? How do they specifically wield it? Now things can become more specific, more personal, *which means more complicated and dimensional.* Maybe you let that person have power over you because they scare you, or inspire you, or take care of you, or are just fun to be around. Maybe they are powerful because you love them? More people tend to follow others out of love rather than fear. So when Leontes begins doing things that go against your better judgment, you might have to keep weighing this against the person who has, up to this point, been someone you've loved dearly. *How do you deal with that context?*

When working on a character, I always think of something my grandmother said about my father: "Look, I don't have to like him, I just have to love him." I think that may be the most profound statement about dealing with human beings that I've ever heard. It bears repeating. "I don't have to like him, I just have to love him." What exactly does that mean? It means that when we love someone we put their actions into a larger context of understanding. You could rephrase my grandmother's observation as, "Look, I don't have to like him, I just have to understand him." The deepest form of understanding is love, which is knowing the full context of why that person is that person and is behaving the way he or she is behaving. That is part of the processing work we need to do between the interpretation of the text and the beginning phases of its realization.

From the Timeless to the Timely

When you ask how a work from the past might relate to you, you are entering into a conversation—whether you like it or not—with time. Time comes to us in two basic manifestations: the timely and the timeless. What we have been talking about is the timelessness of a work, how we are all Hamlets, know Othellos, and fear Macbeths. We are talking about the human condition qua the human condition which, in many ways, seems, in a great work of art, to miraculously transcend time. But there is also the timely, how a play can speak directly to the concerns of today. This is the next level of internal work that we need to do. Not only do we have to translate Shakespeare for ourselves but we also have to translate him for our specific time.

Peter Brook use to say that Shakespeare's plays were like planets. At various points in their orbit they are either closer to or farther from us. I'm not sure if this is astronomically correct, but it sounds good to my vague, semi-Copernican understanding of celestial matters. What Brook's simile suggest is that time makes some plays more immediately relatable to us than others. And so, when we are at war, suddenly Shakespeare's history plays might feel closer to us than, say, his Romances. This is the timely aspect of a classic play: A work from the past can suddenly find itself speaking directly to a present moment. I felt this timely aspect keenly when working on *Timon of Athens*, particularly in the interaction between Timon and his friends, who refuse to help him in a very specific and modern way. One of the things I wanted to do was understand the genealogy of this modern-like indifference, which seemed to be born out of an urban setting. It felt somehow appropriate that the story/myth of Timon was located in an urban world. This is, after all, as Shakespeare makes clear in his title, Timon *of Athens*.

Athens is very much a force, the first truly modern metropolis of the West, which clearly rhymed with Shakespeare's London, and seemed to rhyme with my present-day New York City. I went back to my early journal notes to find the following initial entry on *Timon*:

> In this play we seem to be dealing with an urban consciousness. Man in relation to this new urban landscape and all its contending forces, including this new creature that will grow up to become capitalism. Think about what all this does to us, how it shapes us/deforms us.
>
> June 11, 1996

This became an important energy or dynamic that I wanted the actors to embody and the audience to feel. Here is a later journal entry, written after a certain amount of exposure of the German sociologist Georg Simmel, who wrote on the modern urban experience. My journal is littered with quotes from him: "The metropolis works against our normal psychic strategies of coping, creating a culture that 'habituates oneself to indifference.'"[1] Here's another passage from my journal based on Simmel's theories of modernity and the city:

> Faced with the surprising and shock-like impression of metropolitan life, the city-dweller reacts with the formation of an intellectualized character, with the "rule of reason" and a "purely matter-of-fact attitude in the treatment of people and things." As fundamental features of social interactions, these manifest themselves in blasé attitudes and the outer reserve of city-dwellers, which include an inward slight aversion and latent propensity to reserve antipathy which makes clear that the sphere of indifference are underpinned by an internal withdrawal which is felt as relief and devaluation.[2]

This was the world of Timon's friends, but it was also very much a world that I saw all around me: this modern, disengaged way of being. A world where alienation becomes a form of protection. It reminded me of friends of mine who lived in Los Angeles and would drive to work. Many of them would avoid whole sections of the city that had fallen into destitution. This would sometimes add more than a half hour to their commute, but it was worth it; this way they were spared half an hour of feeling guilty about their lives in comparison to others who were so less fortunate. That was the energy that I wanted our *Timon of Athens* to have: I wanted the audience to leave the theatre and say, "That's no different from today."

11 "The Fall of a Sparrow": Shaping Shakespeare

Play Text as Erector Set

I am not a director who necessarily believes that a Shakespeare play text is sacrosanct. It's ultimately next to impossible to know which text, Quarto or Folio, is actually closest to what Shakespeare's audience would have seen. So the idea of establishing an authoritative text seems like searching for El Dorado. In addition to this brute fact, there is something fundamentally flexible about all these texts. Perhaps this is because they were created with the idea of multiple use. They needed to be adaptable to a wide range of performative possibilities: at the Globe, at an indoor theatre like the Blackfriars, at Court, touring the provinces, and even being performed at some patron's estate (as some think *Midsummer* was first presented). Each of these radically different performative situations put differing demands on the text. As we speculated earlier, touring the provinces probably required a drastically cut text, which may explain *Macbeth*'s brevity; plays that went to Court may not have gone with all their "special effects"; plays that were first performed indoors at a theatre like Blackfriars might go on to favor the eye more than the ear when they moved to an outdoor theatre like the Globe. In short, these plays seem to have something in their very DNA that allows them to be assembled and reassembled for whatever extenuating circumstances they might meet. This does not necessarily give us the right to cut and alter Shakespeare with impunity, but it perhaps explains why it can be done so easily.

The fact remains, in this day and age, that most Shakespeare productions we see are cut. Again, just because this is common practice does not somehow make it all right. This is just one of the realities of our current moment. Finding an audience with the ability to see any play that exceeds three hours is getting harder and harder. I once produced a play, David Ives' *Venus in Fur*, where a reviewer wrote that it was "ninety minutes of good, kinky, fun." I asked my wife, "Which of those four promises is the most enticing to a prospective audience member: 'good,' 'kinky,' 'fun,' or 'ninety minutes?'" Without missing a beat my wife said, "Ninety minutes." Now I am not, in any way, advocating that Shakespeare should be done in ninety minutes, just that this is the attention span of most of today's audiences. It would behoove one to keep this in mind while thinking about preparing a Shakespeare play for today. So, how does one go about cutting Shakespeare? Where does one begin? Well, I suppose we begin at the beginning.

Openings

I think one of the biggest changes that I have experienced in my thirty-odd years of watching and working on Shakespeare's plays is how they are launched. This to me has become the biggest dramaturgical intervention that seems to have happened in my lifetime. Audiences nowadays, thanks no doubt to our sister mediums, want to be thrown into the story immediately. They seem to have less patience for getting to know the world of the play, the characters, or the stakes. They want to get right to the crux of the matter. As a result, I have noticed that most dramaturgical intervention happens in the first ten to fifteen minutes of one of Shakespeare's plays. Even a crowd-pleaser like *Romeo and Juliet* gets a great deal of streamlining in its first twenty minutes. After the jaunty prologue by the chorus (you know the one, "Two households, both alike in dignity. . ."), many productions bypass the top of the first scene, which begins with a bit of obscure wordplay between Samson and Gregory, this encounter lasting a whole of thirty- seven lines. But I would wager that if you were to go see *Romeo and Juliet* tomorrow night, there is a very good chance that you'll never hear a word of that conversation. Most productions dispense with this and start with:

ABRAHAM
  Do you bite your thumb, sir?
SAMSON
  I do bite my thumb, sir.
ABRAHAM
  But do you bite your thumb at us, sir?
SAMSON (to GREGORY)
  Is the law on are side if I say, "Aye"?
GREGORY (to SAMSON)
  No.
SAMSON
  No sir, I do not bite my thumb at you, sir, but I bite my thumb, sir.[1]

Two seconds after this, a fight breaks out between the Montagues and the Capulets. Is this a violation of Shakespeare? I don't think so, since these plays were continually adjusted to suit the needs of the prospective audience. Most audiences today might not be able to fully appreciate the arcane wordplay of Gregory and Samson that begins the show, which, of course, runs the risk of alienating the audience right off the bat, many of whom already have what I call "Shakespeare panic." This usually lasts for the first fifteen minutes of the show, where every single line that a Shakespeare character says (save for the witches in *Macbeth*) seems absolutely incomprehensible, hence the panic that the whole show will be like this and we will have no idea what is going on. This, of course, dissipates; the mind quickly learns not to rely on a word-for-word meaning and just attempts to get the gist of an overall line. Once our minds make this shift in comprehension, the text oddly snaps into focus.

So, now, back to the actors who are playing Gregory and Samson. They have to contend with oblique Shakespearean wordplay *and* the audience's inherent Shakespeare panic. What are they to do? Act big. That's what usually happens: go broad. But I'm not sure being broad in these moments is what an Elizabethan audience would have gotten. For an Elizabethan audience this would have been a slice of life: two youths, laying about, passing the time, cracking snide jokes. Their bit of naturalism becomes, for us, a bit of buffoonery. So you get Shakespeare's words, but not necessarily his intention, which was a bit of verisimilitude to begin the play after the artificial rhyming couplets of the prologue. That's the beauty of the antithesis that Shakespeare creates between the prologue and first scene: it immediately tells the audience, "Ah, this is just how it is on the streets today." This becomes part of the argument for starting the scene with the mock casual, "Do you bite your thumb at us, sir?"

Now here is another example of an opening where the ramifications of such cutting might be more debatable. If you watch Peter Brook's masterful film version of *King Lear* you will see that it opens right away with Lear dividing up his kingdom. But Shakespeare begins the play in an antechamber with the secondary characters of Gloucester, his bastard son Edmund, and the Earl of Kent. That scene begins with a line sure to induce Shakespeare panic in the hearts of even the most stalwart Shakespeare goer. The line:

KENT
I thought the King had more affected the Duke of Albany than Cornwall.[2]

Not the most promising of opening lines when compared to something like "O for a muse of fire. . ."[3] And the scene does not necessarily improve from there. We learn that Edmund is the bastard child of Gloucester, we get a couple of Elizabethan bastard jokes that were probably not all that funny even back then, and we get some more talk about France and Burgundy. You can almost hear the *click click* of the editor's scissors just itching to start cutting, which is exactly what I did when I was organizing a reading of *King Lear* several years ago. The actors assembled at the table, opened their scripts, and the wonderful actor Richard Easton, who was playing Gloucester, exclaimed:

"Where's *my scene*?"
"Well, you see, we needed to implement some cuts—"
"But why would you cut *my scene*?"
"Peter Brook cut it when he did it?"
"Peter Brook is terribly overrated. *Put it back*."
"But —"
"Put it back, dear boy, *the entire play depends on it.*"
"On this scene?"
"Yes. *This very scene.* It announces the theme of the entire play."
"Well—"
"I mean, you know that, don't you?"
"I do." (Actually I didn't.)
"Then what is it?"
"What is what?"
"The theme of *Lear*? Come, come. What is the theme of *Lear*?"
"Well. . . that's a big ques—"
"*Neglect*, my dear boy, *neglect.* That is what the play is about. The danger of neglecting a child or parts of one's kingdom, how that sows discontent and leads to familial and national discord! *Put it back!*"

I put it back. A few years later I saw a terrific version of *Lear* directed by Robert Falls at Chicago's Goodman Theatre. He, like Richard Easton, felt the absolute necessity of beginning the play with this scene. He and his brilliant designer, Walt Spangler, decided to set the scene in a public men's room with Gloucester, Kent, and Edmund relieving themselves against a wall of urinals. A brilliant move that also reminds us of Shakespeare's opening dramatic gambit to start small and intimate before going into the grand theatrics of the court. The audience felt as though they were eavesdropping behind the corridors of power, and it was a brilliant realization of the scene. It gave us the theme of the play, but introduced in the most quotidian and matter-of-fact fashion.

In Shakespeare's Laboratory

The first Shakespeare play that I ever directed was *Timon of Athens*, which, I think it is safe to say, is not one of Shakespeare's best-known plays. Many scholars wonder if it was ever even staged during Shakespeare's lifetime. It is a strange play with a first half that seems to have been primarily penned by Thomas Middleton and a second half that is clearly Shakespeare, but a very unmediated Shakespeare. In many ways, I think the second half of *Timon of Athens* is as close as we are ever going to get to seeing what a real first draft by Shakespeare might have looked like. It is a marvelous mess that Shakespeare, for whatever reason, never decided to clean up. As a result, one scene (Timon and Apemantus) feels like it should be two scenes that need to be interspersed into the fabric of the play's second half, which demands a further reshuffling of scenes to accommodate such a juxtaposition. Working on *Timon* can very much feel like being in Shakespeare's laboratory; although, in this case, Shakespeare is long gone and you've been ask to finish the experiment! It has led me to believe that every young director should be required to work on *Timon of Athens*, since it forces one to be a co-author and emboldens one to try and think like Shakespeare. Whatever trepidation or awe you might have around Shakespeare goes out the window when one works on this play, and it is the only time you will ever, for a moment, feel like an equal. One should savor this moment, learn what it must be like to have to think like Shakespeare, and then return to the finished works of his canon and marvel at his theatrical instincts which are, nine times out ten, nothing short of genius.

Transposing Scenes

When I was doing a production of *Twelfth Night*, there was a period of time when we swapped the order of the opening two scenes. I tried starting the play with Viola coming in ("What country, friend, is this?"[4]) and then followed that by the proper opening scene with Orsino in the throes of melancholy ("If music be the food of love, play on."[5]) We had this huge twenty-foot sweep of blue raked stage that people could literally slide down. I had imagined the first moment of the production being Viola's entrance. You would hear a scream and then see her fall some twenty feet, sliding downward into the playing space, followed by fellow sailors and luggage. I thought to myself, "Now, that's an opening, what an AMAZING way to start the show, get off with a real BANG." During previews we went back and forth, trying out both of these openings: our version (Viola surfing into the space) and Shakespeare's version (Orsino in a melancholic mood). It was difficult to gauge whether one version had a significant impact over the other. We did begin to realize, in a completely non-scientific fashion, that the applause at the end of the show was always louder and longer if we did the opening the way Shakespeare wrote it.

I thought about this for quite some time. Why would Shakespeare's opening, which was not as splashy as mine, ultimately work better for the cumulative experience of the show? I suppose the audience needs to know what the world is and has always been, so that we can properly appreciate its transformation. We need to see that world, before it goes about changing. In this respect, the world of *Twelfth Night* is one of longing and melancholy which is upended with the arrival of Viola. She is the agent of change. It is her unsettled nature that unsettles the world itself. Thanks to her, the gum-stuck machinery of Illyria begins to start up again.

Although act breaks in Shakespeare are misleading and are probably not something he himself demarcated, they are an instructive organizing principle. If we think of scenes and acts like punctuation, then scenes are like commas, a brief pause; whereas acts are like periods, a full stop. When you move from scene to scene you want that transition to feel like the blink of an eye; whereas when you have a transition from one act to another you want a breath before moving. When I was working on *The Winter's Tale*, I mistrusted the punctuation of a major sequence in the play. This was in the third act of the play, whose second scene ends with Leontes devastated by the death of his son and wife. I thought that should be the end of the act. But Shakespeare has one more scene, the comic discovery of the infant Perdita by the Shepherd and his son. I did not trust that you could move from the high drama of Leontes' loss to the low comedy of the Shepherd and his son. I felt that you wanted the sense of a full stop, a breath after the tragedy before you moved to the comedy. I felt this all the more because I wanted to take our intermission between these two scenes. During previews we tried both scenarios. One night the first half of the evening would end tragically, with Leontes devastated by the terrible collateral damage of his jealous rage; the next night we would end the first half of the evening comically with the Shepherd and his son discovering the infant Perdita. What we found, much to my surprise and chagrin, was that Shakespeare's dramaturgical punctuation was correct. The evening worked best when the comic scene followed right on the heels of the tragic one. In fact it was all the more funny and magical for being in such close proximity. This is not only a lesson in the syntax of Shakespeare's scenes, but also a reminder of Shakespeare's genius for antithesis.

Act Breaks and General Shaping

Since we are on the subject of act breaks, where should the intermission fall in a Shakespeare production? Is there a hard-and-fast rule? As you may know from your experiences as a play goer, this shifts from production to production. There is no true golden rule. Again, remember that the idea of an intermission in the middle of a Shakespeare play would have been alien to Shakespeare, whose audience was used to more frequent breaks throughout the evening that may or may not have corresponded with the act breaks we find in Shakespeare's play text.

Perhaps to best answer this, we need to first look at the general, overall development of a Shakespeare play. This could be broken down in the following fashion:

First Movement

Acts 1–3 is roughly the amount of time that it takes for the world as we know it to be irrevocably altered. Usually somewhere toward the end of Act 3:

- Richard II loses his crown.
- Richard III wins his crown.
- The lovers have been realigned.
- Hero is thought to be untrue.
- Desdemona too.
- Hamlet is exiled to England.
- Romeo is banished from Verona.
- Lear loses his mind.
- Timon loses his wealth.
- Leontes and Pericles lose their wives and daughters.

This first movement is about ninety minutes of masterful plotting and by the end of this the audience should be hooked. You may want to streamline these acts to ensure the narrative velocity and engagement. But when we reach our act break, the world as the characters have known it has been forever altered or destroyed; or, in the Romances, a new world is literally discovered. We come back to see:

Second Movement

(After Intermission)

Act 4
How these characters brave these new worlds. In other words:

- A world where I am no longer king.
- A world where I am king.
- A world where I get the lover I want.
- A world where I believe I've lost the one I've loved.
- A world where I am banished forever.
- A world without my sanity, wealth, or family.

Now what? What is life like under the sun of this new reality? These new worlds have another time signature, a different metabolic rate. They have new rules. We must learn them. And as we move closer and closer to the end, these new worlds seem more and more real. This is the final topography of Act 5, which looks at whether our central character(s) can survive or are destroyed by these new conditions.

If this is, in very broad terms, the basic nature of Shakespeare's five-act structure, we can begin to understand why some directors tend to organize the act break somewhere within the third act, when there is a significant shift in the world. There are, of course, instances where we might want to place the intermission earlier. Given the speed of *Macbeth*, we find that we can take the intermission between the end of Act 2 (the death of Duncan) and the beginning of Act 3 (Macbeth becomes King); given the length of *Hamlet*, it can make sense to call the intermission at the end of Act 2 when Hamlet finally decides to take actions ("The play's the thing / Wherein I'll catch the conscience of the king").[6] We come back from the intermission to see how his plan will pan out. But, for the most part, I use the major demarcation point in the play as a way of organizing the performance into two halves. This also means that the first half tends to be longer than the second. Given the nature of the plotting of the first three acts (event to event to event) this can actually feel much faster than the remaining two acts on the other side of intermission. In this kind of structuring one finds that the first half of the evening is going to roughly clock in at about ninety minutes and the second half at about an hour. Usually one needs to find more cuts in the first half to keep it at the bantam weight of ninety minutes and, even though the second half is only an hour, it too will want some internal trimming (usually ten or so minutes which may not seem like so much in clock time, but is an eternity in felt time).

Who's Your Virgil?

As you are working your way through the hell, purgatory, and heaven of preparation, it is always nice to have a guide. After all, even the great Dante had his Virgil. You might want to have someone who can walk alongside you and help guide you through this tricky textual terrain. This can be a dramaturg, a key designer, the lead actor, or all three. The investigation and preparation of a Shakespeare text need not be a journey that you take all on your own. It can be and should be something of a caravanserai.

This is especially true before rehearsals, when you are trying to get a handle on shaping the play for your production. This is something you really should do before rehearsals begin, and this is perhaps the best piece of advice in the entire book. This is so important I will say it again: pre-shape (and cut) the text before rehearsals begin. Why? Because actors get attached to words. They work hard to learn and ground them, and once they do, it is very, very, very hard to take them away. It is also a waste of precious rehearsal time to rehearse a scene or soliloquy that you suspect might not be necessary for your production. So, for everyone's sanity, pre-shape (i.e., cut) the text before rehearsals begin. Of course, there will always be more to do, but the bulk of the work will already have been done.

But, back to potential Virgils, it is helpful to have a guide, or at least someone by your side as you make your journey toward that first day of rehearsal. Some of the best guides I've had throughout my career have been designers like my long-time collaborator Mark Wendland, who has been so instrumental in the way I have thought about taking Shakespeare from the page to the stage. I'll let the next chapter on design explain why.

12 "Brave New Worlds": Designing Shakespeare

Notes Toward World Building

Whenever I am working on a Shakespeare play I always run into at least one person who says, "I hear you're working on *Hamlet*. What are you going to do with it?" And so, if you are a director of Shakespeare, there is a certain segment of your audience that expects you to "*do something* to Shakespeare." Conversely, there is another, equally expectant segment of the audience that doesn't want you to do anything at all. "*Can't you just do the play*," they say with a sigh, or, "*I just want to see Shakespeare.*"

Certainly Shakespeare probably never thought much about this "doing something" to his plays. They were staged without a stick of scenery and in contemporary Elizabethan clothing. In point of fact, if there was any visual interest in Shakespeare's audience it would have been toward what the actors were wearing, since it was usually last year's court fashions. Such wardrobes were often lent out to companies to show off the most fashionable of courtiers' taste in clothes. The King's Men's wardrobe was probably as big a draw as a play by Shakespeare. The biggest nod toward any kind of historical costuming would have been perhaps to drape a white sheet around their Elizabethan garb to suggest that they were antique Romans. For some modern audience members, this sort of approach is fascinating in and of itself. If one were to go to the restored Globe in England, this is the type of production one might see, complete with a jig at the end of each performance, no matter what the play.

But if that is not your inclination as a director or designer, what are your steps toward envisioning a production of Shakespeare? How do you take the kind of work that we have been doing in this book and apply it to what Hamlet will wear, or what kind of throne Claudius will sit upon? Should it even be a throne? Or should it be at the head of modern boardroom table? How do you go about making a series of informed choices? *Aye, there's the rub.* When I started directing Shakespeare, which was very late in my directing career, I did not have any of the points of reference that this book relies upon. Those were learned over two decades of first directing and producing Shakespeare and then, even more daunting, attempting to teach young directors about Shakespeare. In thinking back to those early days of working on Shakespeare, I can see that I approached these texts with a set of questions that emerged and ultimately prompted the points of reference that are covered in the beginning of this book.

I suppose, in those early days of directing, I would characterize my approach as "user-friendly abstraction." At the time I was very much interested in what I called "the unconscious of the play." I wanted to discern what that was and then stage that. Another way I would explain it to my collaborators was to say, if the play were to go to bed and have a dream, what kind of dream or nightmare would it have? I want the production to reflect those subliminal workings. This is why, I suppose, I became so enamored of Wittgenstein's quote about Shakespeare making a kind of dream sense. In fact, if I remember correctly, that quote was the very first thing I shared with the company of actors on the first Shakespeare production that I directed.

In those days I had the great good fortune to be working with the designer Mark Wendland on sets and costumes. We had met in graduate school and began working together professionally shortly after that. We had done about fourteen or so shows together before tackling our first Shakespeare, *Timon of Athens*. This meant we had developed a language of talking to one another about plays that only really made sense to us. Mark would joke and say that his job was like a psychoanalyst: just get me on the couch, ask a bunch of questions, and eventually a concept for the production would emerge. Mark seems to have been born with a humble Socratic curiosity, his questions were like breadcrumbs that would eventually lead us to what we thought the play might mean and, from there, what that meaning might look like. We weren't always right (more on that later) but it would eventually get Mark to the drafting table.

Mark's First Question

"What's the Play About?"

That was always Mark's very first question, usually asked after about a half hour or so of gossiping. I would talk and talk and talk and talk. About what I thought, what I read, what this critic said, what that critic said, what this production did, what that production did, on and on and on and on. This was, I now realize, my first draft of a fourfold technique where I went through every possible interpretative stance (plain, allegorical, analogical, or abstract). And then, after all that explication, Mark would say: "*But what is the play about?*"

And so, the first week or so of work would be about turning all of my babbling into a simple, coherent, and concise one-sentence description. We eventually

settled on the sentence, "*Timon of Athens* is about a man who loses everything."
I think the original version of this sentence was: "*Timon of Athens* is about a man
who systematically loses everything." But the word "systematic" made Mark
nervous. Now someone else might arrive at a sentence like: "*Timon of Athens* is
about a philanthropic man who becomes an absolute misanthrope." That is an
absolutely accurate distillation of the play. It just didn't evoke anything profound
in us. We were very awake to living in the hyper-materialistic world that we know.
The idea of having everything and then losing it felt like very rich terrain for us
and for our audience. It was every person's secret nightmare (especially if you live
in New York) and so it felt ripe for image making. So, in a way, perhaps we need to
rephrase Mark's question a bit. Perhaps what he is really, ultimately asking is, "What
is the play about *to you?*" Having landed on that, we can move to:

Mark's Second Question

"How Do We Tell *That* Story?"

Which really meant: "How do we tell that story *visually?*"
    In those days, story was very important to Mark. This meant that our visual
story ultimately had to have a beginning, middle, and end. But, like Godard, it
didn't have to be in that order. The important thing was the development of the
visual storytelling. My teacher described this process as: "It started here, it ended
there. How did it get there?" It was usually very easy to figure out how the visual
story started (Timon in a world of his possessions) and where it ended (Timon
bereft of those possessions); the tricky part was always how did it get there: step by
step by step. Then the question became, do we have to show every stage of the
development, or can we jump a step or two? For us, the play became a battle
between Timon and his creditors. Both of us were barely making ends meet at that
time in our careers, so the idea of creditors coming to take away what little we
had was very much on both our minds. Our working image/metaphor was that
Timon was a scarecrow and the creditors were like crows, pulling at his straw until
there was nothing left of him. This led to the image of the creditors as figures
dressed in Edwardian coats with bowler hats. How did we get from crows to black-
clad bureaucrats? This was probably one of those free-associational moments.
I have always loved the work of Franz Kafka, whose last name means black crow. It
seemed somehow appropriate that Timon would be besieged by an army of Kafkas.
So we knew it would be these funereal figures that would pick apart Timon's world.
But how? That became the next stumbling block. Do we see them come and
repossess Timon's living room furniture? Ugh. Our notion suddenly seemed so
terribly prosaic. Where was the poetry of such a transformation? This would lead
to my favorite of Mark's questions:

Mark's Third Question

"Do We Have To Be So Literal?"

This is where the dream (or nightmare) work came in. We had identified what the play meant to us: It was about having everything and losing it. Now, how to imaginatively evoke this "everything"? To "evoke" was and remains an immensely important word for us. The theatre is all about evocation, never illustration. As far as we were concerned, if an audience wanted illustration they should go to the movies. So, the problem became: How could we create a *suggestive* rather than a literal image? In short, how can we find the dream image for the play? This led us to what I called the simile game, where we spend the day free-associating with the phrase: "Timon's world is like _____?" Fill in the blank. I will not bore you with the long list of similes we went through; truth be told, I can't remember any, save the one we landed on, which was Timon's world being represented as an enormous, seemingly impenetrable, rectangular box made of metal. (Some of our collaborators thought this looked like a giant money box.) For us, it was an armored abode which protected Timon and his wealth from the outside world. This became our **central image**. The next day Mark brought in a rectangular cardboard box he had made and we spent the next week or so playing "spin the box." We'd rotate the box clockwise and with each orientation we would assign a scene until we had worked our way through the first half of the play.

Mark's Final Question

"Okay, Can You Walk Me Through This Step By Step?"

Or, The Development and Deployment of Scenic Motifs

The major structural conceit or **scenic motif** became the slow stripping away of parts of Timon's box. With each rotation, a major wall panel would be removed until the box was completely disassembled, leaving only its skeletal frame. Each metallic panel was placed upstage to create an ever-evolving wall that ultimately encompassed the entire width of the stage.

Scenic motifs became, for Mark and myself, a kind of visual music or organizing principle whereby we could build the play. And so in structural terms:

- The first half of the play begins with an immense armored box.
- The first half of the play ends with the box dismantled and recombined to build a wall.

- How did it get there? With each spin a part of the box becomes dismantled.

- The remainder of the play was performed in this final configuration.

This also synced up with Lacan's three orders. The Box represented Lacan's **Symbolic Order** (the way of the world). The Dismantling of the Box leads to **The Imaginary Order** (the way Timon's tormented mind now sees the world). Timon dying, exposed to the elements, brings us to the final **Realm of The Real.** Now, with all this in mind, let me walk you through Mark's storyboards, beat by visual beat.

Timon of Athens in Six Storyboard Images

We decided to begin the play by seeing one end of the box where a large pop art portrait of Timon was being painted by the Artist of Act One, Scene One. This box represents Lacan's **Symbolic Order** of the world.

FIGURE 1 *Timon of Athens* (Public Theater 1996). Set sketch by Mark Wendland.

This was the image which greeted audiences as they arrived at the Delacorte Theater in Central Park where the play was performed as part of the New York Shakespeare Festival. The actor playing the artist was on a ladder, applying the finishing touches to his billboard-sized portrait of Timon. A bell rang. The play began with more and more guests assembling before the portrait until, finally, the servants began to rotate the box 180 degrees to reveal:

FIGURE 2 *Timon of Athens* (Public Theater 1996). Set sketch by Mark Wendland.

An opulent dining room with a dining table long enough to seat a company of well-dressed plutocrats. This second image slowly morphed over the rehearsal process, moving more toward a nod to a tableau similar to Da Vinci's *Last Supper* with Timon standing where Christ would be, flanked on either side by his wealthy guests. The guests were all in white linens, the servants in black formal attire. At the end of Timon's party, the box once again rotated to its other opposite end to reveal: Timon's primary creditor.

FIGURE 3 *Timon of Athens* (Public Theater 1996). Set sketch by Mark Wendland.

Our box rotated another 180 degrees, revealing the full metallic exterior of Timon's abode. It is here that our crow-like creditors, decked out in black tails and derby hats, assembled and assailed Timon for what was owed them. More of the metallic box is stripped in this transition, which initiates our decent into Lacan's next order: **The Imaginary**.

FIGURE 4 *Timon of Athens* (Public Theater 1996). Set sketch by Mark Wendland.

The box, having made one full rotation around the stage in a clockwise fashion, would now make four more counterclockwise moves for the next four scenes until we are back to the interior of Timon's abode where his guests have assembled for one final supper. This is Timon's dinner of revenge.

FIGURE 5 *Timon of Athens* (Public Theater 1996). Set sketch by Mark Wendland.

The long dining room table and the chairs of the guests were all on wheels. The servants began to spin the table about, the guests holding on to the table for dear life, as if this were some mad amusement park ride that had gone terribly wrong. Timon ascended the spinning table and started pelting his guests with bread rolls as they spiraled away, one by one, crashing into the upstage wall. At the end of this scene, the remaining panels of Timon's former abode were placed upstage to complete the metallic wall.

FIGURE 6 *Timon of Athens* (Public Theater 1996). Set sketch by Mark Wendland.

The remainder of the play was performed in this strange no-man's land, which could be the woods or the interior of Timon's broken mind. Along with the idea of scenic motifs, another important aspect that Mark and I would look out for was any sort of **visual antithesis**, especially with Shakespeare, whose texts are filled with all manner of antithetical elements. This meant that after such a kinetic first half of the evening, we wanted the second half to be more static in terms of the set. The basic image for the second half of the evening became Timon stuck in this seeming no-man's land, living among the detritus of his former life. These final moments, before his death, ushers in Lacan's **Realm of The Real**. We found, particularly with Shakespeare, that it was very easy to come up with a kind of kinetic scenic life for the first three acts of these plays, especially since they were usually so plot-driven; but by the time we reached Acts 4 and 5 (usually the second half of the evening), the plot would recede and the larger themes of the play would emerge. This shift from plot to theme always made us step back scenically in the latter half of a Shakespeare play and just let the actor and the language do their work.

Costumes for Timon

Because the set of *Timon* (and most of our sets during this period) tended toward abstraction, we needed the costumes to help ground and tell the story. It was through the costumes that we were able to deal with the highly stratified class system of *Timon*. As you can see in Mark's renderings, it was a vaguely Edwardian world. Timon and his friends are dressed in white summer linens. They exude a certain wealth, ease, and privilege. In opposition to this is Apemantus, who wore a rumpled trench coat and looked as though he hadn't shaved or bathed in weeks.

FIGURE 7A Timon   **FIGURE 7B** Friends   **FIGURE 7C** Apemantus
Timon of Athens (Public Theater 1996). Costume renderings by Mark Wendland.

The other characters who rounded out the world were creditors, prostitutes, servants, and thieves. We decided to dress both the creditors and the servants in black. The only color was reserved for Alcibiades' prostitutes, who wore a bright red dress with golden angel wings.

Figure 8A Creditors   **FIGURE 8B** Prostitutes   **FIGURE 8C** Servants
Timon of Athens (Public Theater 1996). Costume renderings by Mark Wendland.

None of the costumes strictly adhered to the Edwardian period, Mark took a series of wonderful liberties in terms of historical accuracy. We wanted a world that felt as though it had one foot in the present and the other foot slightly in the past.

The Perils of Pericles

Our next project for the Public Theater was a production of *Pericles, Prince of Tyre*, which we had initially wanted to do in an immersive fashion (although I'm not sure if the term "immersive theatre" had been coined in 1998; in those days I think we still used the term "environmental theatre"). Regardless, all of our primarily immersive/environmental ideas for the play were politely rejected by the Public Theater. "Where is the audience going to sit?" "You know many of our Shakespeare patrons are quite old?" "Do you know how much it would cost to redo the risers in the Martinson Theater?" Being, at that time, a nice director and designer team, we nodded our heads and went back to the drawing board (literally for Mark). I still wish we hadn't listened to the concerns of the Public and had just done what we wanted to do—but we were young and didn't want to rock the boat. We started again with Mark's four questions:

> "What is the play about?"
> "How what is simple becomes more and more complicated as we move through life."

That became our point of departure; again, this is how the play resonated to us at the time. Our lives were, like *Pericles*, becoming much more complicated than we ever anticipated. It is worth noting that there is nothing wrong with finding the personal rhyme between yourself and the play you are working on. If nothing else, you will forge a strong connection to the material. We also noticed that the play's shifting tonalities mirrored this development from simple to complex, beginning with a kind of picture-book innocence and ending in a deep and dimensional quasi-Christian parable. This observation helped us answer Mark's second question:

> "How do we tell that story?"
> "By creating a world that, act by act, becomes more scenically complex."

The central idea was to create a visual world that got more and more visually rich as we moved through the play. This gave us the central organizing principle to build the production. Let me, briefly, walk you through the basic visual strokes of the story with its ensuing **scenic motifs** and the **visual antithesis** that we discovered along the way.

Pericles in Five Movements

Central idea: to mirror our experience of the ever-changing moment-to-moment textual life of *Pericles*. It felt like a story that moved from simple to complex, from flat to dimensional, from storybook to thick description.

First Movement: Storybook

FIGURE 9 *Pericles* (Public Theater 1998). Set sketch by Mark Wendland.

When the audience arrived at the theatre they were confronted with a large golden wall that functioned like an act curtain. It lived at the very downstage lip of the proscenium and created zero depth. As the play began, different apertures in the wall opened up to reveal a character or characters. Everything was performed in a highly stylized, static, and iconic fashion; like a picture book that was ever so slowly coming to life. With each scene a different aperture would open to reveal another character or situation, and with each opening the actors would become just a little more lifelike. The entirety of the first act was played in this fashion. One could think of this world as representative of Lacan's **Symbolic Order**.

Setting Sail Motif

Transition from Act 1 to Act 2

FIGURE 10 *Pericles* (Public Theater 1998). Set sketch by Mark Wendland.

Scenic Motif: the image of setting sail. We envisioned the company interacting with the set as if it were a giant (abstracted) ship setting off to sea, or in the midst of a storm. The actors appeared, scaled the wall, pulled at ropes, and pushed the set into its next configuration. It was at this point that part of the wall became a severely raked stage for the second movement of the play. From here we move into the **Imaginary Phase** of the play.

Second Movement: Pericles' Adventures

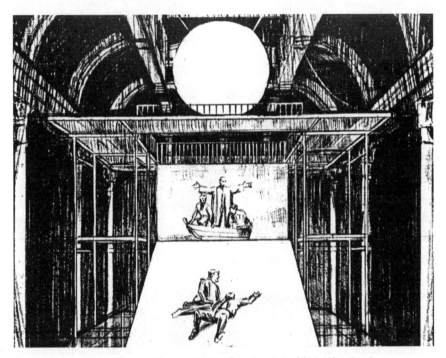

FIGURE 11 *Pericles* (Public Theater 1998). Set sketch by Mark Wendland.

Much of the remainder of the first half of the evening was performed on this steep rake with the actors now exploring a kind of hyper-kinetic movement. The company no longer moved in a slow, stately, storybook manner, but now behaved like puppets set free from their strings. This became our first **visual antithesis** of the evening. The "energy-signature" of this sequence was that of Punch and Judy: big, broad, loud, and manic. This was true of everyone but Pericles, who we thought of as our Alice in this strange and surreal wonderland. It was not until he was wedded to his intended that the madcap dynamic of the act shifted to a more romantic, fairy-tale tone.

Third Movement: Marina in Mytilene

FIGURE 12 *Pericles* (Public Theater 1998). Set sketch by Mark Wendland.

The second half of the production took place in the urban setting of Mytilene which was, as you can see, the most visually baroque of the play. All the elements that we had seen throughout the play are in view, as though the stage had become some storehouse of the play's neglected imagery. Everywhere the audience looked, there would be some leftover object, person, element, or situation. Then with the arrival of Pericles—it all goes away for the scene between Pericles and his daughter, Marina. This is the first time the stage is completely, totally bare, creating our final **visual antithesis** and ushering in the **Order of The Wondrous** which is a variation of Lacan's **Realm of The Real**. Here are two human beings discovering one another. And then:

Final Movement: Wonder

FIGURE 13 *Pericles* (Public Theater 1998). Set sketch by Mark Wendland.

We return to Ephesus, but remain in the realm of the wondrous. Two glass cases were onstage: one represented a toy cityscape of Ephesus and the other a tall pillar that represented the Goddess Diana's temple. It is here that Pericles is reunited with his wife Thaisa.

In many ways, the energy of both *Timon* and *Pericles* was found in the dynamics of their **scenic motifs**: the spinning and disassembling of Timon's metal box or Pericles setting sail. In our next production, we wanted to continue to explore the more subtle nature of **visual antithesis**. This was a production of *Much Ado About Nothing* for Berkeley Repertory Theatre.

Much Ado About Further Antithesis

FIGURE 14 *Much Ado About Nothing* (Berkeley Rep. 2001). Set sketch by Mark Wendland.

In many ways, *Much Ado* was perhaps the most "realistic" of the work I did with Mark. The **central image** was a manor house that became the dominant scenic element of the production. I was struck by the fact that the script seems to indicate that everyone always goes into the house, *except for Benedick*. It is as if he cannot literally or figuratively be domesticated. And so the idea of the house looming like the sword of Damocles over Benedick's head became our representation of **Lacan's Symbolic Order**.

Someone once asked the American painter Jasper Johns what art is, and he said, "Take something, change it, change it again." This seemed to rhyme with Mark's interest in the development of various images over the course of the evening. What is their independent story? How do they change? And so our house landed, moved about the stage to give us different perspectives, broke apart when Hero was suspected of being unfaithful (the crack in the world of the play; which, in Lacanian terms, moves us from the symbolic to the imaginary), and finally was restored in the end. This was also a design where we continued to observe Shakespeare's **visual anthesis** and to developed some of our own. Mark's intuition was that the static quality of the house should be in opposition to something free-form; hence, the birds in flight. Again, we wanted to capture Benedick's dilemma of being free like a bird and his horror of being trapped in domesticity. Another essential anthesis for us was what scenes transpired during the day and what scenes during the night. And so the masked ball, the gulling of Claudio, the Dogberry scenes, Claudio learning of Hero's false death: all of these scenes happened in the dark of night, beneath an enormous moon. Again, Mark was intuitively drawn to the moon as a feminine symbol that, like the house, hovers above the heads of the men. The work with the company became about the antithesis of the freer, more chaotic behavior found at night as opposed to the more mannered and restrained behavior during the day. In the masked ball, which happened at night, everyone was given an animal mask and asked to find moments where they behaved or moved like their animal. Benedick and his "boys" were wolves who entered howling at the moon.

FIGURE 15 *Much Ado About Nothing* (Berkeley Rep. 2001). Set sketch by Mark Wendland.

Figure 16 shows the scene in the orchard where Benedick and Beatrice are gulled into thinking that each loves the other. Here, we are back in the light of day. Again, Mark plays with the antithesis of order (planted orchard trees all in a row) with the more free-form flight of the birds who seem to be startled out of the trees by all this love.

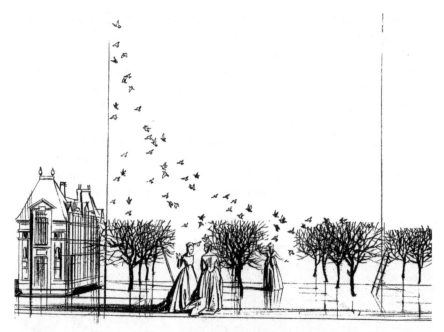

FIGURE 16 *Much Ado About Nothing* (Berkeley Rep. 2001). Set sketch by Mark Wendland.

One of the things that I've always appreciated about Mark's design work, especially for Shakespeare, is how much air or space he gives over to a scene. Although this production probably had more elements (a manor house, trees, birds, moons), Mark instinctively knows that there has to be enough room/air for the language. It is so easy to suffocate a Shakespeare text with "scenery." I suspect that Mark, left to his own devices (i.e., not having me nag at him), would have done the production with far less elements, but I was so excited to finally be in a big theatre with a big budget that I kept pushing him toward more and more stuff on stage. Even so, Mark finds a way to balance it out, to make sure that Shakespeare's words have room to move freely about and do their own evocative work.

Figure 17 shows the final image for the first half our evening. It is the moment where Claudio is led to believe he is seeing Hero being unfaithful to him. It is night, the moon is full, and, as Claudio watches, the house breaks in two, the back half rising to eclipse the moon and reveal a bogus tableau of infidelity. This plunges us into **The Imaginary Order**. The second half of the evening picked up with preparations for the wedding, the wedding itself, and the ultimate disruption of the ceremony which is pictured in Figure 18. This became the second

FIGURE 17 *Much Ado About Nothing* (Berkeley Rep. 2001). Set sketch by Mark Wendland.

big seismic break in the play, the remainder of which was played out at night among the broken house and overturned chairs that had been set up for the wedding guests.

FIGURE 18 *Much Ado About Nothing* (Berkeley Rep. 2001). Set sketch by Mark Wendland.

The final image returned us to the initial wedding tableau where Claudio discovers that Hero is still alive and, even more miraculously, still willing to take his hand in holy matrimony. This marked, for us, the final **Wondrous Order** of the play.

From Conception to Realization

The design of a show, for most theatres in America, must be done in the shop before one even begins rehearsals. This raises several questions: How can you know what you want before you see it in all three dimensions? If you plan everything out in advance, isn't the result going to be rather dead? Doesn't this stop you from being open to the moment at hand? The answer to all these questions is: Yes. But this is how it is in the American theatrical system. If it makes you feel any better, many opera companies will make you tech your show a year in advance, before you've even begun rehearsals with the actual cast. So what is a director to do?

First thing: don't panic. Nine times out of ten, if you've done enough prep work (the studying and explicating of the text that we outlined in the first half of the book), then chances are you are going to be in the right zip code in terms of the world you have created. Have I gotten into rehearsals and realized I had made a terrible mistake? Yes, twice in my life. What happened? We threw the set out and played the work on a relatively bare stage. The great thing about Shakespeare is, at the end of the day, the words and the actors (with those words) can pretty much take care of themselves, as that was the way these plays were originally intended to be performed.

Second, you may want to create space in your design for freedom and improvisation. My dear friend and colleague, Paul Steinberg, one of the great designers of his generation, often says that he designs systems not sets. Paul gives directors a series of discrete scenic elements that can be arranged and rearranged by the director and the acting company.

Personally, I like a certain amount of structure and a certain amount of freedom. When I am storyboarding a scene, I like to know the three big pictures of the scene: opening tableau, ending tableau, and that middle tableau that changes everything (i.e., the event of the scene). All I need is those three pictures in my head. I don't need to know how I get, beat by beat, from picture one to picture two; I can discover that in rehearsal with the actors. This way, I can have my directorial cake and eat it too. I have a certain structure (those three big pictures) and an equal amount of freedom (how to get to those three big pictures) and, all the while, I am open to the fact that we might discover something even better than my three pictures in the process of rehearsing (which is what rehearsing should be all about anyway). And, worst-case scenario, as I said, you can always throw it all away. Believe it or not, Shakespeare's words will take care of themselves. That is your ultimate safety net, so go ahead and take a leap!

EXERCISE #11

Telling the Story of the Play Visually

1st Stage: Decide on the linterpretative bent of your production:

1 Plain Reading

2 Allegorical Reading

3 Analogic Reading

4 Abstract Reading

5 Some combination of the above four

Nowadays, I go through the exercise of examining the play at hand from all four interpretive vantage points, and usually end up with some sort of scenic abstraction that evokes, for me, the secret/unconscious life of the play. I would strongly advocate that playing this interpretative game fully (from all four vantage points) is the best way to ultimately arrive at the most informed approach to realizing a play.

2nd Stage: Answer Mark's four basic questions:

1 What does the story mean to us?

2 How do we visualize that story (i.e. what is its development)?

3 Does that development have to be literal? Can it be metaphoric? Evocative rather than illustrative?

4 With all that in place, can we move step by step through the play's visual paces?

3rd Stage: Begin to develop the following:

1 Finding a **Central Image** (or **Idea**)

2 Developing **Scenic Motifs** (how the central image and other images develop over the course of the evening so that the visual life of the play has a beginning, middle, and end)

3 Thinking about **Visual Antithesis** (how some of these motifs are in opposition to one another, giving the play its dynamic range. In other

words, in order to appreciate color it is helpful to see it in relation to the absolute absence of color)

4th Stage: Shape this into Lacan's three orders
While working in this manner, I slowly discovered that I could help organize the visual development of the play through Lacan's three orders of being. At first I did this sort of work unconsciously, and nowadays perhaps too consciously. The gist of this approach is:

1 Begin in the **Symbolic Order** (how the society is structured)

2 Move into the **Imaginary Order** (how the main character re-sees the world)

3 Resolve in the **Orders of the Real or the Wondrous** (what emerges that both realms have kept at bay, or refuse to see/acknowledge. This usually begins to emerge in the fourth act and ultimately overwhelms the fifth)

This seems to me to be one way that Shakespeare's plays unfold. One can visually score a given production by following such a development.

I am not, as I said at the outset of this section, advocating that directors should follow this process. These questions, techniques, and categories have helped me translate a Shakespeare play from the page to the stage. But every director has to come up with their own unique process that works for them. I think of these elements as tools that become part of a director's tool kit. Please feel free to borrow whatever you might want if it helps you build your production.

13 "The World Must be Peopled": Auditions

Casting is Interpretation

I was working on a production of *Hamlet*. I had done all of this preparatory work on the play, read every book on *Hamlet* that I could get my hands on, and had developed a whole visual world for the production. But, foolishly, I did not have a Hamlet yet. There were three major candidates, and I realized that each candidate not only presented a different Hamlet, but *an entirely different interpretation*. The first candidate would have made for a very emotional Hamlet; he was young and emotionally connected, and the audience would have been deeply invested in his journey, hoping against hope that he would succeed. The second candidate was a very heady, cerebral Hamlet. This Hamlet would be very much about the mind, about ideas and philosophy writ large. The third candidate would be an immensely robust, dynamic, and physical Hamlet, with a deep, resonant voice. There was something about him that felt oddly Elizabethan. He gave one the sense that this is what it must have been like to have seen the role played by Shakespeare's lead actor Richard Burbage. It was clear that none of these Hamlets would fit neatly into my general schema, that I could not simply shoehorn them into my production. I would have to build a *Hamlet* around them, around who they were.

This is true of all the major roles: Hamlet, Othello, Iago, Lear, Macbeth, Lady Macbeth, Antony and Cleopatra, etc., etc., etc. Forgive me for stating the obvious, but: who plays these parts very much determines what the production is. This is particularly important for directors to hear, since many believe that everything circles around them. In the case of Shakespeare, a production is very much determined by the combined efforts of the leading actor(s) and the director. Now, you can work to find a lead actor who fits your vision, or you can build your vision around a lead actor, but what is often difficult is to ask an actor to go against their inherent strengths. Not that there aren't actors who are true chameleons, but such actors are few and far between. I ultimately chose the actor that captured what felt like an Elizabethan Revenger. This was the wonderful Michael Cumpsty. We had first worked together on *Timon of Athens* at the New York Shakespeare Festival, where Michael had proven himself to be a formidable Shakespearean. When it was announced that he would play Hamlet the initial response was, "What a great actor; isn't he a little old to play Hamlet?" In actuality Michael was about the same age that Richard Burbage was when he first performed the role, but in our literal-minded age we tend to want to see a twenty-one-year-old in the role. It is intriguing that not one reviewer actually ended up writing that this was, in any way, a hindrance for the audience. It was clear to all that Michael gave a compelling performance and the issue of age turned out not to be an issue at all. There is something about theatre (not necessarily film) where we are able to make these leaps. Maybe it is the fundamental metaphoric aspect of the medium. For me, an actor does not have to be "classically beautiful" (whatever the hell that means) to be beautiful on stage. In such cases, we respond to an inner radiance that is often more immediate and meaningful. This is, of course, just the tip of the iceberg when it comes to the mysteries of casting.

Meetings and Readings

Nowadays when it comes to certain lead roles (Hamlet, Othello, Iago, Lear, Macbeth, Cleopatra, etc.), it is rare that an actor of note will audition. You are expected to know the actor's body of work and you are asked to do the imaginative math of whether or not the actor is right for the role. In such cases, one usually gets the opportunity to meet with the actor; or, in some instances, the actor might be interested in doing a reading or a workshop. Sometimes, if you are lucky, you can get a meeting and a subsequent reading or workshop, but most of the time it is a meeting that becomes your one opportunity to make an informed decision. What does one look for when it is just a meeting?

I suppose the first, and perhaps the most important thing is: are you engaged in a real conversation? What does that mean? I suppose it means that the actor is actually taking in what you are saying about the character and the world of the play and, of equal importance, you are taking in what the actor thinks. Do you have to be in lockstep agreement? No. But you should share an array of suppositions that you are both interested in getting into a room and testing out. That is the mark of an ideal collaboration, which can be rare. For me, collaboration is everything. Oftentimes I will say to an actor, I think such-and-such moment might be X. Sometimes the actor agrees, sometimes the actor thinks it is about Y. Sometimes their Y is much more interesting than my X and I am intrigued to jettison my own idea and work within their Y.

Now, what happens when you are saying X and the actor is saying Y. Does this mean you can't work with one another? Ah, there's the rub. True collaboration (or at least the most rewarding collaborations that I have encountered) have been when I have wanted X and my collaborator has wanted Y and we both decide to jettison our X and Y and search together for a Z that we can both agree upon. That Z is, nine times out of ten, much more interesting than either of our initial Xs or Ys. So the real question is, can the two of you work together to find that third thing? That Z. If you can, then you might be at the launch of a very special collaboration.

Often, out of such meetings, the actor might agree or want to do a reading or workshop of the play to make sure that our ideas mesh and that we can indeed work well together. In such cases, what are you looking for? The first thing is, perhaps, does the actor literally and figuratively play well with others? Is the actor a true leading man or lady; in other words, not only do they have more lines than everyone else, but can they be a co-leader and set an example for the company in terms of how we all are going to comport and push ourselves? It is not essential, but it is nice to have a co-leader in the room that sets the bar at a certain height for everyone else to emulate. Is this absolutely necessary? No, of course not. But it is nice to see if you have that kind of collaborator.

I am also, of course, interested in the "musicianship" of the actor. I don't mean how good they are with speaking verse (although that is a huge benefit in Shakespeare). I mean that if we think of beats of action as notes in a score, how many beats/notes is the actor capable of playing? We're talking about being alive and present on a moment-by-moment, line-by-line basis; where every moment, every line is awake, unique, and lived. Let's say a scene is made up of 150 beats; how many of those get played? One hundred percent? Fifty percent? Less than fifty? A great actor can not only play every beat but also invents beats that aren't even there! This can be a blessing and curse because if the actor is that "alive" it means you have to surround them with an equally able company, which can be tricky. You see, there are many actors who can play, say, seventy beats in a one-hundred-beat scene. That's pretty damn good; but opposite an actor who can play all one hundred beats, the seventy-beat actor starts to look like a much lesser actor. Often you don't notice the limitations of an actor unless they are playing opposite another actor who is more present than they are. This is why, when you watch the rehearsal process of most Shakespeare plays, it is often the case that the director does very little work with the leading actor, but spends almost all their time on the supporting roles, trying to get them to the level of presentness that the lead actor does naturally (which is why they became leading actors in the first place).

I also try to understand what kind of actors the lead actor responds to, that excites them. Do they like actors who like to change things up? Do they like actors who are more set in their ways and therefore dependable on a night-by-night basis? In such cases, I am trying to figure out what kind of company I need to build around this central artist.

Auditioning Ideas

The audition is not just the place where you audition actors but also where you first audition many of your ideas about the character and the play. It gives you a chance to see whether your ideas make sense, are of interest, and actually activate the imagination of the actors and the playing of the scenes. One of the first things that you usually learn is: whatever you are saying can be expressed in simpler terms. Auditions can help you distill and focus ideas, and can also help you throw things out that aren't working. You often leave an audition process with a much more active and concrete way of talking about your production. You also become the beneficiary of a veritable think tank on each character. You get to see perhaps twenty or so Mercutios do the great Queen Mab speech. Invariably, you find each actor can bring a particular passage or line to life in a way you never thought about before, one that you might end up incorporating even if you didn't cast that particular actor in the role. Finally, it should not be forgotten that you are auditioning as well. A good actor will always have a variety of work options open to them. You want to present yourself and your production in a way that says to the actor that this is the project to join.

Sides: Breadth and Depth

I try to choose rehearsal sides that capture the launch, development, and end point of each character. This also means that the three sides will capture three very distinct facets of the character. Think of Romeo. You want sides that can show his lightness with his friends (his launch), his attraction to Juliet (development), and his grief over the loss of Juliet (end point). If the actor can hit those three very different phases of the character you are in great shape! This gives you three distinct snapshots of the character (you can think of it as their mask, face, and soul). You also probably want one scene that is pretty extensive, such as the balcony scene. Personally, I don't need to see all three sides in the first audition. In fact, in the first audition I usually work with just one side. When the actor first comes in, I'll ask them which side they would like to begin with. Sometimes the actor will say, "Oh, whatever one you want me to start with is fine." I really try to avoid making this decision because what side the actor chooses to begin with often tells me a great deal about their comfort zone, what they feel they do best or have a handle on. I want to start there, to see the actor's place of strength and watch them play within that zip code first.

From the Moment the Actor Enters the Room

The audition process is such a charged environment. It is staggering how much a director learns about the actor before they even begin to read a scene. You are aware of how they enter the room. Are they confident? Relaxed? Nervous? Blasé? All of this is immediately apparent. The stress of auditioning is a good indicator of how an actor deals with stress in general. Chances are, if they are relaxed in this environment, they'll be relaxed during a difficult tech or a first preview.

Now they are in the room, standing before you, perhaps giving you an updated resumé. What happens next is also telling. Do they go right into doing their side? Do they want to talk? Do they have questions? What kind of questions are they? Can the actor read the room? In other words, can the actor sense that this is a director that is comfortable talking? If not, how do they transition to the scene? All of this gives the director a sense of what the actor thinks of themselves as a human being taking up space and whether or not they are comfortable taking up that space. If an actor is uncomfortable taking up space, is this a sign? No. It is natural for a normal human being to be nervous about auditioning. Many actors are simply not good at auditioning. Auditioning, in many ways, is an art form in and of itself, and not indicative of how the final performance will be. This is why, if you can see the actor in an actual show, you can often get a better sense of what they are truly capable of doing. So I never discount anyone who seems nervous in audition, *but I do take note of those who are at ease*, as their ease in such a charged situation tells me something about who they are and how they move through life.

I always look at the resumé before the actor comes in to see if they have worked on an interesting project, perhaps with a colleague or friend of mine. This way I can have a moment to just talk; make a quick human connection in what can seem like a very inhuman transaction. It allows a moment for two human beings to just be two human beings talking, instead one person telling another person, "Do this, do that." I need that moment of human connection. It is as important for me as the side they are about to read. I need to have some initial sense of who the actor is as a person.

Often, before we start the actual audition, an actor might ask, "What do you want in this scene?" I never like answering that question. In that moment, I don't want to see an actor try to do what I think the scene is about, I really want to know what the actor thinks about the scene on their own. I want to see how close it might be with my own understanding of the scene. I also, selfishly, want to see if the actor has an insight into the scene that escapes me. There will be plenty of opportunities for me to impose my ideas onto an actor's process, but in this first encounter, I just want to see what the actor thinks on their own, independent of me.

What Are You Looking/Listening For?

Well, with Shakespeare you're often listening more than looking. First things first: is it clear? Do I understand what the actor is saying? If not, what is causing this disconnect? Is it a voice problem? Or a speech problem? A voice problem is purely about vocal production: perhaps they are dropping the ends of their sentences, or their articulation isn't very good, or their voice is too much in their head register instead of supported by their diaphragm. You have to ask yourself, do I want to hear this voice for two hours? A speech problem is different. This is about whether the actor understands what they are saying and how they are saying it. The "how" is the various rhetorical strategies that the character employs. The most famous in Shakespeare, as we've touched on, is the propensity for antithesis. Is the actor playing the antithesis? The opposition between, say, day and night. Also, does the actor understand what the operative word is? Does the actor speak to the end of the period? Does the actor do their thinking between lines (not such a good thing) or on the line (this tends to work better).

Oh, and then there's the issue of rate of utterance. Is every single line done in the same equally metered-out manner (not such a good thing) or does the rhythm vary from line by line (much preferred and closer to life). After issues of clarity, voice, and speech comes the question of whether or not the language is grounded, whether you believe the actor as the character. My teacher used to break actors into two categories: those who are acting and those who are just being. He preferred those who were just being from moment to moment.

Some directors have a very specific image of what the character should be, and they measure each actor as to how they fit that image. I find this to be somewhat self-defeating. I am personally less interested in the actor being a certain type than the actor being engaging in the role. Sometimes I will be working with a producer who will say something to the effect of, "That actor isn't tall enough to be a king." I always think it is how people treat the actor playing a king that lets you know he's the king, so I don't worry about such things. I'm ultimately looking for the best actor who is open, present, and constantly discovering things.

Sometimes I am asked, "In Shakespeare, what's more important: that they are a good verse speaker or a good actor?" The two don't have to be mutually exclusive; both do exist in actors. But when they don't, I always gravitate to the stronger actor. It has been my experience that teaching verse is always easier to do than teaching acting!

The Adjustment

I find adjustments to be an essential part of the audition process. It is where you really learn if you and the actor are on the same wavelength. Now, to begin with, there are many actors who do not need an adjustment. They might "nail" the speech or the scene, but one of the things that I need to ascertain is whether or not the actor can take a note. In other words, how open are they to input and how adept are they at implementing such input? I will rarely stop an actor once they've begun their side; I wait until the end and then, based on what they've shown, I will ask for one adjustment. Often I will preface this by saying, "That was great. I'd love to give you an adjustment if you don't mind." Sometimes I will add, "It's really not so much an adjustment, but an amplification of what you are already doing." Actors, being the generous souls that they are, always say, "Of course." And then, based on what I saw, I will give an adjustment. It might be something simple like:

> When you get to such-and-such moment, see what happens if it becomes suddenly very serious and then find a moment to drop that seriousness and go back to being light-hearted.

Such an adjustment allows me to see if they can play a simple change and how effective they are at doing it. This particular adjustment has something very specific—"at this moment be serious"—and something very open—"find the right moment to drop the seriousness." I am curious to see the actor follow a specific instruction and then also see what their own instincts are after that. I tend to like to give very specific adjustments, often using verbs:

> When you get to this moment, can you "hurt" him more with your words.

But also, the adjustment does not have to be so exacting, it could be more open:

> Can you find a moment somewhere in the speech to "soothe" him?

With Shakespeare, I might ask the actor, "I'm sorry, I didn't quite understand that line, can you paraphrase it for me?" Here, I want to know if the actor does indeed understand it and how creative they are in "translating" it into our contemporary idioms. Usually that loosens up the line and the intention. Then I'll say, "Do it just like that, only now with Shakespeare's words."

If the actor cannot do the adjustment, I will try again and make sure that I rephrase the adjustment in clearer or more vivid terms. First of all, it is hard to do an adjustment on the spot, and, secondly, I might not have been clear enough in what I was asking. If the actor does it a second time and it still does not work, I might ask for the actor to do it one more time, and I will let go of any nuance or subtlety and just say something like, "Just see what happens if you really yell there."

The great Russian director Grigori Kozintsev once said that if you have to give a note more than three times to an actor, you might as well resolve yourself to either pursuing a new note or a new actor. I'm not sure I would go that far, but it is concerning to me when an actor can't take an adjustment after three attempts. When I encounter something like this, I think to myself, "Perhaps this is not an actor who is in control of their craft, or who is not interested in really incorporating input from others." That does not mean I wouldn't cast them, but if I was faced with the possibility of going with two equally capable actors and one can take the note and one can't, I'm probably going to cast the actor who can take the note.

Second and Third Auditions

A lot of times if I like an actor immediately I'll end the first audition by saying, "I loved what you did, I'd love for you to come back." This way I spare the actor the anxiety of having to wait to hear from their agent. I might also say, "I'd love for you to come back and do this side again, so think about X." And then I'll say, "We'll look at the other two sides that we didn't get to today."

When they come back for the second audition, I always like to start with the side we initially worked on. This is, for me, a nice way to pick up where we left off. I hope that doing this is a nice way to transition into the next phase of work. It also gives me a sense of how the material has hopefully settled within the actor. Often when you give an actor an adjustment on the spur of the moment, it can seem a little forced. Seeing the side again, a day or two later, allows you to see how the adjustment might have grown inside the actor. In addition to seeing how the adjustment has settled, it is also important to note whether the side feels as fresh as the last time. Has the actor discovered new things? Is it exactly as you saw last time? Has it lost its spark? This can sometimes tell you something about the actor's process. Some actors stay open and keep discovering things, others like to fix their performance early on; the question becomes, which type of actor do you enjoy working with?

From here I move to the two remaining sides. If the second side is strong, I might say to the actor, "Would you mind doing the final side?" Having seen both, back to back, I can decide which is the weakest and focus on working on that. The idea here is to get a sense of the actor's overall understanding of the character. If there is one area that is less effective, the remainder of the audition can be used to test whether any adjustments can help with this perceived/potential weak spot. For instance, the actor playing Romeo might be wonderful with the lighter side that deals with his friends, he might be quite winning in the subsequent balcony scene, and yet not quite "on point" for Romeo's last speech over the supposed corpse of Juliet (an admittedly difficult scene if there ever was one). We might work this last scene for a bit, to see if we can get closer to nailing it. If I have one final callback, I might give the actor some things to think about for the final audition.

In that final audition, I ask the actor to do all three sides back to back. I note what (if anything) has grown, what seems fixed, and what might be becoming stale. I particularly want to hear how the weakest of the three side sounds this time. Hopefully, the actor has figured this out by now; if not, I'll try one more adjustment. If that still doesn't work, then I know that this will be the area that we would need to focus on in rehearsal and that it may never quite get to where we want it. At this point I weigh a given actor's pluses and minuses against the other candidates for the role. I have to do this sort of "math" to figure out who might be the best fit. With a role like Romeo (or Juliet for that matter) it is often the case that actors divide into two camps: those who can play the lighter first half and those who can play the darker second half. It is hard to find actors who can comfortably do both. If there is, cast that one! If not, you choose the next best actor and know what the focus of your work is going to be for much of the rehearsal process.

Building a Company

And so, bit by bit, you are building a company. This is usually around a central lead that has already been cast. If that is the case, I often like to have that lead actor be part of the final audition process and perhaps reading with the actors. I am very interested in who the leading actor is interested in; particularly when those actors will be playing opposite the lead in major scenes. I really don't want to make the decision of who is playing Ophelia or Gertrude without seeing what the actor playing Hamlet feels. Does that mean I have to follow whatever the lead actor has to say? No, but it helps to know what they respond to and what is going to make their work more engaging for them. Not every lead actor likes being part of this process, but when they do, I find their input to be immensely helpful.

I'm also trying to tune my ear to the way the lead actor handles the verse. Do they make it sound tremendously colloquial? If so, then I want to surround that actor with other actors who handle the language in a similar fashion, so that they all feel as though they are part of the same world. I want everyone to be roughly in the same zip code. This is particularly important in American productions, where there are such radically different approaches to voice and speech. There are many actors who employ what is called transatlantic speech. This is a kind of speech that sounds as though it exists somewhere between American and English speech. I find this to be particularly artificial, but some directors want this sort of made-up sound. For me, the ultimate common denominator is clarity. I want to understand everyone, I want to believe everyone. I want to forget (after the first ten minutes) that I am hearing "Shakespeare." I want it to sound like people talking today which, believe it or not, is not as hard as it sounds. That's what I'm listening for, that is the group of musicians that I am attempting to assemble. Ultimately, I am looking for a kind of ease of being that radiates out from the language and runs through the body of the actor. I'm looking for a kind of vocal and physical comfort and nimbleness.

Finally, I am looking for a group of people who will "play well with one another" and will work as an ensemble. This means they have the same set of values, that the production is more than a job, that it is an opportunity to continue to grow and discover as an artist, to stretch oneself. I look for people who are generally other-directed and are interested in the "big idea" of the show. I also look for people who aren't trapped in a kind of literalist approach to making theatre, that can imagine taking certain poetic leaps, and that are not afraid of pushing the envelope of representation.

Perceiving Difficulty

What if you perceive that someone "doesn't play well with others"? Then what? Do you not cast them? It is amazing how all it takes is one "difficult" individual to undo an entire process. Not right away, though. It is usually a slow, gradual undoing that begins around the end of the process, just as you are about to move into tech and previews, which is when the "difficult" person is most effective in sowing discord among a group of artists who are at their most vulnerable. That's when a difficult actor can do the most damage, where they can attempt to turn the company against a project. But it is also the case that you can win the "difficult" person over to your side, and they can become a fierce defender of what the group is making. You never quite know. I personally tend to shy away from actors who present this vibe. But I have many colleagues who do not share this ethos and are interested in assembling the most interesting ensemble they can, difficulty be damned. One colleague once told me, "I'm not interested in having a 'nice time' in rehearsals, I'm interested in having a dynamic production." This was an artist who thrived on friction and found friction to be a catalyst for his own work. So, to each their own. There is always a degree of "risk analysis" involved in assembling an ensemble, of finding the right balance. You will very quickly learn what kind of rooms you thrive in and how to fill them appropriately.

Making the Final Choice

At the end of the day: follow your gut. Don't overthink it. Choose the best possible actor for each role. Now, how hard is that?

14 "Resolve You For More Amazement": The First Day of Rehearsal and Beyond

And So

There you are, finally, at the table surrounded by a company of actors about to do the first read-through of the play. Now what? Sit. Listen. And ... be prepared, at any moment, to throw away all of the preparatory work you've done if something better emerges around the table, or at any time in the rehearsal room, or even when it is on stage before an audience. The preparatory work is absolutely essential to prepare you for this moment, but you should never be a slave to it. I always love this one anecdote about the Buddha. He once said that his teachings were like a boat which is meant to get you across a body of water; after you've made that crossing, you don't need to carry the boat on your back for the rest of your life. You leave the boat by the water and carry on.

Our preparation has been the boat that has gotten us to the table. It has given us certain insights that can lead to an interpretation. Peter Brook says that what this really boils down to is a set of surmises. The rehearsal process, for Brook, is the place where you rigorously test out those suppositions to see if they are truly alive, dynamic, and viable. If not, you will find something else. My colleague Anne Bogart says that a director does preparation so that they have something to fall back on if nothing else interesting happens in the rehearsal! The bottom line is that you now know enough to lead a group of collaborators on a journey.

One of the sobering realities of directing Shakespeare is that no matter how much you prepare (*and you must prepare*), no amount of preparation will ever be enough. A play by Shakespeare is a shape shifter, changing with the times, and with those who gather together to work on it. Shakespeare's language traps a certain kind of energy. Once the actors become versed in the particular use of that language—once they grow into it and are able to control it and own it—the energy is released, the genie is let out of the bottle and the energy of those words can manifest a very different play than the one you thought you were working on. It goes from being a play of words to a play of actions, energies, primordial forces at war with one another. But the actors and the director need to arrive at a certain level of competency to get to that place, to be able to release this energy. Then, suddenly, there's a different beast in the room. If you think of a Shakespearean text as a forest, you may go hunting for a deer and what you discover emerging from the thicket of themes can be a ferocious bear. Happy hunting. And with that said, finally, we are truly ready to *begin*.

APPENDIX

"Volumes That I Prize Above My Dukedom": Some Helpful Secondary Texts to Have at Hand

In Alphabetical Order (well, sort of)

Harley Granville-Barker, *Prefaces to Shakespeare* Vols. 1 & 2 (Princeton University Press, 1946): I love these short prefaces by one of the great directors of the early twentieth century. Granville-Barker strikes an extraordinary balance between discussing what Shakespeare is on the page and what he can become on stage. These volumes are not to be confused with **Tony Tanner's** *Prefaces to Shakespeare* (Harvard University Press, 2010), which also happen to be quite amazing in their own right. They are, as far as I'm concerned, the best contemporary one-volume critical analysis of all of Shakespeare's plays. Oh, wait! We also can't forget **Emma Smith's** most recent *This is Shakespeare* (Pantheon, 2019). Ms. Smith gives Shakespeare a much-needed critical dusting-off, returning him to us as fresh and vibrant as he must have been when he first hit the streets of London as a young man on the make.

Geoffrey Bullough, *Narrative and Dramatic Sources of Shakespeare* Vols. 1–8 (Columbia University Press, 1966): Everything you ever wanted to know about the source material for Shakespeare's plays but were afraid to ask. It can all be found here within these extraordinary volumes. As close as anyone may ever come to stumbling upon Shakespeare's library.

Wolfgang Clemen, *The Development of Shakespeare's Imagery* (Harvard University Press, 1951): This little book walks the reader through the major imagery of Shakespeare's great plays. It is like being given a tour of some extraordinary museum of natural history by an ever-patient and expert guide.

Richard Flatter, *Shakespeare's Producing Hand: A Study of his Marks of Expression to be Found in the First Folio* (Greenwood Press, 1948): Flatter was a scholar and Max Reinhardt's dramaturg. He's the granddaddy of First Folio theories.

Neil Freeman, *The Applause First Folio of Shakespeare in Modern Type* (Applause Books, 2001): This book is an invaluable and easily accessible way into the First Folio. It has become the starting point for any work I do when preparing a Shakespeare play text for production.

Frank Kermode, *Shakespeare's Language* (Farrar, Straus, and Giroux, 2000): One of the most beautiful books on the evolution of Shakespeare's language by a master scholar. Also, in terms of a crash course on Shakespeare's times, check out Kermode's concise *The Age of Shakespeare* (Modern Library, 2005).

Peter Lake, *How Shakespeare Put Politics on the Stage; Power and Succession in the History Plays* (Yale University Press, 2017): This is the definitive book on how Shakespeare crafted his history plays to deal with the politics of his time.

Alexander Schmidt, *Shakespeare Lexicon and Quotation Dictionary* **Vols. 1 & 2** (Dover Press, 1971): The cover says it all: "Every word defined and located, more than 50,000 quotations identified." If you want to know how a word like *joy* is used in every single Shakespeare play, then this is the book, or rather books, for you. For those who don't want to lug around two thick volumes (a thousand plus pages), you can always turn to **C.T. Onions'** compact *A Shakespeare Glossary* (Clarendon Press, 1985), which is basically all of Shakespeare's words with definitions cribbed from the *Oxford English Dictionary*. And if you're just interested in all of Shakespeare's naughty bits, then skip these august tomes and go directly to **Eric Partridge's** *Shakespeare's Bawdy* (Routledge, Fourth Edition, 2001). This might as well be subtitled "A Dictionary of Shakespearean Smut." Here you will learn that a word like *crack* not only refers to what can happen to things like a porcelain teacup but also to one's own private parts in the heat of an amorous moment. I'll leave the particulars to Professor Partridge.

George T. Wright, *Shakespeare's Metrical Art* (University of California Press, 1988): This is simply the last word on Shakespeare's metrics. Period. Full stop. Look no further. All you need to know resides within these 368 brisk pages.

NOTES

Introduction

1 William Shakespeare, *The Winter's Tale*, *The Arden Shakespeare Third Series Complete Works*, ed. Richard Proudfoot, Ann Thompson, David Scott Kastan, and H.R. Woudhuysen (London and New York: Bloomsbury Arden Shakespeare, 2021), 3.2.78

2 Ludwig Wittgenstein, *Culture and Value*, ed. G. H. von Wright, trans. by Peter Winch (Chicago: University of Chicago Press, 1980), 89

3 William Shakespeare, *A Midsummer Night's Dream*, *The Arden Shakespeare Third Series*, ed. Sukanta Chaudhuri (London and New York: Bloomsbury Arden Shakespeare, 2017), 4.1.209–14

4 William Shakespeare, *As You Like It*, *Arden Shakespeare Third Series Complete Works*, 4.1.196–200

5 William Shakespeare, *Titus Andronicus*, *Arden Shakespeare Third Series Complete Works*, 3.1.217–18

Part One

Chapter 1: "Now Sir, What is Your Text?"

1 Jorge Luis Borges, *Borges on Shakespeare*, ed. and trans. Grace Tiffany (Tempe, AZ: Arizona Center for Medieval & Renaissance Studies, 2018), 110

2 William James, *Varieties of Religious Experience* (New York: Library of America, 2010), 79

3 Ibid., 80

4 Ibid., 84

5 Ibid., 85

6 Ibid.

7 William Shakespeare, *King Richard III*, *The Arden Shakespeare Third Series Complete Works*, ed. Richard Proudfoot, Ann Thompson, David Scott Kastan, and H.R. Woudhuysen (London and New York: Bloomsbury Arden Shakespeare, 2021), 1.1.18–27

8 Ibid., 1.1.28–35

9 William Shakespeare, *King Richard III, The Applause First Folio of Shakespeare in Modern Type*, ed. Neil Freeman (New York: Applause, 2001), 5.3.249–50

10 Shakespeare, *Richard III, Arden Shakespeare Third Series Complete Works*, 5.3.184

11 James, *Varieties of Religious Experience*, 156.

12 William Shakespeare, *Much Ado About Nothing, Arden Shakespeare Third Series Complete Works*, 2.3.22

13 Ibid., 5.2.26–28

14 Ibid., 5.2.36–40

15 Ibid., 4.1.267–8

16 Ibid., 4.1.269–72

17 Ibid., 4.1.273

18 William Shakespeare, *Julius Caesar, Arden Shakespeare Third Series*, ed. David Daniell (London: Thomson Learning, 2003), 2.1.63–69

19 William Shakespeare, *King Richard II, Arden Shakespeare Third Series Complete Works*, 5.5.8–14

20 James, *Varieties of Religious Experience*, 129

21 William Shakespeare, *Hamlet, Revised Edition, The Arden Shakespeare Third Series*, ed. Ann Thompson and Neil Taylor (London and New York: Bloomsbury Arden Shakespeare, 2016), 2.2.261–9

22 William Shakespeare, *Macbeth, Arden Shakespeare Third Series Complete Works*, 5.3.38–9

23 Ibid., 5.3.22–8

24 Ibid., 5.5.18–20

25 Ibid., 5.5.25–7

26 William Shakespeare, *Timon of Athens, Arden Shakespeare Third Series Complete Works*, 5.2.105–8

27 James, *Varieties of Religious Experience*, 163

28 Ibid., 172–3

29 William Shakespeare, *Pericles, Arden Shakespeare Third Series Complete Works*, 2.2.7

30 William Shakespeare, *The Tempest, Revised Edition, The Arden Shakespeare Third Series*, ed. Virginia Mason Vaughan and Alden T. Vaughan. (London and New York: Bloomsbury Arden Shakespeare, 2017), 5.1.104

31 William Shakespeare, *Cymbeline, Arden Shakespeare Third Series Complete Works*, 5.5.364

32 William Shakespeare, *The Winter's Tale, Arden Shakespeare Third Series Complete Works*, 5.2.16–17

33 Shakespeare, *The Tempest*, 1.2.427

34 Shakespeare, *Winter's Tale*, 5.2.24–5

35 Martin Heidegger, *Basic Questions of Philosophy: Selected "Problems" of "Logic"* (Bloomington: Indiana University Press, 1994), 141

36 Ibid.

37 Shakespeare, *Winter's Tale*, 5.3.63

38 Ibid., 5.3.78–9

39 Shakespeare, *Pericles*, 5.3.40–1

40 Shakespeare, *Winter's Tale*, 5.3.110–11

41 Shakespeare, *Much Ado About Nothing*, 5.2.83–6

42 Ibid., 5.2.87

43 Ludwig Wittgenstein, *Culture and Value*, ed. G. H. von Wright, trans. by Peter Winch (Chicago: University of Chicago Press, 1980), 83

44 William Shakespeare, *Romeo & Juliet, The Arden Shakespeare Third Series*, ed. René Weis (London and New York: Bloomsbury Arden Shakespeare, 2012), 3.5.149

45 Hardin Craig, *A New Look at Shakespeare's Quartos* (Stanford: Stanford University Press, 1961), 4

46 Charlton Hinman, *The Printing and Proof-Reading of the First Folio of Shakespeare*, Volume 2 (Oxford: Oxford University Press, 1963), 191

47 Ibid.

48 Ibid.

49 William Shakespeare, *Applause First Folio of Shakespeare in Modern Type*, iii.

50 William Shakespeare, *Twelfth Night, The Arden Shakespeare Third Series Complete Works*, 5.1.200–1

51 Ibid., 5.1.202–3.

52 William Shakespeare, *Twelfth Night, The Applause First Folio of Shakespeare*, 5.1.210–11

53 William Shakespeare, *The First Quarto of King Lear*, ed. Jay L. Halio (Cambridge and New York: Cambridge University Press, 1994), 5.3.301–6

54 Shakespeare, *King Lear, The Applause First Folio of Shakespeare*, 5.3.409–15

55 Ibid., 1.1.165

56 Shakespeare, *Hamlet*, 4.4.31

57 William Shakespeare, "Hamlet: The First Quarto," *Hamlet: The Texts of 1603 and 1623, The Arden Shakespeare*, ed. Ann Thompson and Neil Taylor (London: Thomson Learning, 2006), 7.115–22

58 Shakespeare, *Hamlet*, 3.1.55–62

59 Ibid., 78

Chapter 2: "And There is Much Music"

1 Fernando Sorrentino, *Seven Conversations with Jorge Luis Borges*, trans. Clark M. Zlotchew (Philadelphia, PA: Paul Dry Books, 2010), 31–2

2 William Shakespeare, *Macbeth, The Arden Shakespeare Third Series Complete Works*, ed. Richard Proudfoot, Ann Thompson, David Scott Kastan, and H.R. Woudhuysen (London and New York: Bloomsbury Arden Shakespeare, 2021), 2.2.63–4

3 Jorge Luis Borges, *Borges on Shakespeare*, ed. and trans. Grace Tiffany (Tempe, AZ: Arizona Center for Medieval & Renaissance Studies, 2018), 87

4 William Shakespeare, *Much Ado About Nothing, Arden Shakespeare Third Series Complete Works*, 2.3.8–21

5 Shakespeare, *Macbeth*, 2.3.54–62

6 William Shakespeare, *The First Quarto of King Lear*, ed. Jay L. Halio (Cambridge and New York: Cambridge University Press, 1994), 5.3.412

7 George T. Wright, "Shakespeare's Metre Scanned," in *Reading Shakespeare's Dramatic Language: A Guide*, ed. Sylvia Adamson, Lynette Hunter, Lynne Magnusson, Ann Thompson, and Katie Wales (London: Arden Shakespeare, 2001), 51–70

8 William Shakespeare, *The Winter's Tale, Arden Shakespeare Third Series Complete Works*, 1.2.186–9

9 William Shakespeare, *Romeo & Juliet, The Arden Shakespeare Third Series*, ed. René Weis (London and New York: Bloomsbury Arden Shakespeare, 2012), 2.2.2–6

10 Anthony Graham-White, *Punctuation and Its Dramatic Value in Shakespearean Drama* (Newark: University of Delaware Press, 1995), 16

11 Ibid.

12 Walter J. Ong, *Orality and Literacy: The Technologizing of the Word* (New York: Routledge, 2002)

13 Graham-White, *Punctuation and Its Dramatic Value in Shakespeare's Drama*, 36

14 Ibid., 38

15 Ibid.

16 Ibid., 38–9

17 Ibid., 42

18 William Shakespeare, *Romeo and Juliet, The Applause First Folio of Shakespeare*, 1.760–1. NB: Spelling has been modernized in all the extracts taken from this source below.

19 Ibid., 1.762–70

20 Ibid., 1.771–5

21 Ibid., 1.776–81

22 Ibid., 1.782–3

23 Ibid., 1.784

24 Ibid., 1.785

25 Ibid., 1.786–92

26 Scott Kaiser, *Mastering Shakespeare: An Acting Class in Seven Scenes* (New York: Allworth Press, 2003), 15

27 Shakespeare, *Romeo and Juliet*, 2.2.33–6

28 Ibid., 2.2.38–49

29 William Shakespeare, *Hamlet, The Arden Shakespeare Third Series*, ed. Ann Thompson and Neil Taylor (London and New York: Bloomsbury Arden Shakespeare, 2016), 1.2.129–37

30 Shakespeare, *Hamlet, The Applause First Folio of Shakespeare*, 1.299–307

31 G. Blakemore Evans, "Shakespeare's Text," in *The Riverside Shakespeare*, ed. G. Blakemore Evans (Boston: Houghton Mifflin, 1974), 39.

32 Shakespeare, *Hamlet, The Applause First Folio of Shakespeare*, 1.308–16

33 Shakespeare, *Much Ado About Nothing, The Applause First Folio of Shakespeare*, 2.432–42

34 Shakespeare, *King Lear, The Applause First Folio of Shakespeare*, 5.349–55

35 Shakespeare, *Romeo and Juliet, The Applause First Folio of Shakespeare*, 1.761–73

36 Shakespeare, *Hamlet*, 1.2.160–4

37 Ibid., 1.2.179–80

38 Ibid., 1.2.185

39 Ibid., 1.2.188–9

40 Ibid., 3.1.114

41 Ibid., 3.1.120

42 Ibid., 3.1.129–30

43 Ibid., 2.2.261–2

44 David Williams, *Collaborative Theatre: The Théâtre du Soleil Sourcebook* (New York : Routledge, 1999), 153–4.

45 Shakespeare, *Hamlet*, 5.1.174

Chapter 3: "Wherefore Are These Things Hid?"

1 William Shakespeare, *Twelfth Night, The Arden Shakespeare Third Series Complete Works*, , ed. Richard Proudfoot, Ann Thompson, David Scott Kastan, and H.R. Woudhuysen (London and New York: Bloomsbury Arden Shakespeare, 2021), 2.5.120

2 Ibid., 2.5.138–40

3 Ibid., 3.4.126

4 William Shakespeare, *The Winter's Tale, Arden Shakespeare Third Series Complete Works*, 1.2.356–8

5 Ibid., 1.2.401–2

6 Ibid., 1.2.430–2

7 Ibid., 2.1.57–8

8 Ibid., 2.1.59

9 Ibid., 2.1.102–3

10 Ibid., 2.3.1–2

11 Ibid., 2.3.173–4

12 Ibid., 2.3.183–7

13 Ibid., 3.3.57

14 Ibid., 4.4.292–3

15 Ibid., 4.4.295–6

16 Ibid. 5.1.72

17 Ibid., 5.1.178

18 Ibid., 5.3.63–5

19 Shakespeare, *The Tempest, Arden Shakespeare Third Series Complete Works*, 1.1

20 Shakespeare, *Hamlet, Arden Shakespeare Third Series Complete Works*, 1.1.1

21 Ibid., 1.1

22 Ibid., 1.5.63–4

23 Ibid., 5.2.316–87

24 Shakespeare, *The Tempest*, 1.2.276–81

25 Ibid., 1.2.287–93

26 Ibid., 3.1.0

27 Ibid., 5.1.54–5

28 Ibid., E.9–10

29 Ibid., E.18–20

30 William Shakespeare, *Much Ado About Nothing, The Arden Shakespeare Third Series*, 2.1.226–34

31 Ibid., 4.2.76–88

32 Shakespeare, *Hamlet*, 5.2.197–201

Chapter 4: "Your Actions Are My Dreams"

1 See Arnold Van Gennep's seminal *Rites of Passage* (Chicago: University of Chicago Press, 2019) and Victor Turner's extension of these ideas, most notably in *The Ritual Process* (London: Routledge & Kegan Paul, 1969)

2 Victor Turner, *Forest of Symbols* (Ithaca, NY: Cornell University Press, 1970), 95

3 Edith Turner, *Communitas: The Anthropology of Collective Joy* (Basingstoke: Palgrave, 2012), 1

4 William Shakespeare, *A Midsummer Night's Dream, The Arden Shakespeare Third Series*, ed. Sukanta Chaudhuri (London and New York: Bloomsbury Arden Shakespeare, 2017), 4.1.191

5 William Shakespeare, *Hamlet: The Texts of 1603 and 1623, The Arden Shakespeare*, ed. Ann Thompson and Neil Taylor (London: Thomson Learning, 2016), 2.2.248

6 Lacan can be notoriously difficult to decipher. Perhaps the best starting place to understand his theories of The Symbolic, The Imaginary, and The Real would be to turn to Dylan Evans, *An Introductory Dictionary of Lacanian Psychoanalysis* (London: Routledge; 1996).

Chapter 5: "Stand and Unfold Yourself"

1 William Shakespeare, *Hamlet, The Arden Shakespeare Third Series*, ed. Ann Thompson and Neil Taylor (London: Bloomsbury Arden Shakespeare), 1.1.1

2 Ibid., 3.2.355–63

3 William Shakespeare, *Othello, The Arden Shakespeare Third Series Complete Works*, , ed. Richard Proudfoot, Ann Thompson, David Scott Kastan, and H.R. Woudhuysen (London and New York: Bloomsbury Arden Shakespeare, 2021), 5.2.299

4 Ibid., 5.2. 300–1

5 William Shakespeare, *The Merchant of Venice*, *Arden Shakespeare Third Series Complete Works*, 4.1.39–42

6 Alfred Simon, *The Elementary Rites of Molière's Comedy*, in *Molière: A Collection of Critical Essays*, edited by Jacques Guicharnaud (New Jersey: Prentice-Hall, 1964), 36

7 William Shakespeare, *Twelfth Night*, *Arden Shakespeare Third Series Complete Works*, 2.3.87–91

8 Ibid., 2.5.34

9 Ibid., 4.6.47–8

10 Ibid., 5.1.338–9

11 William Shakespeare, *Antony and Cleopatra*, *Arden Shakespeare Third Series Complete Works*, 1.5.3–7

12 Ibid., 5.2.287–8

13 Shakespeare, *Hamlet*, 174–84

14 Ibid., 3.1.78–9

15 William Shakespeare, *King Richard II*, *The Arden Shakespeare Third Series Complete Works*, 3.3.72–90

16 Ibid., 1.4.59–64

17 Ibid., 2.1.153–4

18 Ibid., 2.1.155

19 Ibid., 3.2.4–11

20 Ibid., 3.2.145–7

21 Ibid., 3.2.171–7

22 Ibid., 4.1.163–76

23 Ibid., 5.1.16–25

24 Ibid., 5.5.1–2

25 Ibid., 5.5.42–3

26 Ibid., 5.5.61

27 Ibid., 5.5.65–6

28 Ibid., 5.5.45–9)

29 William Shakespeare, *Romeo & Juliet*, *The Arden Shakespeare Third Series*, ed. René Weis (London and New York: Bloomsbury Arden Shakespeare, 2012), 2.3.19–26

30 William Shakespeare, *Macbeth*, *Arden Shakespeare Third Series Complete Works*, 5.3.22–8

31 Ibid., 1.2.16–23

32 Ibid., 1.4.22–7

33 Ibid., 1.3.129–40

34 Ibid., 1.7.1–12

35 Ibid., 1.4.48–53

36 Ibid., 3.1.48

37 Ibid., 3.2.14–16

38 Ibid., 3.2.36

39 Ibid., 3.2.28–9

40 Ibid., 3.2.30–6

41 Ibid., 3.2.37

42 Ibid., 3.2.44–6

43 Ibid., 5.3.40–5

44 Ibid., 5.5.48–51

Part Two

Introduction

1 Jan Kott, *Shakespeare Our Contemporary* (Garden City, NY: Doubleday 1964), 53

2 Elaine Pagels, *The Gnostic Gospels* (New York: Vintage, 1989)

Chapter 6: "To Sing a Song That Old Was Sung"

1 Jorges Luis Borges, *Collected Fictions*, trans. Andrew Hurley (New York: Viking, 1998), 33

2 Ibid., 35

3 Saxo Grammaticus, *Saxo Grammaticus and the Life of Hamlet: A Translation, History, and Commentary*, trans. William F. Hansen. (Lincoln: University of Nebraska Press, 1983), 98

4 Ibid., 106–7

5 William Shakespeare, *Hamlet, The Arden Shakespeare Third Series*, ed. Ann Thompson and Neil Taylor (London: Bloomsbury Arden Shakespeare), 2.2.539–40)

6 John Marston, *Antonio's Revenge*, ed. W. Reavley Gair (Manchester: Manchester University Press, 1999), 13

7 Ibid., 57

8 Ibid., 103

9 Jonathan Bate, *The Genius of Shakespeare* (Oxford and New York : Oxford University Press, 2008), 12

10 Shakespeare, *Hamlet*, 1.1.112–13

11 Carl Schmitt, *Hamlet or Hecuba: The Intrusion of the Time into the Play,* trans. David Pan and Jennifer R. Rust (Candor, NY: Telos, 2009), 16

12 Ibid., 44

13 Ibid., 28

14 Ibid. 25

15 Shakespeare, *Hamlet*, 5.3.343–4

16 Schmidt, *Hamlet or Hecuba*, 24

17 Ibid.

18 Ibid.

19 Robert Burton, *The Anatomy of Melancholy: Volume I: Text*, ed. Thomas C. Faulkner and Nicholas K. Kiessling (Oxford and New York: Oxford University Press, 1989), 162

20 Ibid., 162–3

21 Ibid.

22 Ibid., 171

23 Shakespeare, *Hamlet*, 2.2.539–40

24 Ibid., 3.1.55

25 Ibid., 3.1.82–7

26 Ibid., 5.1.174

27 Ibid., 5.1.258–9

28 Ibid., 3.2.5–14

29 Ibid., 3.2.16–17

30 Ibid., 3.2.17–18

31 Ibid., 3.2.61–7

32 Ibid., 5.2.197–201

Chapter 7: "You Speak a Language That I Understand Not"

1 Martin Lings, *The Sacred Art of Shakespeare: To Take Upon Us the Mystery of Things* (Rochester, VT: Inner Traditions, 1998), 21

2 William Shakespeare, *Hamlet, The Arden Shakespeare Third Series*, ed. Ann Thompson and Neil Taylor (London: Bloomsbury Arden Shakespeare), 1.2.135–7

3 Lings, *The Sacred Art of Shakespeare*, 29

4 Paul Walsh, "His liberty is full of threats to all: Benno Besson's Helsinki *Hamlet* and Brecht's dialectical appropriations of classic texts," in *Re-Interpreting Brecht: His Influences on Contemporary Drama and Film*, ed. Pia Kleber and Colin Visser (Cambridge: Cambridge University Press, 2009), 104–17

5 Margot Heinemann, "How Brecht read Shakespeare," in *Political Shakespeare: Essays in Cultural Materialism, Second Edition*, ed. Jonathan Dollimore and Alan Sinfield (Ithaca, NY: Cornell University Press, 1994), 202–130

6 Ibid., 217

7 Shakespeare, *Hamlet*, 5.2.365–7

8 Walsh, "His liberty is full of threats to all," 108

9 Shakespeare, *Hamlet*, 4.4.46–51

10 Ibid., 4.4.52–65

11 Walsh, "His liberty is full of threats to all," 108

12 Ibid.

Chapter 8: "A Natural Perspective That is and is Not"

1 Michael Almereyda, dir. *Hamlet* (2000; Los Angeles, CA: Miramax)

2 William Shakespeare, *Hamlet, The Arden Shakespeare Third Series*, ed. Ann Thompson and Neil Taylor (London: Bloomsbury Arden Shakespeare), 3.1.133–6

3 Ibid., 3.1.146–8

4 Baz Luhrmann, dir. *William Shakespeare's Romeo + Juliet* (1996; Los Angeles, CA: 20th Century Fox)

5 Jan Kott, *The Bottom Translation: Marlowe and Shakespeare and the Carnival Tradition*, trans.Daniela Miedzyrzecka and Lillian Vallee (Evanston, IL: Northwestern University Press, 1987)

6 Michael Almereyda, "The Bad Sleep Well: Shakespeare's Ghost," *The Bad Sleep Well*, dir. Akira Kurosawa (1960; New York: Criterion Collection, 2006), DVD booklet

7 Akira Kurosawa, dir. *The Bad Sleep Well* (1960; New York: Criterion Collection, 2006), DVD

8 Almereyda, "The Bad Sleep Well"

9 David Williams, *Collaborative Theatre: The Théâtre du Soleil Sourcebook* (New York : Routledge, 1999), 93

10 Ibid., 87

Chapter 9: "Is Not This Strange?"

1 Zygmunt Bauman, *Modernity and Ambivalence* (Oxford: Polity, 1991), 58

2 William Shakespeare, *Hamlet, The Arden Shakespeare Third Series*, ed. Ann Thompson and Neil Taylor (London: Bloomsbury Arden Shakespeare), 3.1.61

3 See Bridget Escolme, *Talking to the Audience: Shakespeare, Performance, Self* (New York: Routledge, 2004), 140–7

4 "Definition of Autism," Autism Awareness Centre Inc., https://autismawarenesscentre. com/definition-autism/

5 Henry Markram, Tania Rinaldi, and Kamila Markram, "The intense world syndrome— an alternative hypothesis for autism," *Frontiers in Neuroscience* 1(1) (Nov 2007): 77–96

6 See Spencer Golub, "Between the curtain and the grave: the Taganka in the *Hamlet* gulag," in *Foreign Shakespeare: Contemporary Performance*, ed. Dennis Kennedy (Cambridge and New York: Cambridge University Press, 1993), 172–3

7 Ibid. 173

8 Ibid. 168–9

Part Three

Chapter 10: "What Say You?"

1 See Georg Simmel, "The Metropolis and Mental Life," *Georg Simmel on Individuality and Social Forms*, ed. Donald N. Levine (Chicago: University of Chicago Press, 1971), 324–40

2 Ibid.

Chapter 11: "The Fall of a Sparrow"

1 William Shakespeare, *Romeo and Juliet, The Arden Shakespeare Third Series*, ed. René Weis (London: Arden Shakespeare, 2012), 1.1.42–9

2 Shakespeare, *King Lear, The Arden Shakespeare Third Series*, ed. R.A. Foakes (London: Thomson Learning, 1997). 1.1.1–2

3 William Shakespeare, *Henry V, The Arden Shakespeare Third Series Complete Works*, ed. Richard Proudfoot, Ann Thompson, David Scott Kastan, and H.R. Woudhuysen (London and New York: Bloomsbury Arden Shakespeare, 2021), 1.1.1

4 William Shakespeare, *Twelfth Night, Arden Shakespeare Third Series Complete Works*, 1.2.1

5 Ibid., 1.1.1

6 William Shakespeare, *Hamlet, The Arden Shakespeare Third Series*, ed. Ann Thompson and Neil Taylor (London: Bloomsbury Arden Shakespeare), 2.2.539–40

INDEX

A Midsummer Night's Dream
(Shakespeare) 2, 75, 80, 81, 82,
83, 84, 85, 87, 91, 94
A Plot/B Plot 73–5
abstract readings 142–3, 145, 147, 148
Castellucci, Romeo/Societas Raffaello
Sanzio, *Amleto* 143–4
Golub, Spencer, *Between the Curtain
and the Grave: the Taganka in
the Hamlet gulag* 146, 147
Hamlet 143, 144, 145, 146, 147
Lyubimov, Yuri, *Hamlet* 143, 145–7
act breaks 161
actional rhymes: 75, 76–7, 78
King Lear 76, 158, 159, 160
Hamlet 76–7
adjustments 193, 194
allegory/allegorical readings 130–1, 132,
134, 135
Hamlet 130, 131, 132, 133, 134
as political allegory (Brecht; Paul
Walsh's essay on Brecht's
dialectical appropriation of
classic texts like *Hamlet*; Margo
Heinemann, *How Brecht Read
Shakespeare*) 132–3, 135
as religious allegory (Martin Lings,
*The Sacred Art of Shakespeare:
To Take Upon Us the Mystery of
Things*) 131–2
Amleth 120–1
analogical readings 136–7, 141
Akira Kurosawa, *The Bad Sleep Well*
(*Hamlet* adaptation) 139–40
Arianne Mnouchkine, *Richard II and
Henry IV* 140

Baz Luhrmann, *William Shakespeare's
Romeo and Juliet* film adaptation
138
Hamlet 137, 138, 139, 140
Michael Almereyda, *Hamlet* film
adaptation 137–8, 139
Romeo and Juliet 138
Antony and Cleopatra (Shakespeare) 88,
97–8
architectonic events 52, 54–6, 61
As You Like It (Shakespeare) 2
auditioning for Shakespeare 192, 187, 190,
194, 195

Bates, Jonathan, *The Genius of Shakespeare*
123–4
Borges, Jorge Louis 1, 2, 9, 32, 119
Brecht, Bertolt 132–3, 135
Brook, Peter 148, 154, 158, 159, 197
building a company 195, 196
Bullough, Geoffrey, *Narrative and Dramatic
Sources of Shakespeare* 199
Burton, Robert, *The Anatomy of
Melancholy* 126, 127

caesura 59
Castellucci, Romeo 143–4
casting 187–8
central image 180, 185
character in Shakespeare 95–6, 96–9, 101,
105, 106, 110
Cixous, Helene 58–9
Clemen, Wolfgang, *The Development of
Shakespeare's Imagery* 199
colon (as notation for a new thought) 38,
39, 41, 47, 48, 49

communitas 83–4
concept to realization 184
core moments 50–1, 57, 59
cores 49, 50, 51, 57, 58, 61, 62
costume design (*Timon of Athens:*
        illustrations) 169, 170, 171, 172,
        173
Craig, Hardin, *A New Look at Shakespeare's*
        Quartos 21
culminating event 54, 55–6
cutting Shakespeare 4, 22, 157, 158, 159

Daines, Simon, *Orthoepia Anglicana* 39
Derrida, Jacques 4, 79
design 4, 92, 146, 151, 152, 159, 164, 165–6,
        180, 182, 184
    central image 168, 180, 185
    costume design 166, 172–4
    Mark Wendland's four basic questions
        166–9, 174
    in relation to Lacan's order of the
        Imaginary 169, 170, 177, 180,
        182, 186
    in relation to Lacan's order of the Real
        and/or the Wondrous 169, 172,
        178, 179, 184, 186
    in relation to Lacan's Symbolic Order
        169, 176, 180
    scenic motifs 168, 172, 175, 176, 179
    set designs 159, 166, 169–72, 175–9,
        180–4
    visual antithesis 172, 175, 177, 178, 179,
        185

Earl of Essex 125–6, 129
Easton, Richard 159
Evans, G. Blakemore 38, 47
events 49, 50, 51, 52, 57, 58, 59, 60, 61, 62
exercises 40, 68
    Exercise #1 Which Shakespeare, Which
        Text? 30
    Exercise #2 Scoring the Play/Event
        Work 60–2
    Exercise #3 Pattern Work 77–8
    Exercise #4 Shaping the Play Using
        Lacan's Three Orders 93–4
    Exercise #5 Developing the Arc of
        Characters: Mask/Face/Soul
        110–11

Exercise #6 Plain Reading Questions
        129
    Exercise #7 Allegorical Reading 135
    Exercise #8 Analogical Reading 141
    Exercise #9 Abstract Reading 148
    Exercise #10 Mixing and Matching 148
    Exercise #11 Telling the Story of the
        Play Visually 185–6

First Folio Practices/Original Practices
        45–6, 47
Flatter, Richard, *Shakespeare's Producing*
        Hand; A Study of his Marks of
        Expression to be found in the
        First Folio 45, 200
Folio 4, 12, 21–9, 38, 39, 40, 63, 119, 156,
        200
    Bad Quarto, Second Quarto, Folio
        27–8
Fourfold reading 4, 113, 116–18
    abstract/ deconstructionist reading 4,
        118, 129, 140, 142–8, 152, 172,
        176, 185
    allegorical/analogic reading 4, 117, 118,
        129, 130–4, 135, 136–40, 145,
        146, 147, 148, 166, 185
    allegorical sense 117, 118
    anagogical sense 117
    Batin 117
    Derash 117
    Hadd 117
    literal sense 117, 118
    Matla/Muttala 117
    moral sense 117, 118
    Peshat 117
    plain reading 4, 117, 118, 119–20, 124,
        129, 145, 147, 148, 185
    Remez 117
    Sod 117
    Zahir 117
Freeman, Neil, Editor, *The Applause First*
        Folio of Shakespeare in Modern
        Type 23
from interpretation to processing 152–4
from seeming to being 101–5, 110

general shaping of Shakespeare text 157,
        158, 159, 161, 164
Godard, Jean-Luc 148, 167

Golub, Spenser 146, 147
Graham-White, Anthony, *Punctuation and Its Dramatic Value in Shakespearean Drama* 38
Granville-Barker, Harley, *Prefaces to Shakespeare* 199

Hamlet (Shakespeare) 12, 14–17, 22, 27–8, 29, 31, 46, 47, 48, 52, 53, 54, 55, 57, 58, 59, 76–7, 80, 85, 88, 89, 90, 91, 92, 95, 96, 99, 100, 101, 107, 108, 115, 116, 118, 119, 120, 122, 123, 124, 125, 126, 127, 128, 129, 130, 131, 132, 133, 134, 137, 138, 139, 140, 143, 144, 145, 146, 147, 187, 188, 195
   analogical reading 137, 138, 139, 140
   Bad Quarto, Second Quarto, Folio 27–8
   cores coming out of events of scenes 57–8
   macro events 54
   Mask/Face/Soul 99–101
   Michael Almereyda, *Hamlet* film adaptation 137–8, 139
   see also abstract reading
Heidegger, Martin 18, 101, 110
Heinemann, Margo 132
Henry V (Shakespeare) 81, 84
Hinman, Charlton, *The Printing and Proof Reading of the First Folio of Shakespeare* 23
historical/political context 124–6

iambic pentameter 20, 29, 34, 35, 49, 56
Imaginary Order (Lacan) 85, 86, 87, 88, 89, 90, 91, 92, 93, 94, 98, 169, 170, 177, 180, 182, 186
inciting event 54, 55, 61
interpretation 115–18
irrevocable event 80, 87

James, William 10, 20, 30
   Alphonse Daudet, *Homo Duplex* 13–14
   Leo Tolstoy 17–18
   Once Born 10–12;
   Reborn/New Birth/Regenerated 17–20
   Sick Soul 15–17
   twice-born 13–15

Varieties of Religious Experience 10, 20–1, 30
Julius Caesar (Shakespeare) 80, 81, 82, 83, 84–5, 87, 91

Kaiser, Scott, *Mastering Shakespeare* 42
Kermode, Frank, *Shakespeare's Language* 200
King James 125–6, 128, 129
King Lear (Shakespeare) 16, 17, 22, 26, 27, 29, 35, 48, 55, 56, 76, 80, 81, 85, 87, 88, 89, 90, 91, 92
Kott, Jan, *Shakespeare our Contemporary* 115–16
Kristeva, Julia, *Black Sun* 17
Kurosawa, Akira 139–40
Kyd, Thomas, *Spanish Tragedy* 122, 123

Lacan, Jacques 85, 86, 90, 93, 98, 169, 170, 172, 176, 178, 180, 186
   the Imaginary 85, 86, 87, 88, 89, 90, 91, 92, 93, 94, 98, 169, 170, 177, 180, 182, 186
   the Real 85, 86, 87, 88, 89, 90, 91, 92, 93, 98, 169, 172, 178, 186
   the Symbolic 85, 86, 87, 88, 89, 90, 91, 92, 93, 94, 98, 169, 176, 180, 186
Lake, Peter, *How Shakespeare Put Politics on the Stage* 200
liminal stage 82, 83, 85
liminality (Arnold Van Geenep and Victor Turner) 81–7
Lings, Martin 131, 132, 134
lively turning 123–4
Ludic Recombination 83–5
Luhrmman, Baz 138
Lyubimov, Yuri 143

Macbeth (Shakespeare) 16, 17, 29, 32, 33–4, 50, 51, 55, 56, 59, 80, 81, 85, 87, 88, 90, 91, 92
macro events 52, 56, 60, 61, 62
Maguire, Mary, *Shakespearean Suspect Texts: The 'Bad' Quartos and their Contexts* 22
Marston, John, *Antonio's Revenge* 122–3
Mask/Face/Soul (Alfred Simon) 96, 98
   Face 96, 97, 98, 99, 100, 101, 102, 104, 105, 106, 107, 108, 109, 110, 111

Mask 96, 97, 98, 99, 100, 101, 102, 103, 104, 105, 106, 107, 108, 109, 110, 111

Soul 96, 97, 98, 99, 100, 101, 102, 104, 105, 106, 107, 108, 109, 110, 111

meetings with actors 188–9

melancholy 119, 126–7

metrics 34, 35, 43

iamb 20, 29, 34, 35, 36, 49, 56, 61;

pyrrhic 35, 36, 56

spondee 35, 36, 56, 60

trochee 34–5, 56, 58, 61

micro events 52–3, 54, 56, 58, 60, 61, 62

Mnouchkine, Arianne 140

Much Ado About Nothing (Shakespeare) 10, 13, 19, 20, 22, 33, 48, 74–5

Berkeley Rep 179, 180, 181, 182, 183

musicianship of the actor 189

Once Born (Wiliam James) 10–12, 13, 14, 15, 16, 17, 18, 20, 30

Ong, Walter J., *Orality and Literacy* 38

Onions, C.T., *Shakespeare's Glossary* 200

openings of Shakespeare's Plays 157–8, 160

Othello (Shakespeare) 80, 85, 87, 88, 89, 91, 92

Pagels, Elaine, *The Gnostic Gospels* 118

Partridge, Eric, *Shakespeare's Bawdy* 200

pattern recognition 3, 4, 63–4, 68, 69, 71, 72, 73, 74, 75, 76, 77, 78, 79, 90, 96, 110, 111, 152

actions 2, 63, 74, 75, 76–7, 78

images 2, 63, 67, 69, 71–3, 78, 79

words 63, 64–7, 68–70, 77, 79

penultimate event 54, 55

Pericles (Shakespeare) 81

Prince of Tyre at the Public Theatre 174

Pierre Menard, Author of the Quixote (by Borges) 119, 120

plain reading 4, 117, 118, 119–20, 129

original sources 120–1

political/historical context 124–6

related genres 122–4

socio/psychological context 126–8

punctuation 24, 25, 26, 38–9, 40, 46, 48, 119, 161

colon 26, 38, 39, 41, 47, 48, 49

comma 25, 38, 39, 40, 161

dash 39

parenthesis 39

period 38, 39, 40–2, 43, 45, 47, 161, 192;

semicolon 25, 39

Quarto 4, 13, 21–3, 24, 25, 29, 30

Bad Quarto, Second Quarto, Folio 27–8

Craig, Hardin, *A New Look at Shakespeare's Quartos* 21

Maguire, Mary, *Shakespearean Suspect Texts: The 'Bad' Quartos and their Contexts* 22

rate of utterance 43, 45

Re-Aggregation Stage 82, 83, 85

Real (Order of Lacan) 85, 86, 87, 88, 89, 90, 91, 92, 93, 98, 169, 172, 178, 186

revenge tragedy 122–4

rhythm of events 56

Richard II (Shakespeare) 11, 12, 14, 22, 101–5

Mask/Face/Soul 101–5

Richard III (Shakespeare) 11–12, 13, 14, 21, 22, 29

rites of passage 81, 82

Liminal Stage 82, 83, 85

Re-Aggregation Stage 82, 83, 84–5, 90

Separation Stage 82, 83, 86

Romeo and Juliet (Shakespeare) 37, 40–2, 43–4, 49, 55, 60, 61, 62, 105–6, 157, 162

soul, secret garden 105–6

rule of the period 40–2, 43, 45

Saxo Grammaticus, *History of the Danes* 120

scenic motifs 168, 172, 175, 176, 179, 185

Schmidt, Alexander, *Shakespeare's Lexicon* 200

Schmitt, Carl, *Hamlet or Hecuba: The Intrusion of Time into the Play* 125–6

Separation Stage (Van Gennep, Victor Turner) 81, 82, 83, 86

set design (illustrations) 169, 170, 171, 172, 175, 177, 178, 179, 180, 181, 182, 183

Sick Soul (William James) 10, 15–17, 18, 20, 30, 109
sides 190, 194, 195
Simmel, Georg 155
Shakespeare, William 9, 28
    character 95–6, 96–9, 101, 105, 106, 110
    First Folio – compositors, kings men 4, 12, 21, 23–4, 25, 26, 27, 28, 30
    Folio vs Quarto 24, 25–7, 28–9
    jealousy 20
    production history/play order 119–20
    punctuation, "blended" texts 24–5, 26
    Quarto 4, 13, 21–3, 24, 25, 26, 27, 28, 30
    speaking verse 2, 3, 4, 20, 21
    the Stuff of Dreams 2
    use of punctuation 38–42, 46
    wonder 18–19
    word usage/additions to English vocabulary/Latin and Anglo-Saxon 31–3
Shakespeare panic 158
Shakespeare's Romances 16–17, 18–20
shaping the text 156–7
Smith, Emma, *This is Shakespeare* 199
speech measures 42–5
Steinberg, Paul 184
Strauss, Claude Levi 79
structure/structuralism (Claude Levi-Strauss, Jacques Derrida) 79–80
Symbolic Order (Lacan) 85, 86, 87, 88, 89, 90, 91, 92, 93, 94, 98, 169, 176, 180, 186

Tanner, Tony, *Prefaces to Shakespeare* 199
The Tempest (Shakespeare) 80, 81, 90, 91

The Winter's Tale (Shakespeare) 18, 20, 73–4, 80, 81, 90, 91, 161
Timeless to Timely: Peter Brook "Plays are like planets" 154–5
Timon of Athens (Shakespeare) 15, 17, 153, 154, 155
    Delacourte Theatre in Central Park, The New York Shakespeare Festival 166, 167, 168, 169, 170, 171, 172, 173, 179
Titus Andronicus (Shakespeare) 3
Tolstoy, Leo 17
transposing scenes 160–1
Turner, Victor 81, 82, 83, 84, 85, 86, 90, 93
Twelfth Night (Shakespeare) 15–16, 25, 160, 161
Twice Born (William James) 10, 12–15, 16, 20, 30

Van Gennep, Arnold 81, 82, 83, 84, 85, 86, 90
visual antithesis 172, 175, 177, 178, 179, 185

Wendland, Mark, designer 164, 166, 169, 170, 171, 172, 173, 175, 176, 177, 178, 179, 180, 181, 182, 183
    Four basic questions 166, 167, 168–9
Wittgenstein, Ludwig 2, 3
wonder 18, 19, 90, 91, 92, 93, 94
Wright, George T., *Shakespeare's Metrical Art* 36

Žižek, Slavoj 88, 92